LAND BIRD COMMUNITIES OF
GRAND BAHAMA ISLAND:
THE STRUCTURE AND DYNAMICS
OF AN AVIFAUNA

ORNITHOLOGICAL MONOGRAPHS

This series, published by the American Ornithologists' Union, has been established for major papers too long for inclusion in the Union's journal, *The Auk*. Publication has been made possible through the generosity of Mrs. Carll Tucker and the Marcia Brady Tucker Foundation, Inc.

Correspondence concerning manuscripts for publication in the series should be addressed to the Editor-elect, Dr. Mercedes S. Foster, Department of Biology, University of South Florida, Tampa, Florida 33620.

Copies of *Ornithological Monographs* may be ordered from the Assistant to the Treasurer of the AOU, Glen E. Woolfenden, Department of Biology, University of South Florida, Tampa, Florida 33620. (See price list on back and inside back cover.)

Ornithological Monographs No. 25, xi + 129 pp.

    Editor of A.O.U. Monographs, John William Hardy

    Special Associate Editors of this issue, Frances C. James, Department of Biology, Florida State University, Tallahassee, and Ned K. Johnson, Museum of Vertebrate Zoology, University of California, Berkeley

    Assistant Editor, June B. Gabaldon

    Author, John T. Emlen, Department of Zoology, University of Wisconsin, Madison, 53706

    First received December 1975; accepted, October 1976; final revision, December 1976

    Issued November 22, 1977

    Price $9.00 prepaid ($8.00 to AOU Members)

    Library of Congress Catalogue Card Number 77-90792

    Printed by the Allen Press, Inc., Lawrence, Kansas 66044

    Copyright © American Ornithologists' Union, 1977

LAND BIRD COMMUNITIES OF GRAND BAHAMA ISLAND: THE STRUCTURE AND DYNAMICS OF AN AVIFAUNA

BY

JOHN T. EMLEN

Department of Zoology
University of Wisconsin

ORNITHOLOGICAL MONOGRAPHS NO. 24
PUBLISHED BY
THE AMERICAN ORNITHOLOGISTS' UNION
1977

TABLE OF CONTENTS

PREFACE	xi
1—INTRODUCTION	1
2—METHODS	2
HABITAT MEASUREMENTS	2
ANALYSIS OF HABITAT DISTRIBUTION	3
BIRD POPULATION MEASUREMENTS	4
WITHIN-HABITAT DISTRIBUTION AND ACTIVITY MEASUREMENTS	4
3—GRAND BAHAMA ISLAND	5
THE ENVIRONMENT	5
Geology	5
Physiographic history	5
Climate	6
Recent history	6
THE BIRDS	7
Geographic distribution of the breeding species	7
Origins and routes of invasion	8
Colonization patterns	10
Turnover rates	11
4—THE HABITATS AND THEIR BIRD COMMUNITIES	12
VEGETATION PATTERNS	12
General description	12
The structure of Grand Bahama habitats	13
Grouping of stands into habitat types	15
Alignment of stands along gradients	19
THE BIRD COMMUNITIES	21
Community structure	21
Bird species diversity	25
Total bird density	28
DISCUSSION—DIVERSITY AND DENSITY CORRELATES	30

5—BIRD DISTRIBUTION THROUGH THE HABITATS — 32

Dynamics of Density Distribution — 32
Concepts and models — 32
Habitat distribution patterns — 33

Habitat Selection — 36
Distribution by types — 36
Distribution along gradients — 36

Dispersion Amplitudes—Specialization — 39
Dispersion of species through the 25 stands — 39
Dispersion by types — 39
Dispersion along gradients — 41

Density—Dispersion Relations — 48

Overlap and Similarity — 51
Measuring overlaps — 51
Overlap and phylogenetic relationships — 52
Overlap and geographic derivation — 52
Ecological spacing — 54

6—THE PINE FOREST COMMUNITY—SEASONAL CHANGES — 55

Procedures and Definitions — 55

Seasonal Changes — 58
The breeding season community — 59
The wintering community — 60
The transient community — 62

Impact of the Winter Migrant Invasion — 63

7—SPATIAL DISTRIBUTION WITHIN THE PINE FOREST — 66

Vertical Distribution—Layers — 67
Vegetative structure and avian utilization at five levels — 67
Population structure in the five layers — 70

Compartment Distribution — 70
Physical characteristics of the compartments — 72
Bird species distribution through the compartments — 73

Population structure in the compartments — 75
 Seasonal changes in spatial distribution — 76
8—GUILD DISTRIBUTION WITHIN THE PINE FOREST — 80
 CONCEPTS AND DEFINITIONS — 80
 PROCEDURES — 81
 THE FORAGING GUILDS OF THE GRAND BAHAMA PINE FOREST — 83
  Ground-gleaning herbivores — 83
  Stem seed pluckers — 94
  Fruit and bud harvesters — 94
  Nectar sippers — 95
  Sap and cambium eaters — 96
  Foliage browsers — 96
  Ground-gleaning carnivores — 96
  Ground pouncers — 97
  Flower probers — 97
  Shrub foliage gleaners — 97
  Shrub stem drillers — 98
  Pine bark and wood drillers — 98
  Bark gleaners — 98
  Pine twig gleaners — 99
  Pine cone probers — 100
  Pine needle gleaners — 101
  Air sallyers — 102
  Air screeners — 103
 GUILD BIOMASS AND FOOD ABUNDANCE — 103
 GUILD STRUCTURE AND COMMUNITY DYNAMICS — 106
  Guild structure and diversity — 106
  Dispersion of species through the guilds — 106
 SPECIES OVERLAP AND COMPETITION — 109
ACKNOWLEDGMENTS — 111
SUMMARY — 112

CONCLUSIONS 115
LITERATURE CITED 115
APPENDIX—SPECIES ACCOUNTS 118

LIST OF FIGURES

Figure		Page
1.	Plant types and foliage compartments	4
2.	Map of the western Bahama Islands	6
3.	Continental and Antillean ranges of the breeding land birds of Grand Bahama	9
4.	Faunal derivation of the breeding land birds of Grand Bahama	10
5.	Map of Grand Bahama Island showing extent of forests and location of survey stands	12
6.	Cross-island profile showing vegetation zones and positions of survey stands	13
7.	Submature pine forests on Grand Bahama Island	14
8.	Young pine forest types and open stands	15
9.	Other Grand Bahama habitat types	16
10.	Distribution of the 25 survey stands on canopy height-canopy cover coordinates	17
11.	Distribution of the 25 stands on habitat gradient diagrams	20
12.	Bird species diversity plotted on habitat gradient diagrams	26
13.	Species number and diversity plotted against foliage height diversity at 25 sites	27
14.	Bird species number and diversity plotted against vegetation density (volume) at 25 sites	28
15.	Total bird density plotted on habitat gradient diagrams	29
16.	Total bird density plotted against total vegetation volume	31
17.	Hypothetical density distribution through habitats of declining quality	33
18.	Decreasing density through 10 favored stands for 34 common species	34
19.	Habitat distribution of Grand Bahama species with respect to tree, shrub, and exposed ground cover	40
20.	Habitat distribution of Grand Bahama species with respect to vegetation height and arboreal foliage volume	42
21.	Habitat distribution of Grand Bahama species with respect to shrub type and shrub plus ground cover foliage volume	44
22.	Permanent resident densities plotted on habitat gradient diagrams	46
23.	Winter resident densities plotted on habitat gradient diagrams	47
24.	Density in preferred stand plotted against dispersion amplitude	51
25.	Ordination of the Grand Bahama bird species for similarity of habitat selection	58
26.	Physiognomic structure and composition of the submature pine forests	59
27.	Temporal limits of the seasonal bird communities of Grand Bahama	62
28.	Monthly changes in size and composition of the pine forest bird communities	63
29.	Geographic sources of the migrant invaders—species	64
30.	Geographic sources of the migrant invaders—numerical representation	65
31.	Relation of avian insect gleaner biomass to food resource levels in 7 compartments	66
32.	Vertical distribution of common species in the pine forests	67
33.	Species diversity and density in 5 equal layers of the pine forests	69
34.	Relative abundance of species in the 5 equal layers	71
35.	Winter invader and permanent resident representation in the 5 equal layers	71
36.	Compartment distribution diagrams for 30 pine forest species	74
37.	Relative abundance of species in the 4 major compartments	75
38.	Relative abundance of species in 16 foraging guilds	85

TABLES

Table		Page
1.	Vegetation measurements in the 25 Grand Bahama habitats	14
2.	Bird densities at the 25 habitat sites—winter 1969	22
3.	Relation of dispersion types and behavior types in Grand Bahama land birds	35
4.	Percent distribution of the 34 common bird species through the 25 survey stands	37
5.	Distribution of species through 7 habitat types on Grand Bahama Island	48
6.	Position and dispersion of 5 pine foliage gleaners along 9 gradients of the pine forest habitat	50
7.	Habitat specialization along 7 gradients for various elements of the Grand Bahama land bird community	50
8.	Overlap in habitat selection in winter	53
9.	Habitat overlap and geographic derivation	54
10.	Habitat overlap and residency status	54
11.	Physiognomic characteristics of the submature pine forests	56
12.	Dominant tree and shrub species in submature pine forests	57
13.	Size, density and biomass of the 4 residency elements in the 3 seasonal pine forest communities	60
14.	Residency status, density, and biomass of member and visitor species in the 3 seasonal pine forest communities	61
15.	Vertical distribution of bird populations in the wintering community of the pine forest	68
16.	Volume and structural characteristics of the major habitat compartments of the pine forests	72
17.	Demographic characteristics of the bird populations in the 4 major compartments of the pine forest	77
18.	Compartment preferences of members of the wintering and breeding communities	78
19.	Guilds and guild provinces recognized in the submature pine forests	82
20.	Foraging guild distributions of members of the pine forest bird community	84
21.	Species densities in the foraging guilds	86
22.	Biomass of each species in the foraging guilds	88
23.	Percent species density composition of foraging guilds	90
24.	Percent biomass composition of foraging guilds	92
25.	Foraging methods of members of the needle-gleaning guild	102
26.	Composition and structure of the 18 foraging guilds of the Grand Bahama forest communities	107
27.	Overlap in guild membership in the wintering community	110
28.	Overlap in guild membership in the breeding season community	111

PREFACE

This monograph had its beginning 24 years ago when I undertook a study of the habitat distribution and structure of several communities of land birds in Central Africa. As I launched into this project it became clear that available techniques were totally inadequate for the quantitative analyses I needed and that it was up to me to develop new ones. Some progress was made that year with a system for describing and measuring habitats (Emlen 1956), but I returned to the States with no solid data on either population densities or habitat relations.

Returning to other research activities, I postponed further fieldwork on these problems until 1967 when I was able to devote a spring semester to a study of the structure and dynamics of the wintering bird communities of a grass-bushland area in southern Texas (Emlen 1972). The vegetative structure was relatively simple here, and besides improving my techniques of habitat description I worked intensively on developing census methods for small land birds, methods that would provide absolute density values by equating variables in transect counts with the detectability characteristics of each species (Emlen 1971).

After testing these habitat measurement and census techniques in a variety of situations, I selected the extensive pineland forests of the southeastern states and neighboring Bahama islands for the type of study I had tried to conduct in Africa 15 years before. The work of William B. Robertson in this area provided a valuable background on ecological conditions and faunal composition (Robertson 1955), and I began the studies described in this monograph in January of 1968.

During the 20 years since the conception of this project, approaches to the study of community ecology have changed considerably. Important new concepts on the niche, competition, and community dynamics have appeared, and emphasis has shifted strongly from descriptive studies to model building and testing. Work in the old pattern seems dimmed by the brilliance of these new studies. But I am repeatedly impressed that the imaginative creations of theoretical ecologists rarely survive long in this modern era of scientific ferment unless they are built on solid empirical data. Most of the speculations and interpretations in this monograph will doubtless be ephemeral as our science progresses; I only hope that the materials on which they are based will prove to be solid and clearly presented.

1—INTRODUCTION

This monograph represents an attempt to analyze the population structure and dynamics of a definitive avifauna. Unlike a typical faunal study it focuses on the densities and ecological distributions of species through the habitats and foraging substrates of the vegetation and undertakes to evaluate and interpret some of the factors underlying community structure and regulation. My approach is descriptive with an attempt to present a broad and balanced picture of the entire system.

I selected an island as the site not because of a particular interest in the problems of insularity, but because an island community is shielded by surrounding water barriers from the confusion of irregular ingress and egress by species that belong only peripherally or really do not belong at all.

As an island site for the study, Grand Bahama was large enough to provide an assortment of habitat types, yet small enough to minimize the confusing effects of regional nomadism and local geographic variation. One type, lowland pine forest, was represented extensively while others were restricted to small blocks or belts adequate to hold only limited populations. Grand Bahama is particularly well situated for observing the extent and impact of seasonal migrant invasions on the structure and integrity of resident communities. Little ornithological work has been done on Grand Bahama, but the avifauna of the region has been well covered during the past 50 years.

The fieldwork was done during the months of January through May in 1968 and 1969. In 1968 I spent alternate 2-week periods on Grand Bahama and in southern Florida censusing the bird populations and plotting their distribution through the vegetation of the pine forests for comparative material. In 1969 I spent the entire period on Grand Bahama, measuring community structures and population densities at 25 survey sites during January, February, and March, and conducting further census and behavior observations in the pine forests in April and May. I returned for brief visits in January and May of 1971 to check several details and to collect material on avian food resources in the pine foliage.

The study covered the small land birds only, those that interacted directly in exploiting the resources of the terrestrial vegetation and its invertebrates. Other members of this trophic assemblage, especially the lizards, should logically have been included. They are a minor element except in the shrubs and ground vegetation, but their omission is due primarily to my limited versatility and lack of time.

The rationale for ecological analysis in this study is to recognize three hierarchical systems of decreasing inclusiveness through which dispersion can be charted: a habitat level, a within-habitat compartment level, and a substrate level. Individual birds are regarded as ranging through the various subdivisions of these systems but concentrating their activities in those subdivisions where conditions are most favorable for their morphological and physiological characteristics. The organization of this monograph is based on this approach. After presenting background material in the first three chapters, I examine across-habitat distribution in chapters 4 and 5, and then compartment and substrate distribution in the pine forest habitat in chapters 6, 7, and 8.

Descriptive material on the bird species with scientific names and quantitative data on ecological and distributional characteristics is presented in an appendix. Nomenclature for North American species follows the A.O.U. Checklist (1957) and supplements (1973); for the Antillean species I have followed Bond (1971).

2—METHODS

SELECTION OF SURVEY SITES

I first surveyed the physiognomic and floristic characteristics of the vegetation of the island to determine the nature and range of habitat variation and to provide a basis for selecting appropriate tracts for intensive study. I then selected 25 tracts representing the full range of variation but each showing maximum internal uniformity of structure over at least 20 ha. Sketch maps of each tract were prepared, and transect routes 0.9–1.8 km in length were laid out bisecting the most typical portion of the tract, avoiding edges, and taking advantage of existing trails and roadways. Three tracts in the submature pine forests that dominated the island were used for intensive studies of within-forest distribution in 1968 (chapters 6, 7, and 8). The other 22 represented various habitat types and, together with the 3 submature forest areas, were used for studies of across-habitat distribution in 1969 (chapters 4 and 5).

HABITAT MEASUREMENTS

The vegetation at each of the 25 sites was sampled along a series of habitat dimensions of presumed importance to the birds. Data were recorded according to a systematic plan in the 3 submature pine forest tracts and less formally for the other 22 tracts. In the 3 submature forests the measurements were made at stations located by random number series within each of 60 blocks (20 in each stand) 66 m long and 90 m wide, evenly straddling the transect route. Each station point served as the center for measurements (trunk diameter, height, crown diameter, crown depth, and distance) of the nearest tree in each of three size classes (emergent, canopy, subcanopy) in each of four radial quadrants. Twenty points surrounding each station point (at 3-m intervals) along 4 equispaced radii) were used for data on tree canopy, shrub vegetation, and ground vegetation. Tree canopy (presence and type) was recorded with a zenith sighting device (Emlen 1967); shrub type, height, crown diameter, and species, and ground cover type, depth, and density were recorded by plumb line contacts. A total of 240 data points was thus obtained for most arboreal dimensions, and 1200 for the others.

Because of time limitations, vegetation evaluations on the other 22 tracts were made by less systematic sampling, pacing, and subjective comparison with diagrammatic representations of canopy cover. A shorthand system (Emlen 1956) was used in which vegetation type, foliage type, foliage density, canopy height, canopy cover, and patchiness were recorded in formulae representing the tree, shrub, and ground cover strata.

For within-habitat distribution studies the vegetation in all stands was apportioned into compartments based on plant type, vertical zone, and horizontal zone in the tree, shrub, and ground cover strata (Fig. 1). I recognized 7 plant types in the forest from dead stumps and emergent pines (towering above the dominant canopy) to ground cover, 5 vertical divisions or levels in each plant from the lower stem to upper crown, and 5 horizontal divisions arranged as concentric zones around each plant from the tree trunk or shrub core to the periphery and the empty space around and between plants. Any point in the entire space between the canopy top and the ground is thus assignable to 1 of 175 compartments in this system. In practice, many compartments were nonexistent, undetectable, or unmeasurable, and for data analysis the number was reduced by combinations and eliminations to 11.

The volume of standing vegetation (number of m^3 of space containing plant stems of foliage) was calculated for the 3 vegetation strata and the 11 recognized compartments of each stand. Viewing the average tree crown as a vertical cylinder with rounded top and bottom, I multiplied the mean crown depth in meters by 0.75 by the canopy cover in m^2 per ha for each tree class to give a volumetric density value in m^3 per ha. A similar procedure was used for the shrub and ground vegetation strata. Volumes for all compartments per ha were derived by calculating the percent representation of each in its stratum and multiplying by the stratum volume. Volume of the air space between plants was obtained by subtracting all compartment volumes from the total space between ground surface and tree tops. Values for bark and wood surfaces on tree trunks and stumps were calculated in surface units (m^2) by multiplying mean trunk circumference in the upper and lower half of trees by the trunk lengths.

The complexity of the habitat is important as a comprehensive environmental parameter in community studies but is difficult to reduce to a simple, meaningful index. In this study I followed the procedure introduced by MacArthur and MacArthur (1961), using the density of vegetation in three horizontal layers corresponding to the trees, shrubs, and ground cover as the basis for calculating an overall habitat diversity index. Because of marked differences in texture and screening characteristics of the foliage in the three layers on Grand Bahama, however, and because of the presumed importance of twigs and stems as perching substrates, I used the presence or absence of standing vegetation in blocks of volumetric space as the basis of measurements rather than the leaf surface or foliage screening measures adopted by the MacArthurs. The information theory equation ($H' = p_i \log^e p_i$) was used to calculate the index values. Natural logarithms were used in all diversity calculations.

Analysis of Habitat Distribution

The relative positions of the 25 stands with respect to three basic habitat features—canopy height, canopy coverage, and foliage type—are graphically displayed in Figure 10. The groupings of symbols in this figure provide a relatively objective basis for recognizing 7 habitat types useful in general discussions of species distributions. This approach of plotting stand positions on bicoordinate grids was also used as the basis for tracing the quantitative distribution of species and of various community attributes along selected habitat gradients (Fig. 11). Density or index values for a species are simply entered at the coordinate position

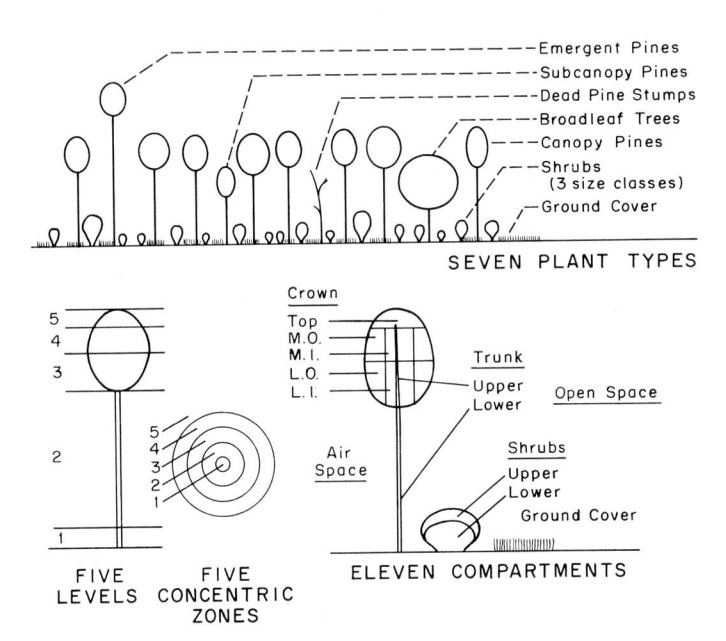

FIGURE 1. Plant types and foliage compartments used in structural analyses of the forest habitat. M.O. = middle outside, M.I. = middle inside, L.O. = low outside, L.I. = low inside.

of each stand in these diagrams. The resulting patterns provide graphic portrayals of density and attribute distributions along the selected gradients.

BIRD POPULATION MEASUREMENTS

Population densities for all bird species were obtained from transect counts converted to absolute values by applying locally determined detectability coefficients based on the lateral distribution pattern of detection points (Emlen 1971). All counts were started within a half hour after local sunrise and extended for from 1.2 to 2.1 hours. I always walked the transects alone, covering the route without deviations at between 1.0 and 1.6 km/hr. All detections, visual or auditory, were recorded.

WITHIN-HABITAT DISTRIBUTION AND ACTIVITY MEASUREMENTS

In addition to identifying each bird and estimating its lateral distance from the trail, I was able to record basic information on activity and position within the habitat for most of the detections tallied on the census transects. These observations included activity when first detected (whether foraging, singing, resting, being agressive), plant type in which located, vertical position (level) in the plant, radial position (zone) in the plant, and height above the ground. Weather conditions (temperature, cloud cover, wind direction and speed, wetness of vegetation) were also recorded for all trips afield.

Close attention to the task of detecting and recording all birds encountered on the morning transect counts precluded sustained observations of behavior and foraging methods. Unscheduled observation time later in the day was used for such work as well as for measuring vegetation, finding nests, and mapping territories. In these unscheduled observations I recorded the basic information described above plus data on age of the subjects, presence and activity of conspecific and allospecific associates, the foraging perch, the food substrate, and the foraging method. After an observation or series of observations in one place I evaluated the local habitat selection by recording the type, size, and density of foliage within approximately 1 m of the bird, and the proportion of tree cover, shrub cover, and exposed ground cover within an estimated 36-m radius (1 acre).

I used spaced observation units rather than seconds of continuous observing on the assumption that they would give a more balanced and representative picture of foraging activity by a population. In order to further suppress biases related to atypical local conditions or individual idiosyncrasies, I attempted to distribute observations as widely as possible in these activity observations. Where one individual or an uncommon species remained for continuous observation, I spaced the entries at a minimum of ½ min, and limited the record to 5 entries in a series. For compartment distribution analyses, the bias inherent in selected observation situations was avoided by using only the transect count tallies.

3—GRAND BAHAMA ISLAND

The Environment

Geology.—Geologically, Grand Bahama Island is a long low ridge of oolitic limestone of Pleistocene age, rising at its highest point to only about 10 m above sea level. The ground surface is heavily eroded with innumerable pits and deep solution holes. Soil is essentially absent, the organic materials deposited from the vegetation leaching or settling to the bottom of the holes.

Physiographic history.—Being a tectonically stable border ridge of the Little Bahama Bank (Fig. 2), the surface area of Grand Bahama expanded many fold when sea levels were low during the Pleistocene glacial epochs and alternately shrank to zero or nearly zero during the interglacial period of high sea level. Thus the terrestrial flora and fauna were probably annihilated repeatedly by marine inundation, the last such episode, according to data from southern Florida, ending about 80,000 years ago (Alt and Brooks 1965). No direct land connections except with neighboring Abaco Island have existed since the tertiary. During the Pleistocene ice advances, however, the broad low surface of the Little Bahama land mass, of which Grand Bahama is a part, extended to within 50 km of the Great Bahama land mass to the south which, in turn, approached to within 35 km of Cuba. All of this complex has been separated from the peninsula of Florida since at least tertiary times by the deep and relatively wide (105 km) rapidly flowing current of the Florida straits.

Since emerging from the deep seas of the Sangamon interglacial period (80,000 years ago) Grand Bahama Island has fluctuated in size from its present 1200 km^2 or smaller to 16,500 km^2, the area of the Little Bahama Bank of which it is a part. Estimates of a sea-level subsidence to the −120 m mark during the last Wisconsin ice advance (about 15,000 years ago) (Milliman and Emery 1968)

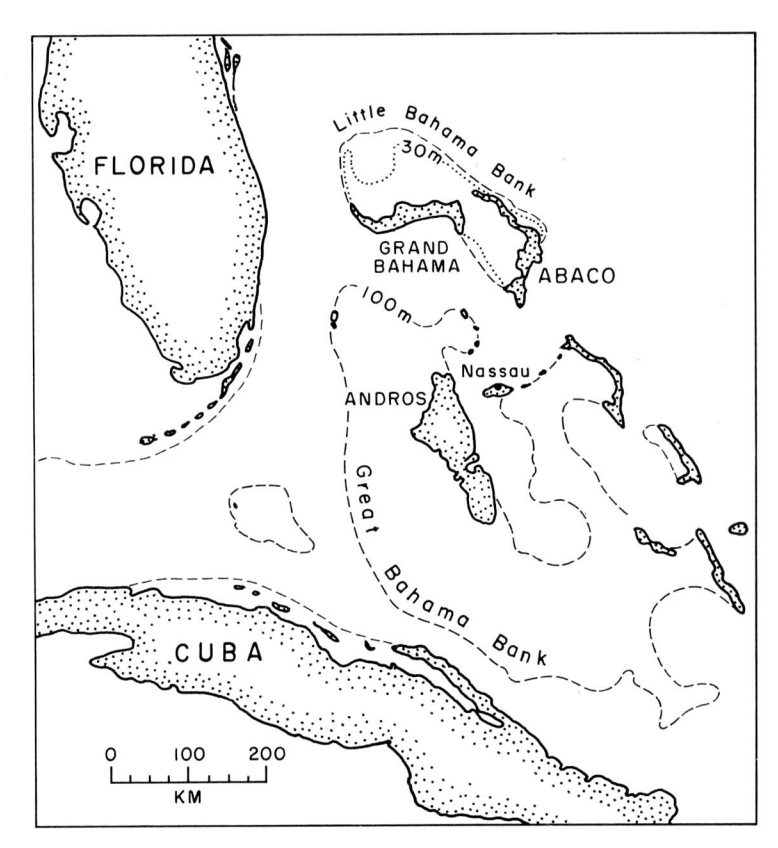

FIGURE 2. Map of the western Bahama Islands showing their position with relation to neighboring land masses and to shallow "banks" that mark the extent of the island areas during Pleistocene glacial periods.

would indicate an expansion to about 15,000 km² at that time. Since then the sea has been rising slowly, reaching a stage of −7 m about 4,000 years ago (Scholl et al. 1969). At this level the island of Grand Bahama must still have been six or eight times its present size and formed a continuous land mass with neighboring Abaco Island. The major shrinking in size has occurred over the past few thousand years during which sea levels have been rising at about 0.5 m per 1,000 years (Scholl et al., op. cit.).

Climate.—The climate of Grand Bahama Island is subtropical with temperatures ranging from a mean of 20.3°C in January to 28.2 in July (data from the Freeport airport). Annual rainfall averages 1,216 mm and occurs throughout the year with about twice as much in summer as in winter. The trade winds produce a dominant southeasterly air flow varying in direction and intensity under the influence of cyclonic disturbances to the north. Hurricanes occur occasionally in late summer, the most recent severe storms hitting the island in 1941 and 1949.

Recent history.—Grand Bahama was almost undisturbed and essentially unpopulated until 1929 when extensive timber cutting was initiated. Most of the timber was stripped from the island for mine props or pulp during the late 1940's and 1950's, but reproduction has been rapid since that time, and no extensive cutting other than local clearance for real estate development has been done since 1959. Stands cut between 1946 and 1949 were 10 and 12 m high in 1968 and possessed a lush shrub understory on the south half of the Island, less lush on the north half. Stands cut during the 1950's showed various stages of recovery reflecting mean growth rates of roughly 0.5–0.6 m per year. Height, density, and understory vegetation are secondarily influenced by irregular ground fires and occasional crown fires. A few small tracts of pine were apparently denuded by salt water encroachments during storms.

The principal method used in timber cutting in the 1940's and 1950's was to remove all trees other than saplings and a few tall scattered stems (about five trees per acre) used for anchoring the hauling gear and supposedly as seed trees for forest reproduction. The remaining small trees and brush were then usually levelled and burned. This procedure has resulted in rather even-aged stands with a scattering of slender relic "emergents" above the dominant young canopy. One patch of about 4.4 km^2 on the north side was completely cleared and kept open for habitation and farming during the early lumbering period. Abandoned for 10–12 years, it is now vegetated with bracken, coarse forbs, and tall grasses, and except for the narrow coastal strips and a few urban areas and golf courses, constitutes the only open land on the island.

Further disturbances caused largely by real estate operations since 1959 include the construction of the city of Freeport-Lucaya west of the Island's center, now covering about 30 km^2, and a network of unpaved development roads penetrating in an irregular network into nearly one-half of the Island's interior.

The Birds

At the time of this study (1968–69) there were apparently 33 species of land birds excluding birds of prey breeding on Grand Bahama Island. Thirty of these were permanent residents, and three were summer residents migrating in from winter ranges to the south. An additional 34 species moved in from the north during the winter season, and 8 more were present briefly as transients during the spring migration period.

Geographic derivation of the breeding species.—Grand Bahama, an oceanic island, contains no relict continental species in its breeding fauna and has been populated entirely by over-water colonization from the neighboring continents and islands. Because of the relative recency of its final emergence as an island capable of supporting a terrestrial fauna, it presents a good opportunity to study the geographic origins of its colonists. The two primary sources are obviously the North American continent to the north and west and the Antillean Islands to the south. The nearest land on the continent is 105 km away across the deep and geologically ancient Florida straits (Fig. 2). Cuba, the nearest and also the largest of the Antilles, lies about 500 km away, but one large "stepping stone" (Andros Island) and a series of smaller ones have been continuously available for dispersing birds since Grand Bahama's emergence. The water barriers to the south and north of Andros were about 35 and 50 km wide respectively at lowest sea level 15,000 years ago, and are 190 and 180 km wide at the present time.

Abaco Island, lying about 30 km to the east of Grand Bahama, is merely another ridge on the Little Bahama Bank, and, not surprisingly, has a very similar avian fauna.

Origins and routes of invasion.—In the absence of a direct record of invasions and colonizations, the present geographic ranges of the members of the fauna provide the best available indication of origins and routes of invasion. The direction and extent of the ranges of each of the 33 members of the breeding land bird fauna are graphically portrayed in Figure 3. Circles to the left of the central circle in this diagram indicate continental affinities; circles to the right indicate Antillean affinities. The degree of shading in each lateral circle reflects the closeness of phylogenetic relationship of the related forms in each of four increasingly remote regions. Information incorporated in these diagrams, together with analyses of avian dispersal in the area by Chapman (1891) and Bond (1963), provides a basis for tentative deductions on the geographic derivation of each member of the Grand Bahama community. The deductions are presented in code form at the right of each species diagram in Figure 3. A graphic representation of the deduced origins and routes of invasion is presented in Figure 4.

Of the 32 species (exluding the introduced House Sparrow), 7 are best represented by conspecifics or other closely related forms on the continent to the northwest and are accordingly considered to have arrived directly from North America. Two of these, the wide-ranging Mourning Dove and the Blue-gray Gnatcatcher, have apparently developed no taxonomically recognized morphological changes since colonizing Grand Bahama (C_0). Four, the Hairy Woodpecker, the Brown-headed Nuthatch, the Yellow-throated Warbler, and the Pine Warbler have been recognized by taxonomists as subspecifically distinct on the island (C_1), and one, the Bahama Yellowthroat, is considered to have evolved to full species status (C_2).

The ancestors of 11 of the community members appear to have come from North or Central America relatively recently but reached Grand Bahama by way of the Greater Antilles. All of these have changed morphologically in the course of their Caribbean peregrinations. The sequence of events in the course of their history of dispersal requires considerable speculation, but three species, the Cuban Nighthawk, Northern Mockingbird, and Yellow Warbler, apparently subspeciated in the Greater Antilles before spreading north into the Bahamas ($C_1 A_0$); one, the Ground Dove, has several distinct races in the West Indies, all different from the continental forms, and probably has subspeciated at least twice in reaching Grand Bahama ($C_1 A_1$). Five species are found in the Greater Antilles as well as in the Bahamas and belong to superspecies or sibling species groups also occurring on the North American continent. Their ancestral dispersal routes thus probably included early invasions of the Greater Antilles where they speciated before spreading northward to the Bahamas. Two of these, the Black-whiskered Vireo and Olive-capped Warbler, show no further morphological changes en route to the northern Bahamas ($C_2 A_1$). Two species, the Bahama Swallow and the Thick-billed Vireo, I regard as belonging to superspecies groups with specifically distinct representatives on several Antillean islands as well as the Bahamas. Ancestors of the Grand Bahama forms probably speciated several times en route to their present range ($C_2 A_2$). The interpretation of the Bahama Swallow (*Cal-*

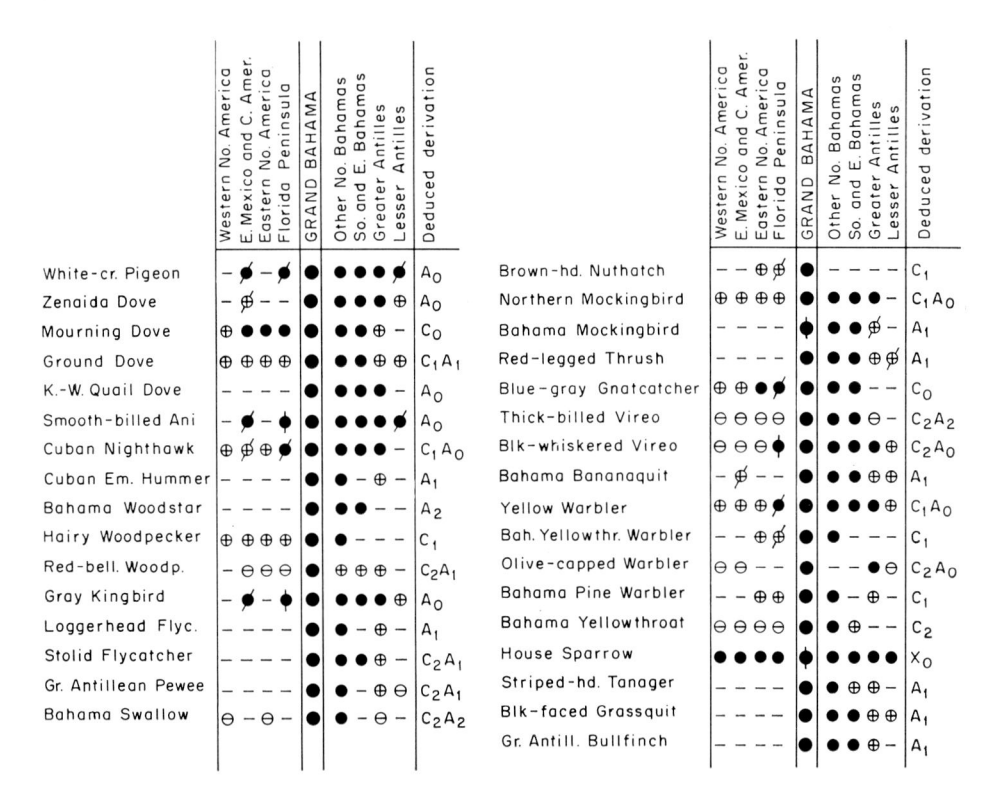

FIGURE 3. Continental and Antillean ranges of the breeding land birds of Grand Bahama Island. The presence of the same or related forms (same subspecies, species, superspecies) is indicated at four increasingly remote stations in each of the two directions. (Except for the Bahama Swallow, taxonomy follows Bond (1971) and the AOU Checklist (1957) and supplements thereof (1973). My deductions concerning the geographic derivation of each form on Grand Bahama are indicated by symbols at the right of the diagrams. Symbols for degree of relationship are: Solid circle = same subspecies; circle with cross = same species, different subspecies; circle with horizontal line = same superspecies, different species; diagonal line cutting circle = limited occurrence; vertical line cutting circle = recent colonizer. Symbols for deduced derivation are: C = North American continental origin, A = Antillean origin, CA = Continent via Antilles. X = introduced by modern man, /1 = subspeciated with invasion, /2 = speciated with invasion, /0 = no change recorded.

lichelidon) as congeneric with *Lamprochelidon* is based on a composite of taxonomists' opinions (L. Short *in litt.*).

The 14 species classed as of Antillean origin belong to genera that probably derived at an early period from ancestral forms in either Central or South America (Bond 1963). Five of these, the White-crowned Pigeon, the Zenaida Dove, the Key West Quail Dove, the Smooth-billed Ani, and the Gray Kingbird, now have dispersed ranges in the West Indies and show no taxonomically recognized changes in their northward extension into the Bahamas (A_0). Nine species have undergone taxonomically recognized changes in the Bahamas; eight of these, the Cuban Emerald Hummingbird, Loggerhead Flycatcher, Bahama Mockingbird, Red-legged Thrush, Bahama Bananaquit, Striped-headed Tanager, Black-faced Grassquit, and

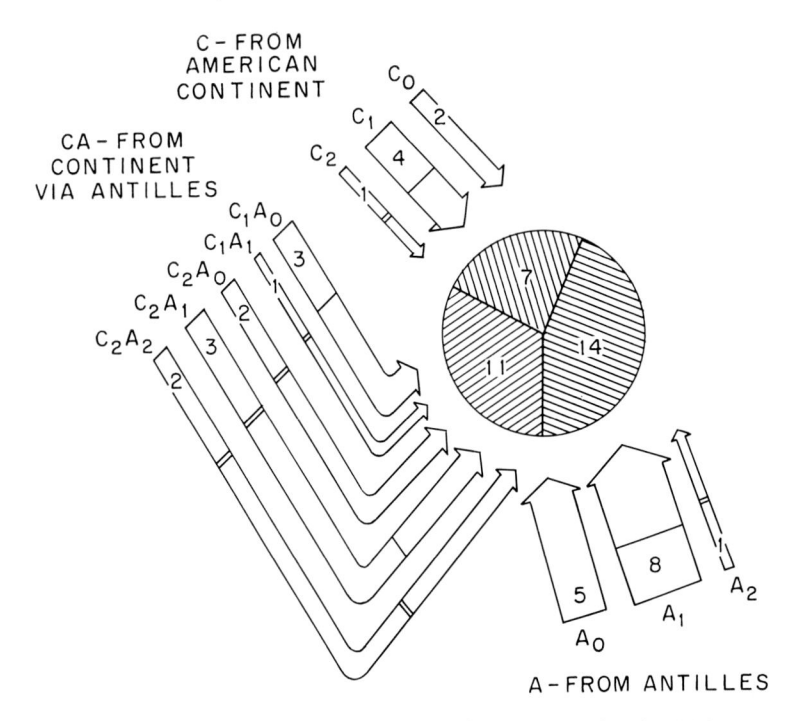

FIGURE 4. Faunal derivation of the species comprising the breeding land bird fauna of the Grand Bahama Island. Each arrow represents a group of species. The width of the arrow indicates the number of species in the group. A cross line on the arrow shaft shows that subspeciation has occurred; a double line, that full speciation has occurred. The symbols at the base of each arrow match those used in Figure 3.

Greater Antillean Bullfinch, to the subspecies level (A_1) and one, the Bahama Woodstar, to the species level (A_2).

Colonization patterns.—Generalizations based on patterns of dispersion through island chains can provide suggestions on colonization histories and sequences. Of the seven species colonizing Grand Bahama directly from North America only two have pushed farther into the Antilles than the first few northern Bahama Islands (cf. Fig. 3) and these two, the Mourning Dove and the Pine Warbler, occurring as distinct subspecies in the Greater Antilles, may have reached those sites by an earlier invasion or a separate invasion from Central America. Such patterns of limited and essentially unbroken penetration of the island chain suggest recent invasion, i.e. an early stage in taxon dispersion as visualized by Ricklefs and Cox (1972) in their taxon cycle model for archipelagos. From the other direction, the Southeast, Grand Bahama is at the end of a long island chain of dispersion. The 25 species considered to have come by this route tend to show the extended and broken distribution patterns that characterize advanced stages in the taxon cycle of Ricklefs and Cox.

These observations suggest that members of the Antillean faunal element have, in general, a longer history in the northern Bahama Islands than those of the North American element. Other factors must be considered, however, especially the vegetation patterns through the Bahamas and the habitat characteristics of the bird species. Pine forests dominate Grand Bahama and the other northern islands, while brushy vegetation cover the islands to the south and east. With the exception of the Mourning Dove, a highly eurytopic species, all seven of the colonizers from North America are pine forest inhabitants on Grand Bahama, even the Gnatchatcher and the Yellowthroat, which elsewhere are characteristically broad leaf forest and marshland birds respectively. This does not conform with Ricklef and Cox's generalization that recent (stage I) colonizers tend to occupy open, coastal, or disturbed habitats. On Grand Bahama these habitats are, in fact, occupied by species belonging to the Antillean element, species that according to the island penetration and broken distribution criteria, should be in advanced stages of the taxon cycle.

More direct evidence that the bird species of the North American element of pineland birds did not invade the northern Bahamas until quite recently comes from fossil pollen data indicating that pines were uncommon in the southern Florida vegetation until about 5,000 years ago (Watts 1971). The conditions of rising sea levels and permeable limestone rock associated with this spread of pine forests in Florida must have also existed and could have produced similar effects on the Little Bahama Bank. Bahamian Pines (*Pinus caribaea*) probably reached Grand Bahama from the south (Howell 1972), but whether the present forests were established before the postglacial period of sea level elevation is unknown. Avian fossil materials from New Providence Island (Brodkorb 1959) indicate that arboreal bird species and hence trees were present on the Great Bahama Bank to the southeast during the last glacial stage of the Wisconsin glaciation.

Turnover rates.—The faunal history of an island such as Grand Bahama is of course more than a progressive succession of colonizations. Many extinctions and replacements have undoubtedly occurred over the millenia, and some species may have had a history of repeated extinctions and recolonizations. MacArthur and Wilson (1967) proposed that the number of species present on an island at a given time reflects an equilibrium between the colonization rate related particularly to distance from colonization sources, and the extinction rate related particularly to island size. Recent studies on previously surveyed islands off southern California (Diamond 1969), in the South Pacific (Diamond 1970), in the Virgin Islands (Robertson 1962), the Cayman Islands (Johnston 1975), and on Mona Island near Puerto Rico (Terborgh and Faaborg 1973) suggest that a considerable number of both extinctions and new colonizations have occurred on all of these islands during the past 50–75 years. Such data, if accurate, suggest that turnover rates of roughly 1.0–1.5% per year may be representative for islands of the size and position of Grand Bahama, but other observers (Lynch and Johnson 1976, Lack 1976) have challenged these values as artifacts of modern human intervention.

Historical data do not exist to permit direct estimates of colonization or extinction rates on Grand Bahama. One species, the West Indian Red-bellied Woodpecker, listed as an uncommon species in coastal scrub forest by Bond in 1936, was apparently missing in 1968–69, and two species not noted by Bond, the Mourning Dove and House Sparrow, were present locally and in small numbers

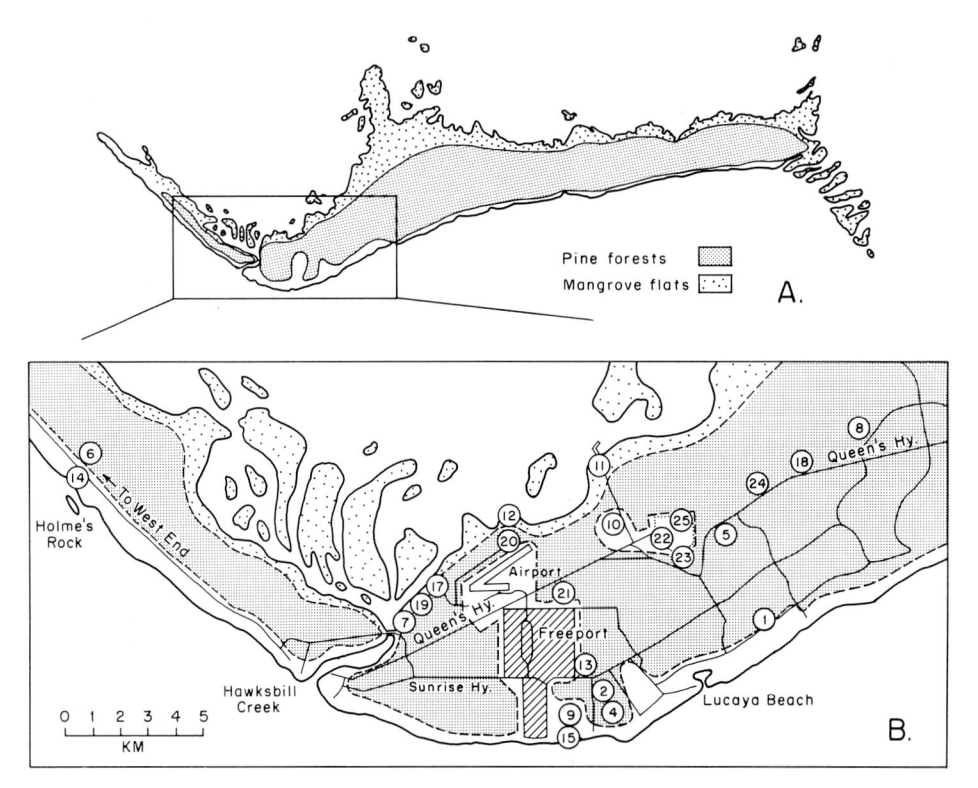

FIGURE 5. Map of Grand Bahama Island showing in A the distribution of pine forests and mangrove flats and in B the location of the 25 stands surveyed in this study.

in the latter years. The Bahama Mockingbird, not reported on Grand Bahama by Bond, was collected in 1960 (Schwartz and Klinikowski 1963) and was seen by several amateur observers during the early 60's and by me in 1969.

4—THE HABITATS AND THEIR BIRD COMMMUNITIES

The term bird community is used in this chapter to designate all the birds that co-occupy an area of habitat at a particular season and hence interact directly with each other. The fauna of Grand Bahama Island is thus composed of an array of communities differing both spatially and temporally. Variation is continuous along both axes, but I have assigned a series of spatial categories on the basis of localities or vegetation types, and of temporal categories on the basis of the arrival and departure periods of seasonal migrants. In this chapter I examine the spatial distribution of the birds present on the Island between 10 January and 31 March 1969 while the winter migrants were still present, i.e. the wintering communities.

VEGETATION PATTERNS

General description.—Most of the interior of Grand Bahama Island (roughly 80% of the land surface) is covered with moderately dense forests of Caribbean

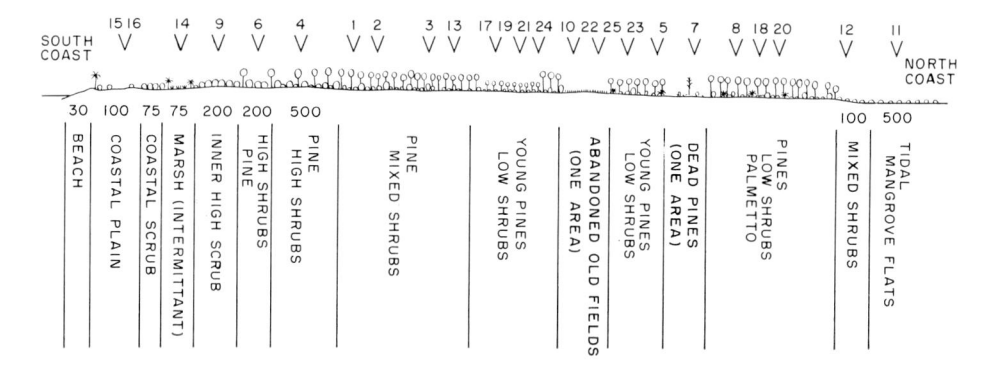

FIGURE 6. Cross-island profile (schematic) transecting the major vegetation zones and types; approximate average widths of zones are given in meters. The positions of the 25 survey stands with respect to the vegetation zones are indicated above the diagram; the numbers correspond to those in Table 17 and the map in Figure 5.

Pine (*Pinus caribaea*). Much of this forest was clear cut during the late 1940's and early 1950's, but the very rapid growth has restored the appearance of submature forest over most of the area. Broad tidal flats with open, low mangrove scrub separate the pine forests from the sea on the north or leeward side of the island. The higher windward front on the southern shore supports a series of parallel vegetation belts generally progressing from a narrow beach backed by low sand dunes and occasional palms, through a narrow coastal strip of halophytic grasses, herbs, and low dense shrubs and a strip of dense 3-m-high broad-leaf scrub with pockets of cattail marsh to a wider band of 4–5 m scrub that blends back into the pines. The distribution of these major vegetation types is mapped in Figure 5 and shown in a cross-island profile in Figure 6.

Photographs in Figure 7 depict conditions in the submature pine forests as they appeared in 1968; those in Figure 8 show the vegetation in recently cut forests and in one older stand. Vegetation features of other habitat types are shown in Figure 9.

The structure of Grand Bahama habitats.—Measurements and evaluations of habitat features considered to be significant to birds are presented in Table 1 for each of the 25 stands surveyed in this study. Included are features of each of the three strata in the vegetation plus an index of overall habitat complexity or diversity. The figures in each case are averages for conditions within the stand.

Mean tree height varied from 2 m in a recently cut stand (stand #24—est. 4 yrs.) to 16 m (max. 22 m) in the oldest of the submature forests (#1—est. 30+ yrs.). Trunk diameters in these two stands averaged 5.5 cm and 28 cm (max. 35 cm) respectively. Old cut stumps rarely exceeded 35 cm in diameter at any site, suggesting that this approximates the maximum size attained locally by the Carib Pine in undisturbed forests.

Except for two badly disturbed sites and one marginal pine-broadleaf thicket, tree canopy cover varied from 19–45% with densities as great as 60% in patches of up to ½ ha. In several stands there were 2 distinct height classes reflecting 2 major disturbances spaced 8–10 years apart. In such cases the lower stratum

TABLE 1
VEGETATION MEASUREMENTS IN 25 GRAND BAHAMA HABITATS

#	A[1]	Percent cover T[2] Sh[3] G[4]	D[5]	Pine trees Age classes M[6] A[7] Y[8]	Ht[9]	Vol.[10]	C[11]	Shrub stratum Size classes T[12] M L	Foliage types B[13] P F G	Vol.[14]	Ground cover Vegetation types G[15] H V L	Vol.[16]	Tot. vol.[17]	V.H.D.[18]
1	30+	38:29:33	567	32: 4: 2	16.0	11,571	46	1: 4: 5	6:1:2:1	4,035	2:0:2:6	900	16,506	0.742
2	25	36:37:27	612	1:35: 5	11.2	10,962	58	2: 5: 3	6:2:1:1	6,011	2:0:2:6	1,100	18,073	0.836
3	22	37:35:28	552	2:32: 3	10.3	11,266	56	1: 3: 6	6:3:0:1	4,250	1:0:3:6	1,000	16,516	0.781
4	25	20:68:12	299	10: 6: 5	12.0	6,090	85	2: 1: 8	6:2:2:0	5,593	4:4:1:1	(900)	12,583	0.899
5	12	30:28:42	448	5: 0:25	5.0	9,135	40	0: 0:10	3:6:0:1	2,164	7:3:0:0	—	12,199	0.711
6	—	2:78:20	45	0: 2: 1	9.0	609	80	6: 3: 1	8:0:2:0	25,000	1:7:1:1	(500)	26,109	0.195
7	5	1:40:59	16	1: 0: tr	14.0	305	40	0: 0:10	5:5:0:0	1,652	3:3:3:1	(400)	2,357	0.816
8	27	45:38:17	672	5:40: 0	11.0	13,702	70	0: 0:10	6:3:0:1	3,837	3:2:2:3	(900)	18,439	0.701
9	—	0:90:10	0	0: 0: 0	—	0	90	8: 1: 1	10:0:0:0	18,500	1:6:0:3	(400)	18,900	0.098
10	25	0: 2:98	0	0: 0: 0	—	0	1	0: 0:10	10:0:0:0	200	9:0:1:0	8,000	8,200	0.098
11	—	0:40:60	0	0: 0: 0	—	0	40	0: 0:10	9:0:0:1	2,100	—	(100)	2,200	0.198
12	—	0:54:46	0	0: 0: 0	—	0	54	0: 1: 9	9:0:0:1	2,850	—	200	3,050	0.254
13	20	31:34:35	463	1:30: 0	8.0	9,440	50	0: 0:10		2,884	—	(900)	13,224	0.519
14	—	0:48:42	0	0: 0: 0	—	0	58	4: 5: 1	5:0:0:5	7,500	8:2:0:0	5,000	12,500	0.673
15	—	0:12:88	0	0: 0: 0	—	0	12	2: 4: 4	6:0:0:4	1,100	7:2:1:0	8,000	9,100	0.367
16	—	0:12:88	0	0: 0: 0	—	0	12	2: 4: 4	6:0:0:4	1,100	7:2:1:0	8,000	9,100	0.367
17	8	22:57:21	329	2: 0:20	4.0	6,699	60	0: 1: 9	4:5:0:1	3,350	1:5:4:0	(900)	10,949	0.866
18	20	36:32:32	538	1:35: 0	10.0	10,962	50	0: 0:10	3:6:0:1	2,596	3:2:4:1	—	14,458	0.685
19	8	6:47:47	90	2: 0: 4	4.0	1,827	50	0: 0:10	5:4:0:1	2,662	3:3:3:1	(600)	5,089	0.962
20	25	25:52:23	373	15: 5: 5	12.0	7,613	70	0: 0:10	6:3:0:1	3,746	3:3:3:1	(1,000)	12,359	0.859
21	8	26:37:37	388	1: 0:25	4.0	7,917	50	0: 4: 6	6:3:0:1	4,086	3:2:5:0	(600)	12,603	0.805
22	20	tr: 6:94	2	tr: 0: 0	12.0	100	6	2: 3: 5	10:0:0:0	700	9:1:0:0	9,000	9,700	0.300
23	8	19:59:22	284	1: 0:18	4.0	5,786	73	tr: tr:10	5:5:0:0	4,651	—	(900)	11,337	0.911
24	4	36:33:31	538	6: 0:30	2.0	10,962	52	0: tr:10	5:5:0:0	2,900	3:2:3:2	(600)	14,462	0.659
25	20	tr: 2:98	2	tr: 0: 0	14.0	100	2	1: 3: 6	10:0:0:0	200	2:0:0:8	11,000	11,200	0.018

was generally quite dense (35–40%) while the older trees produced a 10–20% canopy.

The shrub understory of pinelands varied considerably between sites in composition height and density, differences presumably being attributable to substrate water, fire history, and perhaps windborne moisture. North of a line running longitudinally down the middle of the island, shrubs were generally low, relatively sparse, and often dominated by Palmetto (*Thrinax microcarpa*). South of this line and especially near the south coast the shrub stratum was relatively tall and lush with many Tamarinds (*Lysiloma*) century plants (*Agave*), and only a few palmettos.

Broadleaf shrubs reached their greatest height and richness behind the dunes along the south coast where one study area (#9) was located. Here, often in standing fresh water, they formed nearly impenetrable closed canopy thickets or "coppets" 3–5 m high, from which pines were largely or completely excluded. Where the water was brackish the typical mixed coppets with *Metopium, Bumelia, Torrubia, Ilex, Rapanea, Annona*, etc. gave way to monotypic thickets of red mangrove (*Rhizophora*).

Grass dominated in the ground stratum in roughly inverse proportion to tree and/or shrub canopy except in one case (#25) where bracken fern replaced the grass, probably in response to recent burning.

An index of overall habitat complexity, expressed as vegetation height diversity (VHD), is presented in the last column of Table 1. It was highest in the pine forest stands where all three strata were well represented. It was lowest in the open or shrub habitats. Dense foliage in the closed canopy thickets tended to shade out the ground vegetation to produce a nearly one-stratum (shrub) situation.

Grouping of stands into habitat types.—The three vegetational features most commonly incorporated into the descriptive names applied to avian habitats by ornithologists: canopy height, canopy cover, and foliage type of the dominant stratum, are presented graphically in Figure 10 for the 25 stands studied on Grand Bahama Island. Canopy cover and height of the dominant stratum are plotted on the x and y axes respectively, and the foliage type, a complex multidimensional feature, is indicated qualitatively by symbols. The numbered symbols representing

---

←

[1] Age in years (A) estimated from sample ring counts and historical records.
[2-4] Proportion of the area covered by trees (T), shrubs without trees (Sh), and ground vegetation or bare ground alone (G).—expressed as percents.
[5] Tree density (D = number per hectare).
[6-8] Proportion of age classes: M = mature (DBH > 20 cm), S = submature (DBH, 10–20 cm), and Y = young (DBH < 10 cm).
[9] Canopy height (Ht.). (Top of canopy of the best represented age class.)
[10] Volume of space occupied by pine foliage (m³/ha).
[11] Total shrub cover (C) as percent of ground surface covered by shrubs. (The value in column 3 is the percent of surface with shrubs not covered by tree crowns.)
[12] Proportion of shrub size classes in tenths. Shrubs > 2 m are classified as tall (T), less than 1 m as low (L).
[13] Proportion of foliage types in tenths (B = broadleaf), (P = palmetto), (F = ferns), (G = grasses).
[14] Volume of space occupied by shrubs (Vol.). Sum of area × depth of each height class (m³/ha).
[15] Proportion of vegetation types in ground stratum in tenths. (G = grass, H = herbs, V = vines, L = litter, F = ferns).
[16] Volume of space occupied by ground cover (Vol.). Area × mean depth (m³/ha).
[17] Total volume of standing foliage in m³/ha. (Sum of columns 10 + 14 + 16).
[18] Habitat Diversity (vegetation height diversity—$H' = \sum p_i \log_e p_i$) where p_i is the proportion of m³ of habitat space containing standing vegetation that falls in the ith layer of three horizontal layers below the tree top level—a ground layer 1 m deep (0.1 m), a shrub layer 4 m deep (1–5 m), and a tree layer 7 m deep (5–12 m).

FIGURE 7. Submature pine forests on Grand Bahama Island. A, general view in stand 2 (20–25 years, medium density N38/35+ BP8/5, 5/10, 2/10+ GVB); B, stand 3 (20–25 years, medium+ density N36/38+ BP10/2, 4/8, 2/10+ BVG; C, shrub stratum in stand 2; D, ground cover in stand 2. (For explanation of descriptive code see Emlen 1956).

FIGURE 8. Variant pineland types. A, an area with high tree density (near 3); B, pine-coppet transition (4); C, a medium-dense stand with palmetto in understory (18); D, young pines in recently cut stand (24); E, an old stand (portion of 1); F, old dead trees and scrub in cut and flooded area (7).

FIGURE 9. Other Grand Bahama habitats. A, coastal beach with tall grasses and dense shrubs (16); B, brushy marsh with tall grasses and cattails (14); C, dense broadleaf thicket (coppet) behind the coastal dunes (9); D, tidal flats with mangroves (11).

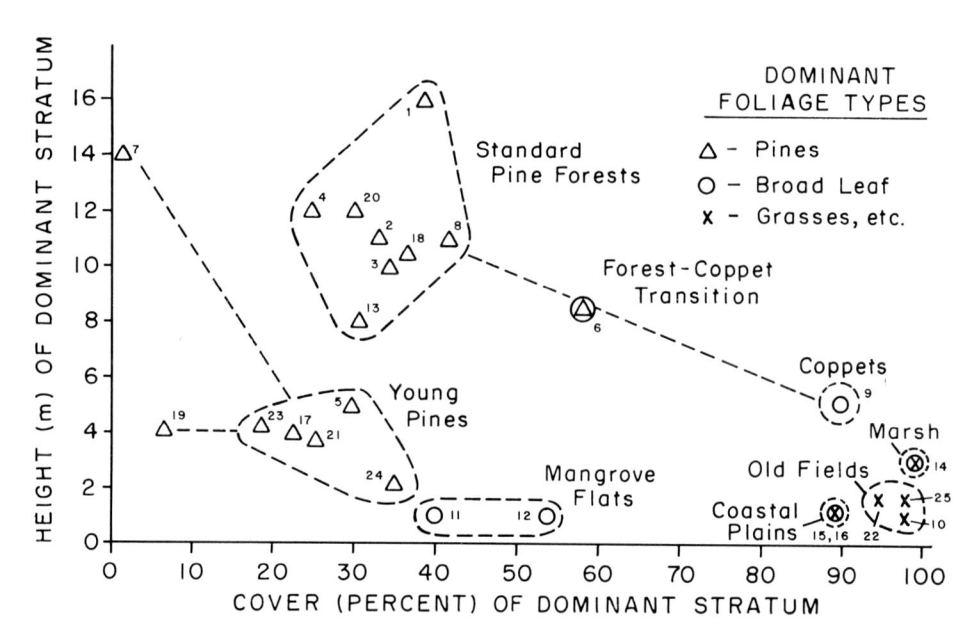

FIGURE 10. Delineation of the major habitat types on Grand Bahamas as determined by the distribution of the 25 survey stands on canopy height and canopy cover coordinates and by foliage types (indicated by symbols).

the 25 stands in this diagram fall into 7 rather distinct clusters corresponding to subjectively conceived vegetation types considered in the first few paragraphs of this chapter. Two man-created types, lawn (golf courses) and urban development, are not covered in this study.

Alignment of stands along gradients.—Diagrams similar to those used for delineating habitat types in Figure 10 are presented for seven additional variable features of potential significance to birds in Figure 11. The triangle at the top provides 3 axes for positioning each of the 25 stands with respect to the relative amounts of tree, shrub, and ground cover exposed to the sky. The middle and lower rectangles show tree height matched with pine vegetation volume, and understory foliage type matched with understory vegetation volume. By plotting these values on two or more axes, an appraisal of combination dimensions on the diagonals can also be made. Besides revealing the structural relationships of stands to each other in terms of specified dimensions, these diagrams can be used as bases for plotting habitat distributions of bird species (see Figs. 19, 20, 21) and of various community attributes (see Figs. 12 and 15).

In the triangle diagram of Figure 11, three open field sites (10, 22, 25) and two coastal plain sites (15, 16) appear in the lower left corner, hugging the base line (no trees) but variously displaced to the right (showing increasing amounts of shrub cover). The two mangrove flats (11 and 12) fall near the center of the base line, the marsh (14) with a mosaic of cattail and brush lies a little farther to the right, and the thicket site or coppet (9) falls in the lower right corner. The 16 pine forests are scattered over the heart of the triangle where trees, shrubs, and ground cover are all well represented. A site in the transition between forest

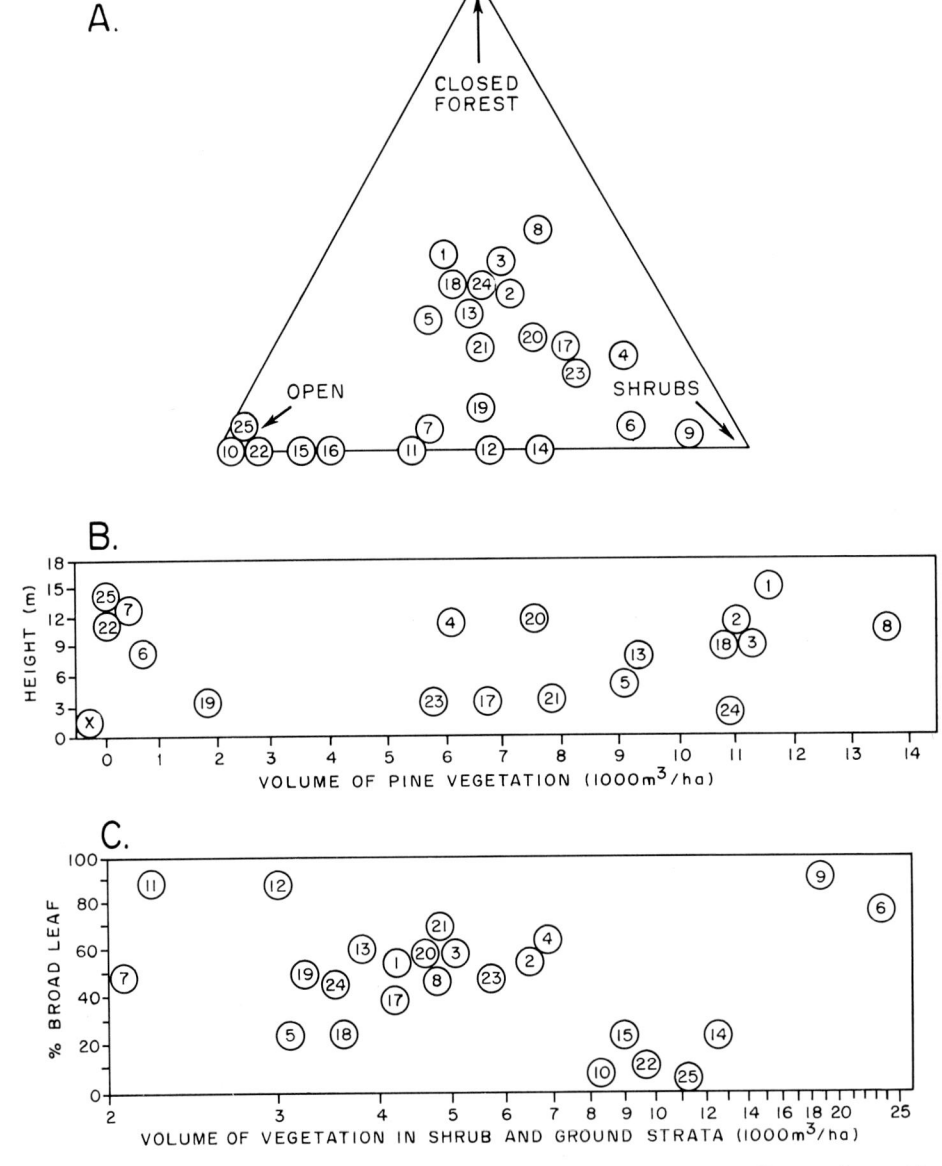

FIGURE 11. Position of the 25 survey stands along seven habitat gradients. A, position with respect to the proportions of tree cover, shrub cover and ground cover open to the sky; B, position with respect to volume of standing pine vegetation (1000 m³/ha) and tree height (of dominant age class); C, position with respect to volume of shrub and ground cover vegetation (1000 m³/ha), and foliage type (percent of total ground cover that has broadleaf foliage vs. grass, palmetto, ferns, etc.).

and coppet (6) appears below and to the right, while a stand that failed to regenerate after lumbering (7) lies below and near the base line.

In the central diagram of Figure 11 forest sites with high pine foliage volume appear in the right half while fields, marshes, and mixed coppets with only scattered pines are clustered at the left. Seven sites where there were no pine trees are represented by a single circle with an x at the lower left corner.

Tree height (vertical axis) in general reflects the time intervals since the last drastic lumbering at the site. Tree densities decline as individual crowns broaden with age so that canopy cover generally remains at between 25 and 40%, and standing vegetation volume at around 1,000 m^3 per km^2 through the growth cycle. Thus, while canopy height increases rather constantly with time for 20–30 years, pine vegetation volume is relatively independent of tree age and reflects a variety of other environmental factors.

In the lower rectangle of Figure 11 vegetation volume is represented horizontally on a log scale, and foliage type, expressed as the ratio of broad-leaves to all other foliage (palmetto, grasses, ferns, etc.), on the ordinate. The highest vegetation volumes occurred in the coppets and coppet-pine transition stands (9 and 6) appearing at the right end of the rectangle and high on the broadleaf scale. Not far to the left of these, but low on the vertical scale, are the circles representing the marsh habitat (14), dominated by cattails, and the two abandoned fields dominated by bracken fern (25) and tall grass (22). The two beach tracts (15 and 16, but combined and labelled 15), and the old field (10), characterized by relatively short and sparse grass, are centrally located along the base line of the long axis. Pine forests had relatively light understory vegetation and are clustered to the left of center. The two mangrove sites (11 and 12) with low vegetation volumes and high broadleaf ratios, appear at the upper left.

The Bird Communities

The bird species found in each of the 25 stands are listed in Table 2 with their population densities. The distribution of species across the stands in this table is examined in the next chapter. Only the community attributes of structure, diversity and density, as revealed by reading down the columns are considered here.

Community structure.—Community structure was analyzed with respect to species composition and the proportions of migrant and permanent resident elements in the membership.

Numerical dominance was held by the Palm Warbler in 12 of the 25 communities including most of those in pine forests, one on a mangrove flat (12), and one on the coastal strip (16). Other winter residents held the top numerical position in 8 more communities: the Common Yellowthroat in the marsh (14), one coastal strip (15), and one old field (22); the Catbirds in the coppet community (9), and an old field with dense bracken fern (25), the Grasshopper Sparrow in a grassy field (10), the Yellow-rumped Warbler in a pine stand (4), and the Northern Waterthrush in one mangrove community (11). Five communities had permanent resident species at the top: the Cuban Emerald Hummingbird dominated in three young pine stands (19, 21, 25), the Striped-headed Tanager in the coppet-pine transition community (6), and the Olive-capped Warbler in one tall pine community (8).

There are four seasonal residency elements in the Grand Bahama avifauna: nonmigratory permanent residents (hereafter designated PR), winter residents or invaders moving in from northern breeding grounds for the winter months

TABLE 2
Density (Individuals/km²) of Each Bird Species at the 25 Habitat Sites on Grand Bahama Island—Winter, 1969

Species	Coef. of detectability	Seasonal status[1]	1 p² 6.7³	2 p² 8.1³	3 p² 6.7³	4 p² 8.3³	5 Y² 4.1³	6 Th² 5.8³	7 Y² 5.6³	8 p² 5.5³
White-crowned Pigeon	.30	P	—	—	—	—	—	2.3	—	—
Mourning Dove	.25	P	—	—	—	—	—	—	—	—
Zenaida Dove	.20	P	2.9	15	—	12	—	10	—	—
Ground Dove	.20	P	6.0	—	3.0	17	—	3.5	—	—
Key West Quail Dove	.20	P	—	—	—	—	—	—	—	—
Smooth-billed Ani	.60	P	—	—	—	—	—	21	—	—
Cuban Emerald Hummingbird	.14	P	21	46	200	59	173	123	52	293
Bahama Woodstar	.12	P	—	—	—	—	—	—	5.8	18
Hairy Woodpecker	.35	P	16	11	10	11	17	24	4.0	12
Yellow-bellied Sapsucker	.22	W	5.4	6.8	5.5	—	—	—	—	10
Gray Kingbird	.60	S	—	—	—	—	—	—	—	—
Loggerhead Flycatcher	.30	P	9.8	1.7	4.0	4.8	9.7	2.3	—	2.3
Stolid Flycatcher	.30	P	—	—	2.0	—	—	7.0	—	—
Greater Antillean Pewee	.30	P	6.0	18	4.0	9.7	23	18	2.3	2.3
Bahama Swallow	.35	P	—	—	—	—	—	—	—	—
Brown-headed Nuthatch	.25	P	48	—	17	—	—	—	—	40
Gray Catbird	.18	W	—	69	20	145	—	188	—	—
N. Mockingbird	.65	P	—	2.3	—	9.7	—	2.1	—	—
Bahama Mockingbird	.60	P	—	—	—	—	—	—	—	—
Red-legged Thrush	.18	P	3.3	5.5	—	1.5	—	3.8	—	—
American Robin	.50	W	—	—	—	—	—	—	—	—
Blue-green Gnatcatcher	.25	P	46	62	28	60	23	00	2.8	2.8
Thick-billed Vireo	.36	P	20	36	3.3	42	33	65	—	1.9
Black and white Warbler	.17	W	14	15	7.0	14	—	4.1	—	—
Worm-eating Warbler	.10	W	—	—	—	—	—	—	—	—
Orange-crowned Warbler	.12	W	—	—	4.9	—	—	—	—	—
Parula Warbler	.12	W	—	21	—	24	—	5.8	—	—
Yellow Warbler	.20	W	—	—	—	—	—	—	—	—
Magnolia Warbler	.15	W	—	—	—	—	—	4.6	—	—
Cape May Warbler	.12	W	—	25	—	53	—	12	—	—
Black-throated Blue Warbler	.12	W	—	—	—	—	—	5.8	—	—
Yellow-rumped Warbler	.20	W	3.0	99	12	313	20	55	15	15
Black-throated Green Warbler	.12	W	—	4.2	—	—	—	—	—	—
Yellow-throated Warbler	.20	P/W	54	40	24	56	34	11	—	47
Olive-capped Warbler	.25	P	148	42	57	—	120	7.0	—	316
Pine Warbler	.30	P	66	36	20	23	81	18	14	72
Prairie Warbler	.15	W	20	26	16	55	—	23	—	—
Palm Warbler	.24	W	168	723	425	167	231	66	110	249
Ovenbird	.12	W	4.9	—	—	4.0	—	18	—	—
Northern Waterthrush	.15	W	—	—	—	—	—	—	—	—
Common Yellowthroat	.15	W	48	9.9	—	29	13	14	—	—
Bahama Yellowthroat	.20	P	27	20	15	37	63	18	16	65
Wilson's Warbler	.12	W	—	—	—	—	—	—	—	—
Redstart	.15	W	—	30	8.0	19	19	—	—	—
Red-winged Blackbird	.60	W	—	—	—	—	—	—	—	—
Bananaquit	.20	P	39	111	128	109	39	52	7	44
Stripe-headed Tanager	.20	P	15	50	51	49	44	159	3.5	72
Greater Antillean Bullfinch	.15	P	—	—	—	—	—	25	—	—
Black-faced Grassquit	.15	P	16	6.6	8.0	55	—	97	—	58
Savannah Sparrow	.12	W	—	—	—	—	—	—	—	—
Grasshopper Sparrow	.12	W	—	—	—	—	—	—	—	—
Lincoln Sparrow	.12	W	—	—	—	—	—	—	—	—
Total of species (S)			24	27	24	26	16	32	11	18
Bird species diversity (H')			2.60	2.21	2.10	2.61	2.34	2.81	1.67	2.17
Total density (D)			807	1532	1073	1479	943	1164	232	1320
Permanent res. (species)			17	16	16	16	12	21	9	15
Permanent res. (density)			544	503	574	656	660	767	67	1046

TABLE 2 (Continued)

Species	9 p/Th² 2.5³	10 F² 3.1³	11 Mn² 4.6³	12 Mn² 4.2³	13 p² 1.4³	14 Msh² 4.7³	15 C² 1.4³	16 C² 1.2³	17 Y² 4.6³	18 p² 7.7³
Winter res. (species)			7	11	8	10	4	11	2	3
Winter res. (density)			263	1029	499	823	283	397	165	274
White-crowned Pigeon	5.4	—	—	—	—	—	—	—	—	—
Mourning Dove	—	—	—	30	—	—	—	—	—	—
Zenaida Dove	—	—	—	—	—	—	—	—	—	2.7
Ground Dove	—	—	—	—	3.8	—	83	—	—	—
Key West Quail Dove	—	—	—	—	—	—	51	—	—	—
Smooth-billed Ani	—	—	—	—	—	5.7	—	—	—	—
Cuban Emerald	58	9.4	—	—	10	12	70	—	31	70
Bahama Woodstar	—	11	—	—	—	—	—	108	87	4.3
Hairy Woodpecker	55	3.7	2.5	5.4	2.1	2.5	—	—	—	6.0
Yellow-bell. Sapsucker	44	—	—	—	6.6	—	—	—	—	—
Gray Kingbird	—	—	—	1.6	—	—	—	—	—	—
Loggerhead Flycatcher	5.4	—	—	—	4.9	—	—	—	8.7	5.3
Stolid Flycatcher	—	—	—	—	—	—	—	—	—	—
Greater Ant. Pewee	—	—	—	—	7.3	—	—	—	—	10
Bahama Swallow	—	—	—	—	—	61	—	4.2	—	—
Brn.-hd. Nuthatch	—	—	—	—	5.8	—	—	—	—	25
Gray Catbird	314	7.2	—	—	—	54	28	—	—	—
N. Mockingbird	—	7.8	—	1.5	—	1.3	4.3	4.9	—	—
Bahama Mockingbird	—	—	—	—	—	—	—	—	—	—
Red-legged Thrush	54	—	—	—	—	—	—	—	—	5.6
American Robin	—	—	—	—	—	1.7	—	—	—	—
Bl.-g. Gnatcatcher	207	—	—	—	8.8	10	—	—	3.5	2.1
Thick-billed Vireo	202	—	—	—	—	35	—	—	2.4	1.5
Black and white Warbler	28	—	—	—	—	—	—	—	—	—
Worm-eating Warbler	—	—	—	—	7.3	—	—	—	—	—
Orange-crowned Warb.	—	—	7.3	—	—	—	—	—	—	—
Parula Warbler	108	—	—	—	—	—	—	—	—	—
Yellow Warbler	—	—	13	—	—	—	—	—	—	—
Magnolia Warbler	—	—	—	—	—	—	—	—	—	—
Cape May Warbler	—	—	—	—	—	—	—	—	—	—
Black-throated Blue Warbler	—	—	—	—	—	—	—	—	—	—
Yellow-rumped Warb.	186	13	—	80	11	146	14	32	8.5	21
Blk.-thr. Gr. Warb.	14	—	—	—	—	—	—	—	—	—
Yellow-throated Warbler	8.1	—	—	—	3.7	—	—	—	4.3	3.4
Olive-capped Warb.	—	—	—	—	30	20	—	—	10	240
Pine Warbler	—	4.3	—	—	15	—	—	—	41	24
Prairie Warbler	151	8.7	—	—	—	17	19	—	5.8	—
Palm Warbler	67	75	33	110	37	25	267	850	167	67
Ovenbird	108	—	—	—	—	—	—	—	—	—
Northern Waterthrush	97	—	35	19	—	125	—	—	—	—
Common Yellowthroat	202	—	29	58	—	228	445	237	29	—
Bahama Yellowthroat	143	6.5	—	14	3.7	—	14	—	26	31
Wilson's Warbler	13	—	—	—	—	—	—	—	—	—
Redstart	97	—	—	—	—	5.7	—	—	—	3.5
Red-winged Blackbird	—	—	1.5	96	—	31	—	5.3	—	—
Bananaquit	267	—	8.7	33	7.3	30	139	—	4.4	8.0
Stripe-headed Tanager	154	—	—	—	15	—	—	—	—	24
Greater Ant. Bullfinch	43	—	—	—	—	—	—	—	—	—
Black-faced Grassquit	3.2	—	—	6.3	19	34	—	—	—	14
Savannah Sparrow	—	—	—	—	—	—	69	—	—	—
Grasshopper Sparrow	—	139	—	—	—	—	—	—	7.3	—
Lincoln Sparrow	—	—	—	—	—	23	—	—	—	—
Total of species (S)	27	11	8	12	18	19	13	7	15	20
Bird species diversity (H')	2.89	1.77	1.74	2.01	2.61	2.30	1.94	0.96	1.98	2.09
Total density (D)	2677	286	130	455	198	854	1226	1246	436	568
Permanent res. (species)	13	6	2	7	14	10	6	3	10	17
Permanent res. (density)	1205	43	11	92	136	220	361	122	218	476
Winter res. (species)	14	5	6	5	4	9	7	4	5	3
Winter res. (density)	1472	243	119	363	62	634	865	1124	218	92

TABLE 2 (CONTINUED)

Species	19 Y² 3.7³	20 p² 1.3³	21 Y² 2.2³	22 F² 1.9³	23 Y² 3.1³	24 Y² 3.4³	25 2.0³	Freq.	Total⁴ 25.99
White-crowned Pigeon	—	—	—	—	—	—	—	2	0.27
Mourning Dove	—	38	—	—	—	—	—	2	1.68
Zenaida Dove	—	—	—	—	6.5	—	—	6	3.35
Ground Dove	—	31	7.0	—	—	—	—	8	4.05
Key West Quail Dove	—	—	—	—	—	—	—	1	0.80
Smooth-billed Ani	—	—	—	—	—	—	—	2	0.85
Cuban Emerald Hummingbird	49	89	347	157	325	108	55	22	93.57
Bahama Woodstar	28	—	286	117	76	25	16	12	21.17
Hairy Woodpecker	—	45	8.3	—	—	17	—	18	9.91
Yellow-bellied Sapsucker	—	—	—	—	—	—	—	6	3.18
Gray Kingbird	—	—	—	—	—	—	—	1	0.07
Loggerhead Flycatcher	—	21	—	—	—	5.0	—	13	3.60
Stolid Flycatcher	—	—	—	—	—	—	—	2	0.50
Greater Antillean Pewee	—	31	9.7	—	—	30	—	13	7.57
Bahama Swallow	—	—	—	34	—	—	165	4	6.83
Brown-headed Nuthatch	—	—	—	—	—	—	—	5	8.48
Gray Catbird	—	—	87	100	—	—	651	11	58.33
N. Mockingbird	—	—	6.6	62	2.0	—	62	11	4.15
Bahama Mockingbird	—	—	—	—	—	—	3.2	1	0.07
Red-legged Thrush	—	—	—	—	—	8.3	—	7	3.44
American Robin	—	—	—	—	—	—	—	1	0.08
Blue-green Gnatcatcher	—	38	2.3	—	—	30	7.7	17	29.00
Thick-billed vireo	—	17	16	11	43	38	11	17	22.64
Black and white Warbler	—	—	—	—	—	—	—	6	4.54
Worm-eating Warbler	—	—	—	—	—	—	—	1	0.40
Orange-crowned Warbler	—	—	—	—	—	—	—	2	0.67
Parula Warbler	—	—	—	—	11	—	—	5	6.75
Yellow Warbler	—	—	—	—	—	—	—	1	0.60
Magnolia Warbler	—	—	—	—	—	—	—	1	0.27
Cape May Warbler	—	—	—	—	—	—	—	3	6.75
Black throated Blue Warbler	—	—	—	—	—	—	—	2	1.58
Yellow-rumped Warbler	11	157	222	30	20	7.5	—	23	66.50
Black-throated Green Warbler	—	—	—	—	—	—	—	2	0.67
Yellow-throated Warbler	—	16	29	—	13	31	—	15	21.75
Olive-capped Warbler	—	75	17	—	5.2	334	—	14	72.00
Pine Warbler	—	62	24	—	48	60	—	16	27.87
Prairie Warbler	—	—	—	27	—	—	39	12	16.67
Palm Warbler	50	208	410	317	399	19	80	25	214.79
Ovenbird	—	—	—	—	—	—	—	4	4.17
Northern Waterthrush	—	—	—	—	—	—	—	4	10.26
Common Yellowthroat	—	21	9.6	520	17	—	128	17	50.07
Bahama Yellowthroat	5.5	31	36	—	117	61	154	21	32.15
Wilson's Warbler	—	—	—	—	—	—	—	1	0.33
Redstart	—	41	—	—	—	—	—	8	8.46
Red-winged Blackbird	—	—	—	20	—	—	—	5	5.84
Bananaquit	—	47	15	30	46	91	167	22	55.00
Stripe-headed Tanager	—	79	—	10	13	114	—	15	36.75
Greater Antillean Bullfinch	—	—	—	—	—	—	—	2	2.07
Black-faced Grassquit	—	125	—	27	8.7	51	—	16	24.00
Savannah Sparrow	—	—	—	17	—	—	16	3	1.58
Grasshopper Sparrow	—	—	—	—	—	—	16	3	4.83
Lincoln Sparrow	—	—	—	—	—	—	—	1	0.33
Total of species (S)	5	19	17	15	16	17	15		
Bird species diversity (H')	1.36	2.67	1.95	2.02	1.91	2.31	1.98		
Total density (D)	144	1172	1553	1479	1141	1030	1561		
Permanent res. (species)	3	15	13	8	12	15	9		
Permanent res. (density)	83	745	824	448	703	1003	641		
Winter res. (species)	2	4	4	7	4	2	6		
Winter res. (density)	61	427	729	1031	438	27	920		

[1] Seasonal status: p = permanent resident, W = winter resident or visitant.
[2] Vegetation types: p = submature pine, Y = young pine, Th = low tree thicket, F = old field, Mn = mangrove flat, Msh = Marsh, C = coastal shrub and grass as plotted in Figure 10.
[3] Km of transect.
[4] Totals: the density values in this column are for the total of areas covered by census transects—the sums of the densities in individual stands.

(hereafter designated WR), summer residents wintering elsewhere (SR), and in-transient migrants (transients) encountered only in passage between their summer and winter homes (Tr). Only the first two of these elements were present during the January–March period of this 1969 across-communities study.

The ratio of PR to WR species varied widely over the 25 communities (Table 2). In numbers of species the PRs outnumbered the WRs in 20 communities including all of those in pines, equalled them in one coppet and one mangrove community, and were outnumbered in the other mangrove and both coastal strip communities. In terms of total population (densities for all species combined), PRs dominated in closed, wooded habitats but were dominated by WRs in open situations. PRs outnumbered WRs in the young pines 1.86:1, in the submature pines 1.35:1, and in the coppet communities 1.08:1. They were outnumbered by WRs in the old fields 1.98:1, in the marsh 2.88:1, in the coastal strips 4.12:1, and in the mangrove communities 4.68:1.

Bird species diversity.—The diversity of a bird community may be expressed simply as the number of species present (S), or it may be refined to incorporate information on the evenness or equitability of abundances among the member species (H') (MacArthur and MacArthur 1961). Measured as number of species (S) diversity in the Grand Bahama communities averaged 17.3 species and ranged from 5 in a sparsely foliaged, recently disturbed young pine stand (19) to 32 in the densely foliaged, tall shrub thicket or "coppet" (6) (Table 2). Using the information theory measure of diversity (H'), which incorporates equitability of distribution along with species number, diversity ranged from 0.96 bits in one of the coastal strip communities (16) to 2.89 in a mixed coppet (9). H' diversity values for the 25 communities are presented in Figure 12 in a form that shows the relation of diversity to each of the 7 selected parameters plotted in Figure 11. Trends can be seen towards high diversity in shrub-dominated stands and in stands with high vegetation volume.

Bird species diversity is plotted against habitat diversity (both S and H') in Figure 13. The habitat diversity index for this graph (VHD—see footnote for column 18 in Table 1) showed a weak positive correlation with both the S and the H' indices of bird species diversity, weaker than might have been predicted by current diversity theory (MacArthur and MacArthur 1961). The major deviants contributing to this poor correlation were, on one side, the coppet and the coppet-pine stands (9 and 6) which were essentially one-stratum habitats because of the suppression of the ground vegetation by a very dense and tall shrub canopy. On the other side, the two most deviant sites were the heavily disturbed (recently cut and slashed) pine stands (19 and 7) with vegetation that, despite its overall sparsity, had fairly equal shrub and ground strata plus a few trees. The conditions at these sites suggest that BSD might show a better correlation with overall foliage volume than with vegetation diversity.

When bird species diversity is plotted against vegetation volume (Fig. 14) a significant correlation is found. The correlation is particularly clear for species richness (Fig. 14A).

Comparisons of bird species diversity across habitat types as delineated in

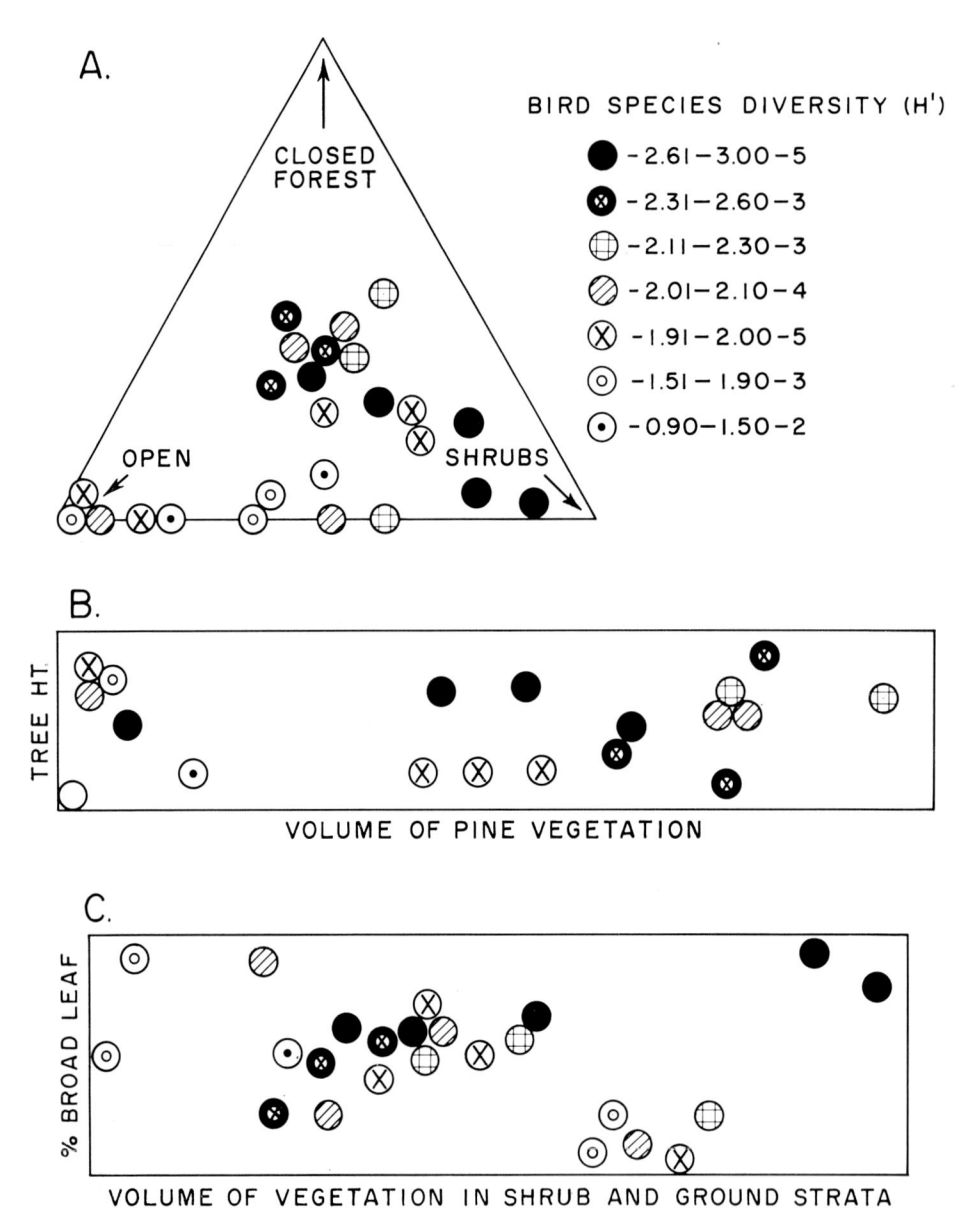

FIGURE 12. Distribution of bird species diversity (H′) along 7 habitat gradients. Symbols indicate the diversity level in each of the 25 stands, as identified by position in Figure 11.

Figure 10 provide further insights into community structure and dynamics. Diversity (H′) was highest in the coppet and pine-coppet community type (2.85), followed by the standard pine (2.38), the marsh (2.30), young pine (2.10), old field (1.92), mangrove (1.87), and coastal strip (1.45) communities. This sequence suggests a progression toward low habitat stability, or at least frequent

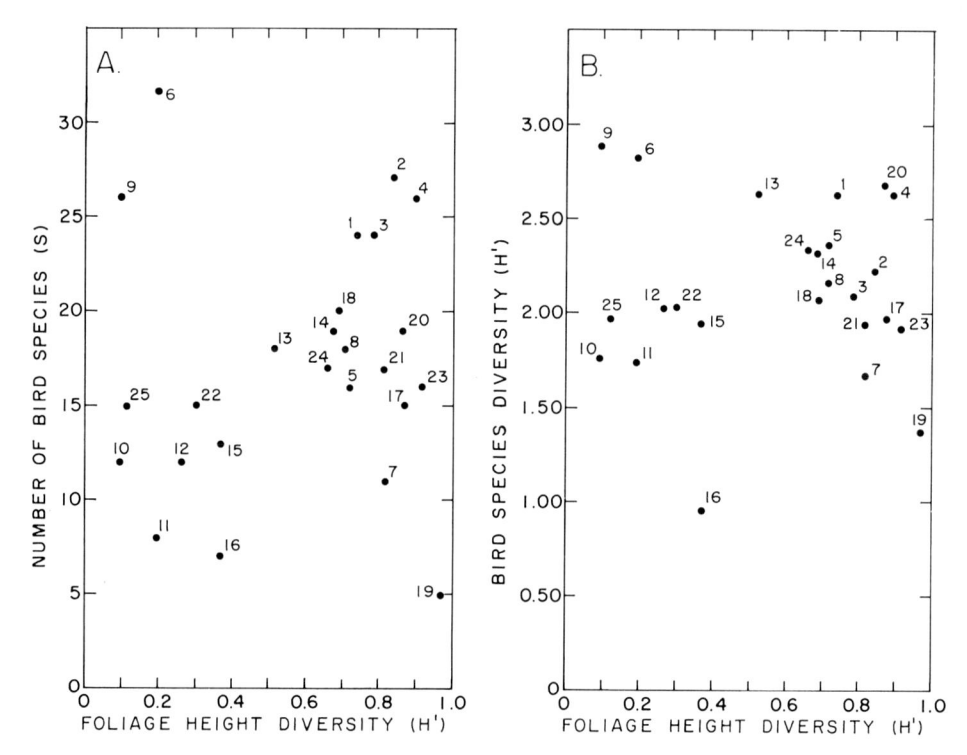

FIGURE 13. Bird species diversity vs. vegetation diversity in the 25 survey sites. A, species number (S) plotted against foliage height diversity (H') ($r = 0.085$, $P > 0.05$); B, bird species diversity (H') plotted against foliage height diversity (H') ($r = 0.006$, $P > 0.05$).

disturbances, either natural or artificial. Had the series been extended to include urban development and lawns it seems likely that the trend would have continued.

All of the preceding figures on bird species diversity are for the complete wintering communities, i.e. the permanent residents plus the winter invaders. With the departure of the WRs each spring, the diversity, of the Island's avifauna is reduced by about one third. This decrease is most pronounced in the mangrove and coastal strip communities, where 29% and 56% of the wintering species are WRs, and least in the submature and young pine communities where only 28% and 25% are WRs. The magnitude of these seasonal changes is considered again in the next section on total population density, and examined in detail for the pine forest community in later chapters.

Total bird density.—The size of an avian community may be expressed in terms of total population density (the sum of all species densities) or of community biomass. Population density values are useful in studies of community structure and dynamics and are emphasized in the present across-community comparisons. Biomass values including adjustments for variations in food use rates with body size, are most appropriate for analyses of consumer-resource relationships as considered in later chapters of this monograph.

Calculated total density values for the 25 Grand Bahama communities ranged

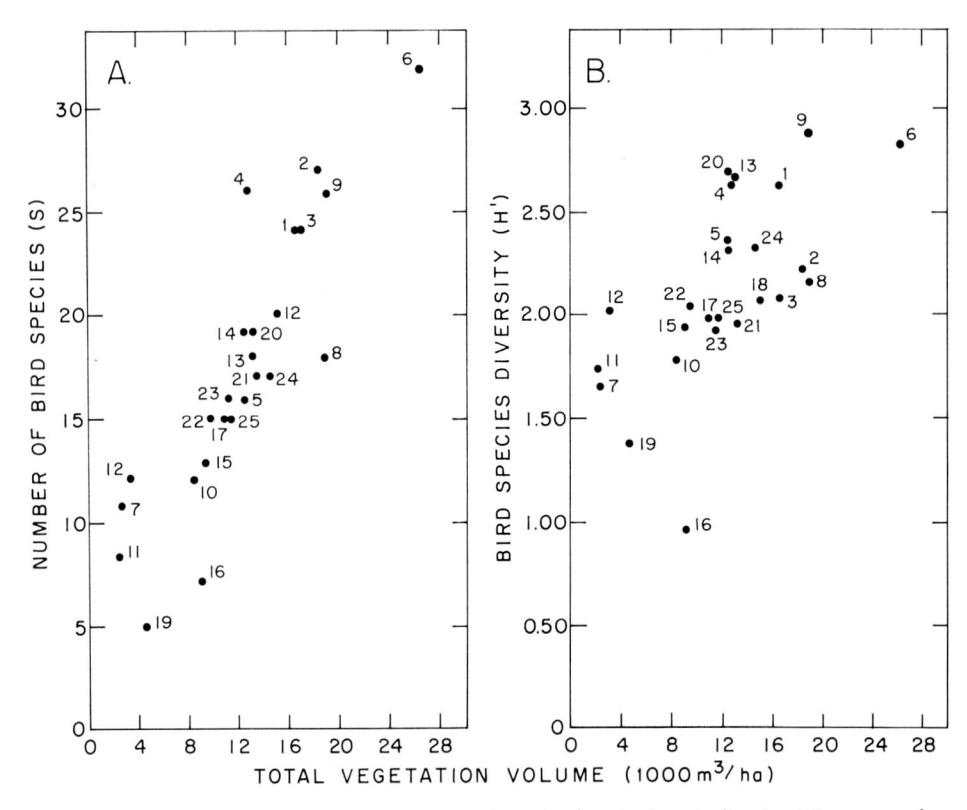

FIGURE 14. Bird species diversity vs. vegetation density (volume) in the 25 survey sites. A, species number (S) plotted against vegetation volume ($r = 0.878$, $P < 0.01$); B, bird species diversity (H') plotted against vegetation volume ($r = 0.683$, $P < 0.01$).

from 130 birds per km² (53 per 100 acres) in a mangrove community (11) to 2,677 (1,084 per 100 acres) in the coppet community (9) (Table 2). Sixteen of the 25 stands supported densities between 800 and 1,600 birds per km². Environmental factors associated with these wide differences were explored by both the habitat type and gradient approaches. Densities were highest in the coppet habitat type with 1,921 birds per km² (778 per 100 acres), followed in order by the coastal plains, old field, submature pines, brushy marsh, young pines, and mangroves, the later with only 293 birds per km² (Table 2).

The effect of human disturbance on total population densities was clearly visible in the pine forests. With timber cutting operations, submature forest communities averaging 1,006 birds per km² were, in effect, replaced by young pine communities with 767 birds per km². This is essentially what must have happened on a vast scale in the Grand Bahama forests during the 1940's and 1950's, followed by a return to the higher densities as the forests recovered in the 1960's. Figuring on this basis, 17 of the 21 permanent resident forest species were reduced by the Grand Bahama Island timber cutting operations, 3 of them completely eliminated on the cut areas, while 4 species increased. The effect on the winter invader

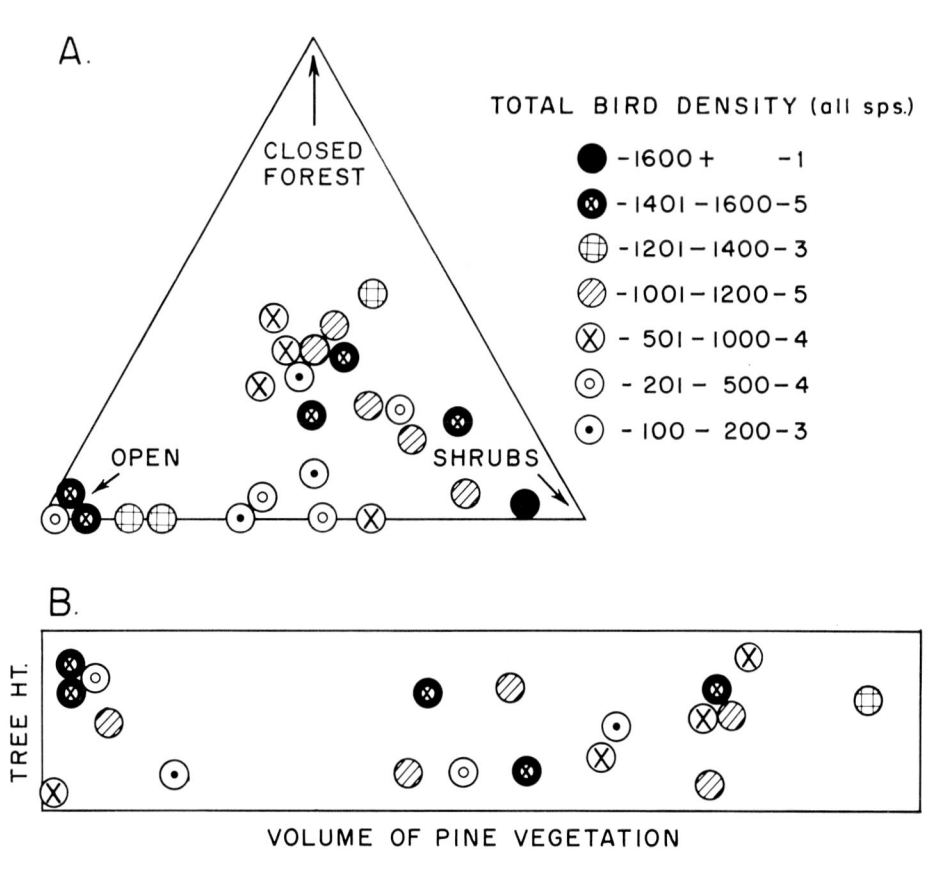

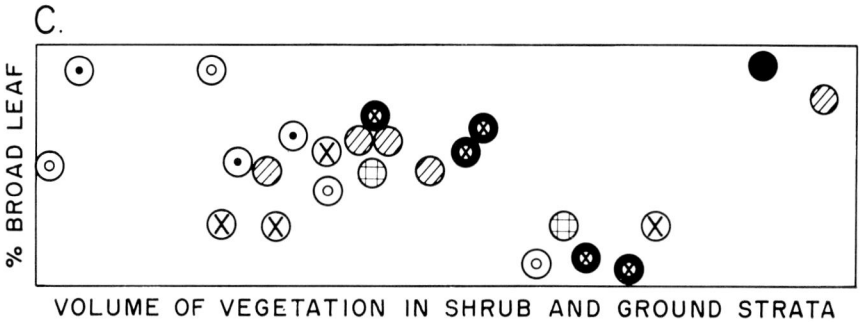

FIGURE 15. Distribution of total bird density (all species) along 7 habitat gradients. Symbols indicate the density level in each of the 25 survey stands. The position of the stands along the 7 gradients is taken directly from the calibrated diagrams in Figure 11 where they are identified.

species was even greater with 13 or 14 reduced, 8 of them locally eliminated, while 1 species benefitted (see Table 3b).

In the diagrams showing overall population density along a series of habitat gradients (Fig. 15) several trends can be detected. The central basal portion of the triangular diagram again shows that open (treeless) stands with low shrubs supported few birds, and that densities increased with herbaceous (to left), shrub (to right), and arboreal (upward) cover. These trends can also be seen on the horizontal axis of the lower rectangle in the figure where total volume of shrub and ground vegetation is plotted on a logarithmic scale.

As a more direct test for the apparent positive relationship between total population density and the volume of the vegetative substrate, I plotted these two functions against each other in Figure 16. The positive correlation in this graph ($r = 0.354$) is not significant at the 0.05 level.

Discussion—Diversity and Density Correlates

Insofar as environmental complexity implies a wide variety of niches capable of supporting a varied assortment of bird species there is logic in the predicted correlation between bird species diversity and habitat diversity. MacArthur and MacArthur's (1961) index of habitat diversity (FHD) has been used by many investigators (MacArthur et al. 1966, Karr 1968, Recher 1969) and has served to demonstrate the predicted relationship in a wide variety of situations. But other investigators have failed to find the expected correspondence using FHD and have turned to other indices based on plant growth forms (Tomoff 1971) or some aspect of horizontal heterogeneity (Cody 1968, Willson 1974, Roth 1976).

In the data presented in this paper the variable showing closest correlation with bird species diversity in the Grand Bahama habitats was total foliage volume, a a factor apparently reflecting the amount rather than the complexity of vegetation in a stand. The amount of foliage in habitats has also been examined with positive results by Willson (1974). Her measure of vegetation quantity was the sum of the percent cover in each of three vegetation strata (PCVS), rather than the total space occupied by standing vegetation. In discussing her results Willson pointed out that an increase in PCVC generally implies an increase in habitat diversity as well as vegetative mass since additional strata or layers are inevitably included with high PCVC values. My total foliage volume is, in the same way, an indicator of the structural complexity of the vegetation as well as of volume *per se*. As I measured it, foliage volume incorporates the full range of vegetative variation found in all of the compartments and foraging substrates of the stand. A small volume stand such as a field or mangrove flat may for instance have only one compartment, while a high volume stand may incorporate many compartments distributed along both the vertical and horizontal planes. Thus habitat diversity may still be and probably is the biologically significant variable behind BSD, my measures of foliage volume merely being a more sensitive indicator of habitat complexity than FHD in the Grand Bahama habitats. If this interpretation is correct, the best index of habitat complexity for avian community studies may indeed be one based on some sort of inventory and quantitative appraisal of the compartments or guild provinces present in a stand.

In much the same way that the structural complexity of a habitat, measured as the diversity of structural units present, is thought to determine the number of species in a community, the total quantity of structural or substrate units, regard-

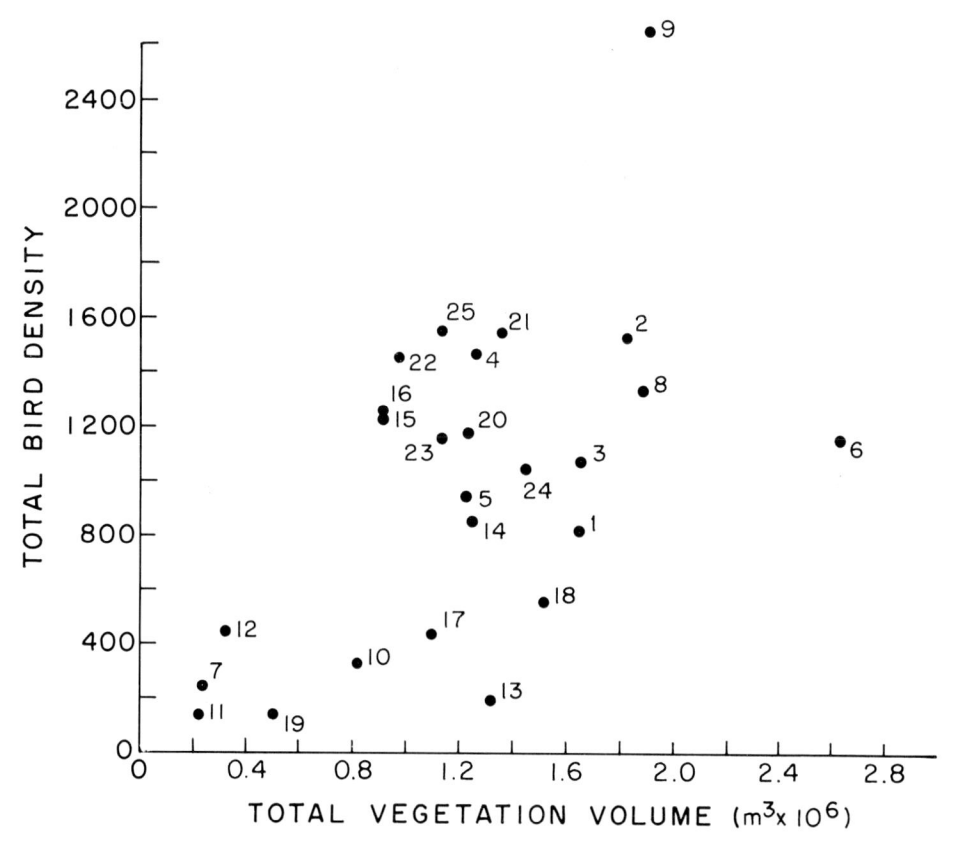

FIGURE 16. Total bird density (all species) plotted against total vegetation volume in the 25 survey stands ($r = 0.354$, $P = 0.082$).

less of diversity, might be expected to determine the number of individual birds the habitat will support. The logic behind this proposition rests on two assumptions: (1) that there is at least a rough relationship between the abundance of foraging substrate units and the abundance of avian food organisms, and (2) that food abundance is an important determinant of population density. My Grand Bahama data showing a better correlation of vegetation volume with species numbers than total density (Figs. 13 and 14) clearly do not support this proposition. They cannot, of course, be taken to disprove it, but they suggest that more caution may be desirable in accepting some of the basic assumptions of popular consumer-resource and carrying capacity models. They also suggest that it may be more profitable to examine density-environment relations at finer levels of community organization than the habitat level considered in this chapter. An examination of this problem at the guild level is undertaken in Chapter 8.

5—BIRD DISTRIBUTION THROUGH THE HABITATS

The quantitative data collected on the bird communities of Grand Bahama (Table 2) offer an exceptional opportunity to examine the dynamics of density dispersion through the habitats and to evaluate the nature and mode of action of density-related social factors in population regulation and distribution. They also provide a basis for analyzing the distribution patterns of all species, evaluating dispersion amplitudes and overlaps, and examining spacing characteristics.

Dynamics of Density Distribution

Concepts and models.—A widely accepted theory of habitat distribution in birds and other mobile organisms (Lack 1933, 1940, Svärdson 1949, Hilden 1965) visualizes individuals as selecting among the array of available habitat patches in an area on the basis of individual experience and/or of innate responses that align preference with survival and reproductive success. At the population level such individual responses result in movements toward and density increases in the habitats with qualities best suited for the species' particular requirements.

The basic factor in habitat quality for birds is the physical substrate (the vegetation) as it determines the abundance and accessibility of key resources, particularly food. But other factors including the presence of other birds and particularly of conspecifics may detract heavily from the overall quality of the habitat and effect a net value far below the potential of the physical environment.

The detracting or suppressive effect on overall habitat quality of the population of birds already in residence on an area varies with the density of that population (Fretwell and Lucas 1970). It may increase progressively with some function of density as numbers advance towards the resource-determined carrying capacity of the habitat (as in the logistic model of population regulation), or it may be minimal at low densities and then appear rather abruptly and completely at some social saturation threshold level (as in the territory models of Kluyver and Tinbergen 1953, Tinbergen 1957, Brown 1969, and others). In the first instance habitat selection may be regarded as a single response to the overall quality of the environment, reflecting a balance of positively valent substrate features and negatively valent density characteristics. In the second instance habitat selection would appear to be completed in two stages: first, a positive response to physical substrate features and then a withdrawal imposed by the aggressive behavior of resident birds. When this occurs displaced individuals must move on (spill over) to successively inferior sites until they find one not already filled to the saturation level.

The dynamics of these two systems of population dispersion and density regulation are depicted diagrammatically for a series of hypothetical habitat patches arranged in order of decreasing substrate quality in Figure 17. Diagram A (free dispersion) shows the theoretical distribution of densities (solid bars) in the absence of significant density factors, a purely hypothetical situation in which populations should be free to increase by ingress or reproduction until they approximate the resource-determined carrying capacity of the habitats. Diagram B (modified free dispersion) shows the distribution of densities where movement towards the better habitats is suppressed as some function of the density of the birds already present and the resource-determined carrying capacity. The bars indicating density levels in this series decline less precipitously than in the free dispersal

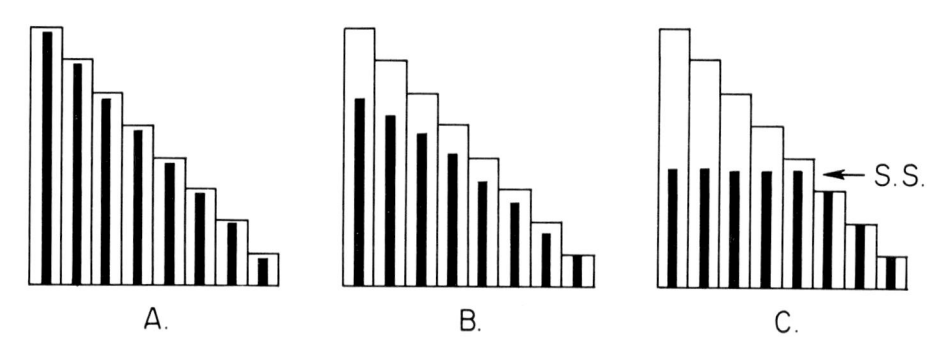

FIGURE 17. Three alternative models depicting hypothetical density distributions and regulating mechanisms through a series of habitats arranged in order of decreasing intrinsic quality. The height of each column represents the carrying capacity in terms of physical features. The height of the solid bars within each column represents the presumed density level attained under the assumptions of each of the three models: A, established residents have no direct effect on immigrants; B, established residents lower the attractiveness of the habitat for prospective immigrants; and C, established residents actively repel prospective immigrants as they arrive.

model. Diagram C (socially restricted dispersion) shows the distribution of densities where movement into the best habitats is arrested rather abruptly at a threshold level determined by the saturation of available space with aggressive territory holders. The bars in diagram C form a plateau of roughly equal densities (through the high quality habitats and down to the point where the resource-determined carrying capacity is less than the social saturation level of the species).

Population regulation and dispersion by the social restriction process (Fig. 17, model C), while generally associated with and best illustrated in territorial species and the breeding season, need not be restricted to these situations. Indeed, data on habitat distribution in members of the Grand Bahama wintering community suggest that it may have featured in a number of both permanent resident and winter resident species during the January–March period of study in 1969.

Habitat distribution patterns.—The density data obtained for the 25 stands and presented in Table 2 are organized in the form of histograms for each of the common species (> 3 birds/km^2) in Figure 18. In each case the stand with the highest density is shown at the left with the next nine stands aligned to the right in order of decreasing density. The variety of patterns in these histograms suggests that the various mechanisms of density regulation and dispersion (see Fig. 17) may differ considerably among the 34 species represented. Some show steep initial declines suggestive of model #1 (FD) while others have at least indications of a plateau of moderately high densities like that shown in the third (SRD) model. As a test for the applicability of my empirical data to those models I attempted an independent and largely subjective evaluation of the aggressive and localization characteristics of each species. Four categories were established: localized and aggressive (LA), localized and passive (LP), nomadic and aggressive (NA), and nomadic and passive (NP). The histograms in Figure 18 are grouped according to this classification with 14 species of type LA at the top,

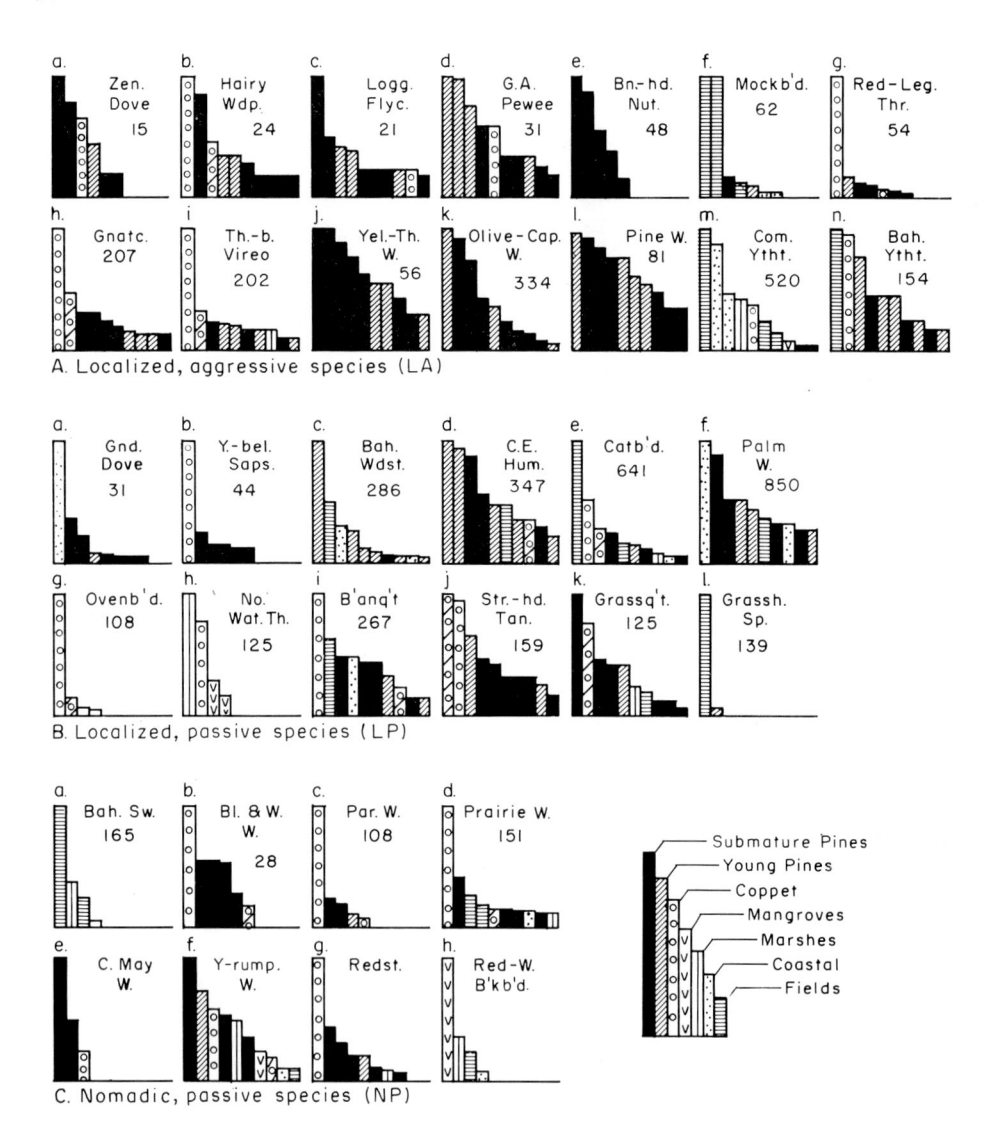

FIGURE 18. Histograms showing relative densities in descending order through the 10 favored stands for each of the 34 common (≥ 3 birds/km²) species. Bar heights are relative to the density in the most favored stand, the first bar. The vegetation type of the stands is indicated by shading. Species histograms are arranged in three groups on the basis of aggressive behavior.

12 of type LP in the center, and 8 type NP at the bottom. No birds were assigned to type NA.

Most (13 of 14) of the birds placed in the localized and aggressive category (LA) are permanent resident species showing traces of territorial behavior, and, in some cases, the beginnings of breeding activity. The one winter resident species in this group (Common Yellowthroat) showed evidence of localization and occasional aggressiveness suggestive of winter territorialism. Six of the 12 species in the localized and passive group (LP) were permanent residents, late nesters,

TABLE 3
RELATION OF DISPERSION TYPES (3 MODELS) AND BEHAVIOR TYPES (AGGRESSIVENESS AND LOCALIZATION) IN GRAND BAHAMA LAND BIRDS

Dispersion model[1]	Behavior type[2]			
	LA	LP	NA	NP
Free dispersion (FD)	6	6	0	6
Modified free dispersion (MFD)	3	3	0	2
Socially restricted dispersion (SRD)	5	3	0	0

[1] For description and graphic portrayal see Figure 17.
[2] LA = localized and aggressive, LP = localized and passive, NA = nomadic and aggressive, NP = nomadic and passive.

and/or weakly territorial species. The other 6 were nonflocking winter migrants of which individuals were seen or mist-netted (Fluck *in litt.*) repeatedly in the same localities over periods of days or weeks. All but one of the 8 in the third group, the nomads, were winter resident species; most of them occurred in flocks that seemed to drift irregularly. The single permanent resident species assigned to this category, the Bahama Swallow, was still ranging widely at this season.

The relation of localization and aggressive characteristics to dispersion patterns is presented in Table 3. Species were assigned to the three dispersion models of Figure 17 according to the amount they spilled over from their preferred habitat type to a second type. If the drop in density to the second type was greater than 50% the species is assigned to the FD model (Fig. 17A), if it was less than 50% but more than 20% it was assigned to the MFD model, and if it was less than 20% it was assigned to the SRD model. This is admittedly crude since there is doubtless considerable variation in the distinctiveness of these habitat types from the birds' viewpoint. A positive relation is indicated for the 26 localized species (LA and LP) with 8 (31%) falling into the SRD patterns; while none of the 8 nomadic species fell into this pattern. Similarly 5 (36%) of the 14 aggressive species fell in the SRD patterns while only 3 (15%) of the 20 passive species did so.

The division points for these assignments are, of course, quite arbitrary, and a definite effect of either density or social factors is still undemonstrated in any of the species. But I suggest that the extent of overflow into secondary habitat types and beyond is indicative of social factors in at least some of these species unless responses to physical habitat features are far less specific than commonly assumed in considerations of habitat selection. Furthermore, the association of aggressiveness and localization with heavy overflow seem to support the contention that social behavior is a critical factor in at least some of the dispersion from preferred habitat types.

Another aspect of density distribution, conspicuous in many of the diagrams in Figure 18, is the irregular order of habitat types in the sequence of declining densities from left to right. Thus a simple habitat type such as submature pines may appear at the head of a series, in the middle, and at the lower end, with stands belonging to several other types intruding in the sequence (as in the Loggerhead Flycatcher—diagram Ac). Such situations are difficult to reconcile with the assumption underlying all the models of Figure 17 that birds tend to move initially towards stands of the physical type best suited to their special requirements. The spatial proximity of inferior stands to stands of high quality and density could contribute to this irregular sequence of types, or it is possible that my selection of canopy height, canopy cover, and foliage type as key criteria for delineating habitat types was poorly conceived and quite unrepresentative of the real situation. Finally one must remember that the habitat types were based on physical factors alone and do not reflect other modifying factors such as the presence of other species.

Habitat Selection

Distribution by types.—The habitat type(s) preferred by each species are indicated in Table 5 by a line under the highest density value(s) in each row. Top preference was unevenly distributed among the 7 types; 22 of the 52 species preferred the densely-foliaged, and essentially one-layered coppet habitat, a type found on only a few hundred hectares on the entire island. Only 8 species favored the widespread standard pine habitat; smaller numbers reached top density in each of the other five types.

Permanent residents as a group outnumbered winter residents in the three forest habitats but were outnumbered by them in the four open habitats. Among the 20 common (> 3.0 birds per km^2) PR species, 8 were most numerous in one or the other of the 2 pine habitats, and only 3 in one or another of the 4 open habitats. By contrast, 7 WR species favored open habitats, and only one favored the pinelands.

Distribution along gradients.—Density distribution along the seven habitat dimensions represented in the diagrams of Figure 11 is plotted for all the common species together with other distributional data in Figures 19, 20, and 21. I had thought these plottings might reveal clear patterns of distribution from which central tendencies and variances could be calculated for identifying critical dimensions and revealing areas of competition between related or convergent species. Most of the patterns are diffuse, however, the birds dispersing widely and irregularly over large portions or the full range of conditions available to them along each dimension. Obvious specialists such as the shrub-oriented Bullfinch or the grass inhabiting Savannah Sparrow present more restricted clusters of points along certain dimensions, but these cases are exceptional.

Permanent residents as a group increased with pine canopy cover (upward in the triangle diagram) and pine-shrub cover (up and to the right), while the winter residents decreased along these gradients (Figs. 22 and 23). Differences between PR and WR components were slight along the pine vegetation volume axis, but WR species tended to select stands with taller trees (vertical axis in the central rectangle). The tendency noted earlier (chapter 4) for high overall densities to accompany high total vegetation volumes (see Fig. 15) was more pronounced in the PRs than in the WRs.

The partial habitat segregation of permanent and winter resident populations

TABLE 4
PERCENT DISTRIBUTION OF THE 34 SPECIES WITH TOTAL DENSITIES GREATER THAN 3.0 BIRDS/KM^2 THROUGH THE 25 STANDS.

	1	2	3	4	5	6	7	8	9	10	11	12	13	14	15	16	17	18	19	20	21	22	23	24	25	H'	J'
Zenaida Dove	6	31	–	24	–	20	–	–	–	–	–	–	–	–	–	–	–	6	–	–	–	–	13	–	–	1.63	0.91
Ground Dove	4	–	2	11	–	2	–	–	–	–	–	–	3	–	54	–	–	–	–	20	5	–	–	–	–	1.41	0.68
Cuban Emerald Hummingbird	1	2	8	3	7	5	3	12	3	T	–	–	T	T	3	–	1	3	2	4	15	7	14	5	3	2.69	0.91
Bahama Woodstar	–	–	–	–	–	–	1	2	–	2	–	–	–	–	–	14	11	1	4	–	37	15	10	3	2	1.96	0.79
Hairy Woodpecker	6	4	4	4	7	10	2	4	22	1	1	2	1	1	–	–	–	2	–	18	3	–	–	7	–	2.45	0.85
Yellow-bellied Sapsucker	7	9	7	–	–	–	–	13	56	–	–	–	9	–	–	–	–	–	–	–	–	–	–	–	–	1.39	0.78
Loggerhead Flycatcher	12	2	5	6	11	3	–	3	6	–	–	–	6	–	–	–	10	6	–	25	–	–	–	6	–	2.36	0.93
Greater Antillean Pewee	3	10	2	6	13	10	1	1	–	–	–	–	4	–	–	–	–	6	–	18	6	–	–	17	–	2.25	0.88
Bahama Swallow	–	–	–	–	–	–	–	–	–	–	–	–	–	23	–	3	–	–	–	–	–	13	–	–	61	1.01	0.73
Brown-headed Nuthatch	35	–	13	–	–	–	–	29	–	–	–	–	4	–	–	–	–	18	–	–	–	–	–	–	–	1.43	0.89
Gray Catbird	–	4	1	9	–	11	–	–	19	T	–	1	–	3	2	3	–	–	–	–	5	6	–	–	39	1.82	0.78
Northern Mockingbird	–	1	–	6	–	1	–	–	–	5	–	–	–	1	3	3	–	–	–	–	4	37	1	–	37	1.62	0.65
Red-legged Thrush	4	7	–	2	–	5	–	–	67	–	–	–	–	–	–	–	–	7	–	–	–	–	–	10	–	1.23	0.63
Blue-Gray Gnatcatcher	7	9	4	9	4	15	T	T	32	–	–	–	1	2	–	–	1	1	–	6	4	–	–	5	1	2.23	0.83
Thick-billed Vireo	3	6	1	7	6	11	–	T	35	–	–	–	–	6	–	–	T	T	–	3	3	2	7	7	2	2.19	0.83
Black-and-White Warbler	17	18	9	17	–	5	–	–	34	–	–	–	–	–	–	–	–	–	–	–	–	–	–	–	–	1.64	0.92

TABLE 4 (CONTINUED)

	1	2	3	4	5	6	7	8	9	10	11	12	13	14	15	16	17	18	19	20	21	22	23	24	25	H'	J'
Parula Warbler	—	12	—	14	—	3	—	—	64	—	—	—	—	—	—	—	—	—	—	—	—	—	7	—	—	0.92	0.67
Cape May Warbler	—	28	—	60	—	13	—	—	—	—	—	—	—	—	—	—	—	—	—	—	—	—	—	—	—	0.93	0.84
Yellow-rumped Warbler	T	7	1	21	1	4	1	1	12	—	—	5	—	10	1	2	1	1	1	11	15	2	1	T	—	2.47	0.86
Yellow-throated Warbler	15	11	6	15	9	3	—	13	2	—	—	—	1	—	—	—	1	1	—	4	8	—	4	8	—	2.44	0.90
Olive-capped Warbler	10	3	4	—	8	T	—	22	—	—	—	—	2	1	—	—	1	17	—	5	1	—	T	24	—	2.01	0.81
Pine Warbler	11	6	3	4	13	3	2	12	—	1	—	—	2	—	—	—	7	4	—	10	4	—	8	10	—	2.58	0.93
Prairie Warbler	5	6	4	14	—	6	—	—	37	2	—	—	—	4	5	—	1	—	—	—	—	7	—	—	10	2.08	0.84
Palm Warbler	3	14	8	3	4	1	2	5	1	1	1	2	1	T	5	16	3	1	1	4	8	6	7	T	2	2.75	0.88
Ovenbird	4	—	—	3	—	13	—	—	81	—	—	—	—	—	—	—	—	—	—	—	—	—	—	—	—	0.67	0.48
Northern Waterthrush	—	—	—	—	—	—	—	—	35	—	13	7	—	45	—	—	—	—	—	—	—	—	—	—	—	1.18	0.85
Common Yellowthroat	2	T	—	1	1	1	—	—	10	—	1	3	—	11	22	12	1	—	—	1	T	26	1	—	6	2.09	0.77
Bahama Yellowthroat	3	2	2	4	7	2	2	7	16	1	—	2	T	—	2	—	3	3	1	3	4	—	13	7	17	2.66	0.89
Redstart	—	13	4	8	8	—	—	—	43	—	—	—	—	3	—	—	—	2	—	18	—	—	—	—	—	1.65	0.79
Red-winged Blackbird	—	—	—	—	—	—	—	—	—	—	1	62	—	20	—	3	—	—	—	—	—	13	—	—	—	1.03	0.64
Bananaquit	3	8	9	8	3	4	T	3	19	—	1	2	2	3	9	—	T	1	—	3	1	2	3	6	12	2.67	0.90
Stripe-headed Tanager	2	6	6	6	5	19	T	8	18	—	—	—	2	—	—	—	—	3	—	9	—	1	2	13	—	2.35	0.89
Black-faced Grassquit	3	1	2	10	—	18	—	11	1	—	—	1	4	6	—	—	—	3	—	24	—	5	2	10	—	2.31	0.85
Grasshopper Sparrow	—	—	—	—	—	—	—	—	—	86	—	—	—	—	—	—	5	—	—	—	—	—	—	—	10	0.51	0.47

revealed in these data could theoretically serve to disperse the exploitation pressure on the resources of the island during the winter and early spring months. However, I saw no direct evidence of WR species displacing PR species from preferred habitats. In fact, the Ground Dove, Zenaida Dove, and Bahama Swallow, the three PR species that showed partial seasonal movements between habitat types, all moved out to join the WRs in the open habitat in winter.

Dispersion Amplitudes (Specialization)

The degree of specialization a species in its selection of habitats as exhibited in its spread through a series of stands or along a habitat gradient could theoretically have an important bearing on its interactions with other species, its population stability under changing conditions, and its overall success as a member of the avifauna.

Dispersion of species through the 25 stands.—Species varied greatly in the nature and extent of their dispersion through the 25 stands in this study (see Table 2). Nine species were recorded in only one stand while one, the Palm Warbler, was encountered in all 25 of the stands in densities ranging from 19 to 850 birds per km^2. Relative population strength in each stand in percent total representation is shown in Table 4 for each of the 34 species with overall densities greater than 3.0 individuals per km^2. From these values information theory indices of distributional amplitude (H') (Table 4, last 2 cols.) were calculated on the assumption that both the number of habitats occupied and the relative density of birds in them should be incorporated in an index to be applied to considerations of species overlap and community dynamics. Amplitudes ranged from 0.51 and 0.67 respectively in the ecologically restricted Grasshopper Sparrow and Ovenbird to 2.69 and 2.75 in the ubiquitous Cuban Emerald Hummingbird and Palm Warbler. Equitability ($J' = H'/H'$ max) was consistently rather high (≥ 0.75) for the species with 10 individuals per km^2 regardless of the amplitude value.

Dispersion by types.—The uneven representation of habitat types in the sample of stands surveyed creates strong biases in the measures of distributional amplitude presented above. For instance, a bird specialized for pine foliage might easily disperse through all of the 13 stands containing 100 or more pine trees per hectare (see Table 1), while a species adapted to brushy marsh situations would have only one stand to select from. An analysis of spread through the seven habitat types delineated in Figure 10 was therefore made in which means were calculated for the standard pine stands and other multi-represented types so as to equate them with the lightly represented types such as the marsh.

Dispersion through the seven habitat types differed greatly from species to species (Table 5). Among the 28 permanent resident species 2 were encountered in all 7 types while 6 were found in only one type each (column 8); distributional amplitudes (H') varied from 0–1.75 and averaged 0.77. Winter resident species showed similar dispersion patterns with 3 of the 24 occurring in all 7 types and 6 limited to a single type; distributional amplitudes ranged from 0 to 1.72 and averaged 0.54.

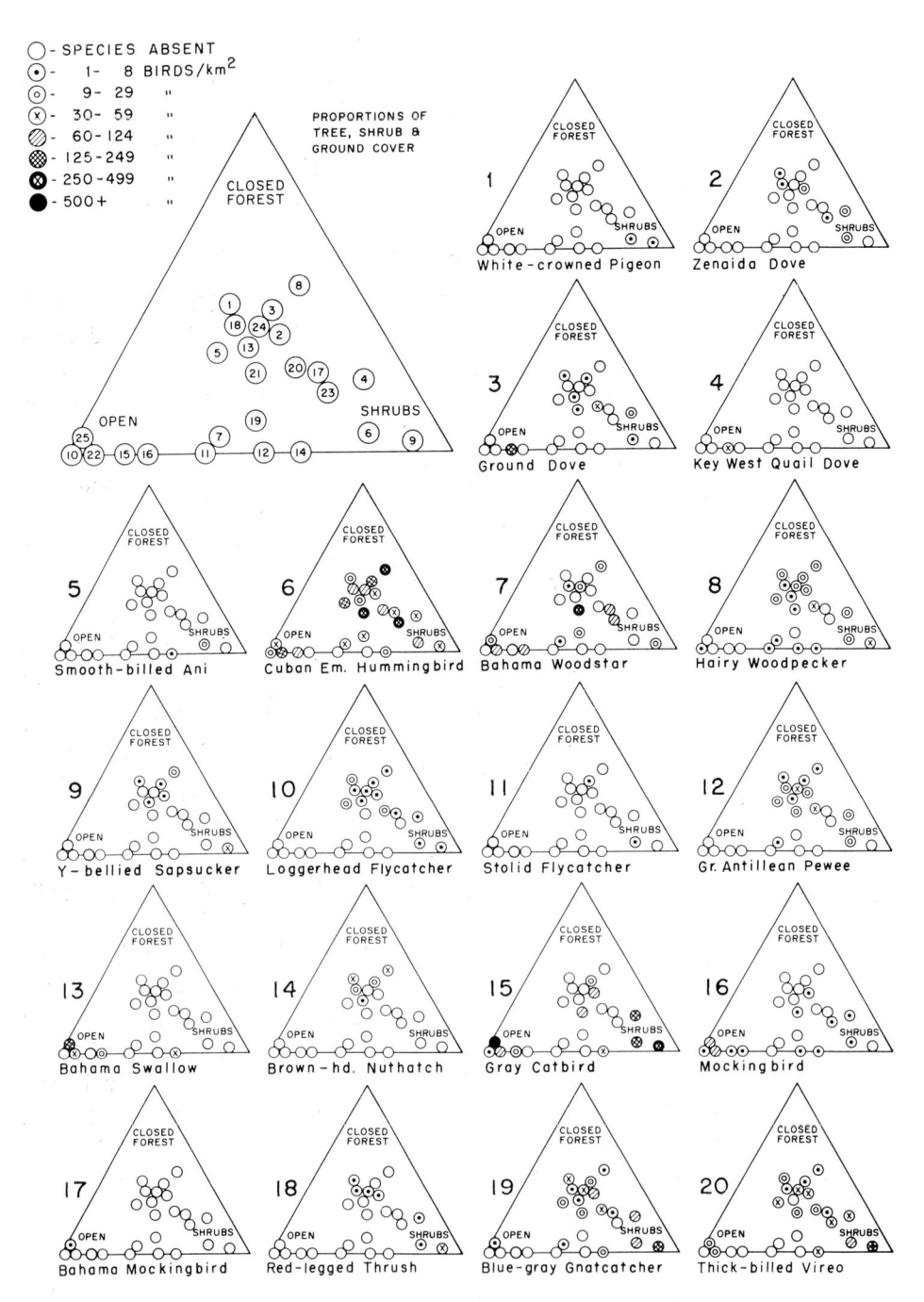

FIGURE 19. Winter distribution of 44 species with respect to vegetation type. The 25 circles in each diagram represent the 25 survey stands, positioned with respect to the relative amounts of trees, shrubs, and ground cover open to the sky. The circles (stands) are identified by number in the large diagram at the head. The population density (in 8 density classes) is indicated for each stand by symbols in the circles. A key to the symbols is shown at the head. Further explanation is given in the legend of Figure 11.

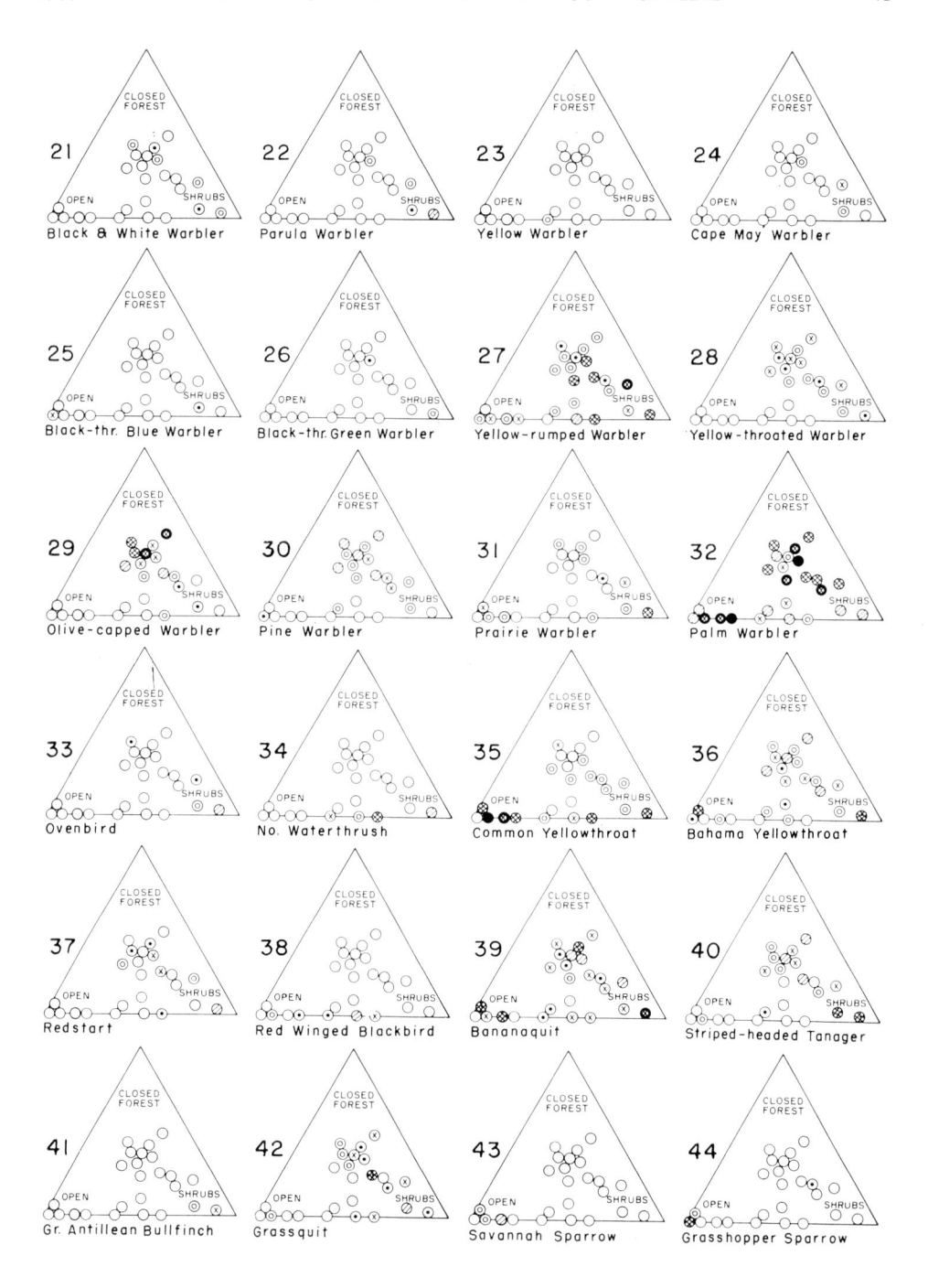

Dispersion along gradients.—Dispersion along the seven selected habitat dimensions and several combination dimensions are graphically portrayed for most species in the diagrams in Figures 19, 20, and 21. The broad and irregular density distributions seen in most of these diagrams indicate a general absence of close environmental restriction with respect to the dimensions adopted and, show the

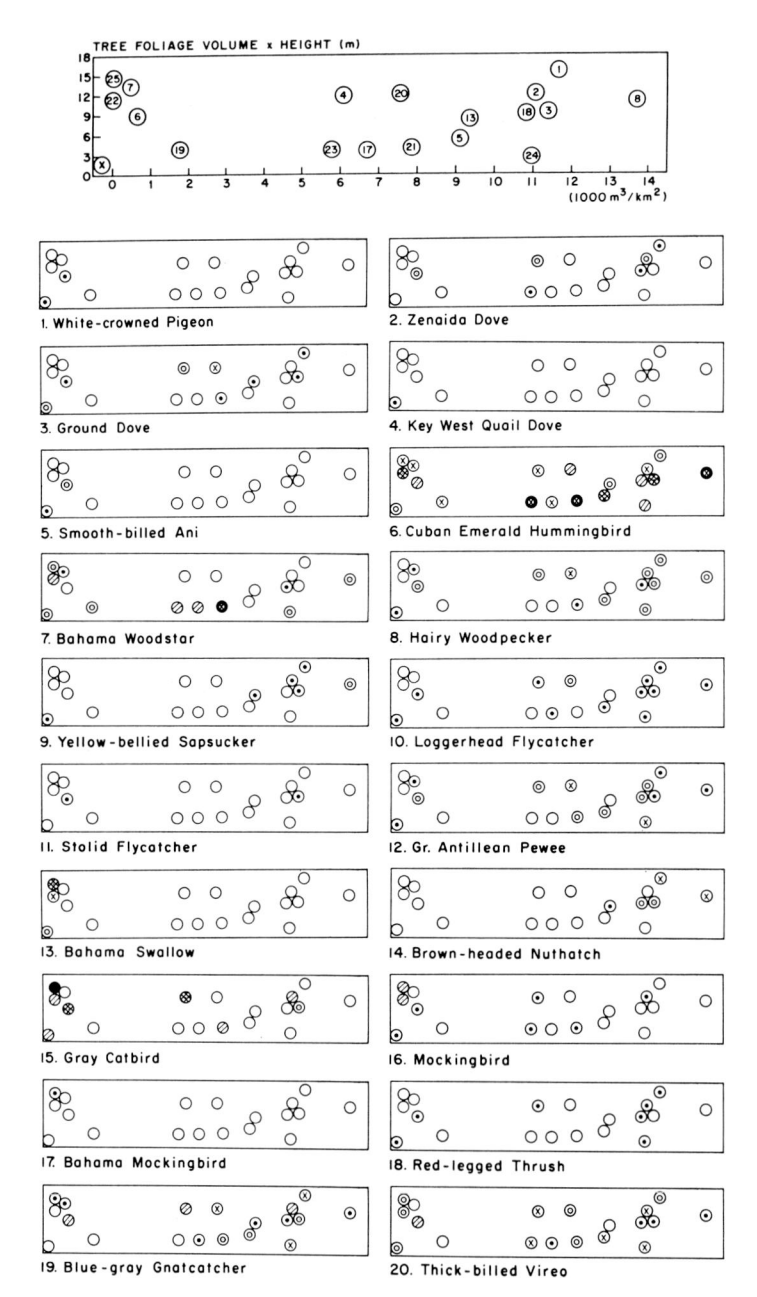

FIGURE 20. Winter distribution of 42 species with respect to vegetation height (vertical axis) and volume of pine foliage (horizontal axis). For explanation see Figures 11 and 19.

futility of attempting to apply traditional statistical methods for determining variance from the centers of distribution. Standard analytical methods were applied, however, to the distribution of five pine forest specialists with limited dispersion along nine pine forest gradients (Table 6). Centers of distribution along each

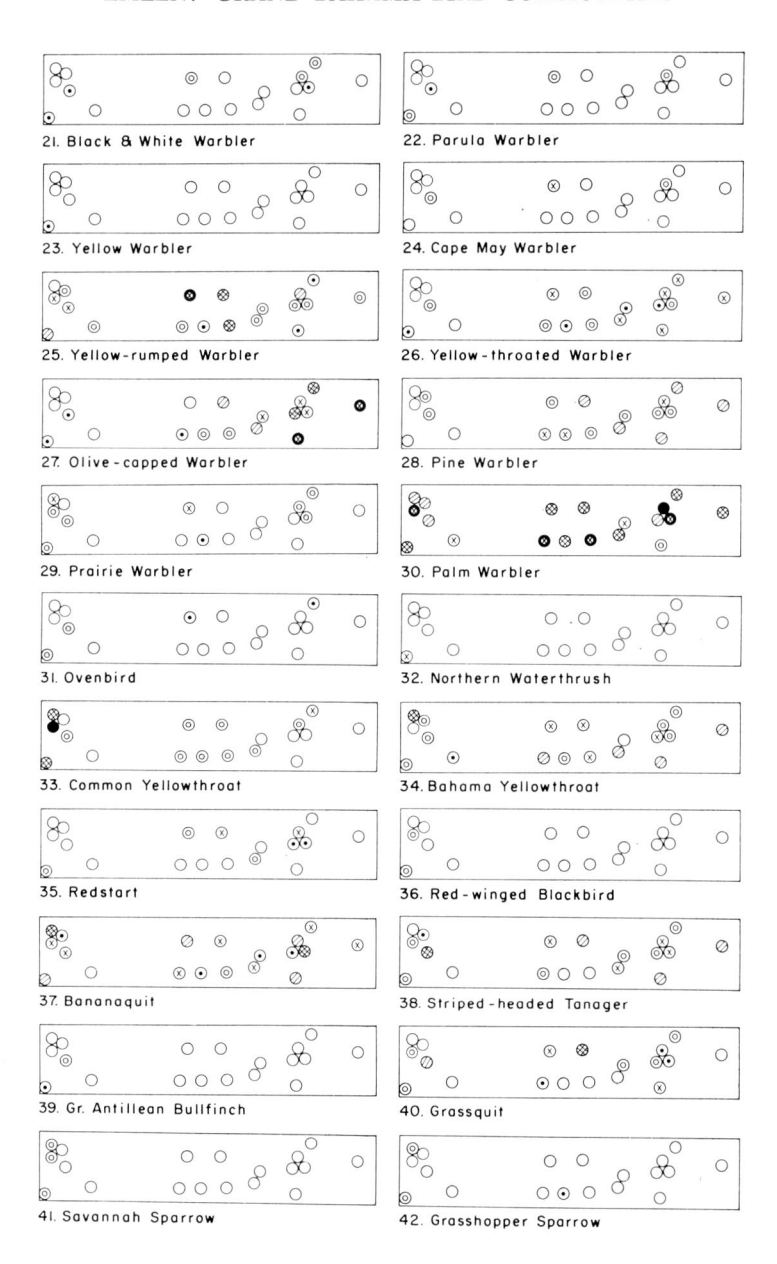

21. Black & White Warbler
22. Parula Warbler
23. Yellow Warbler
24. Cape May Warbler
25. Yellow-rumped Warbler
26. Yellow-throated Warbler
27. Olive-capped Warbler
28. Pine Warbler
29. Prairie Warbler
30. Palm Warbler
31. Ovenbird
32. Northern Waterthrush
33. Common Yellowthroat
34. Bahama Yellowthroat
35. Redstart
36. Red-winged Blackbird
37. Bananaquit
38. Striped-headed Tanager
39. Gr. Antillean Bullfinch
40. Grassquit
41. Savannah Sparrow
42. Grasshopper Sparrow

dimension were calculated for these species as means by weighting the value of each stand's position on the gradient (multiplying it by the bird density) and dividing the resultant mean by the highest value available to the birds, i.e. that of the stand positioned highest on the gradient ($X = [f(x)/N]/ \times $ Max.). The measure of dispersion is the standard deviation from the actual mean (not the percent value), divided by and represented as a percent of the mean (C.V. $= \sigma/\bar{X} \times 100$) so as to allow for comparisons between species. Mean population densities for the pine stands and other (not pine) stands are given at the bottom of the table for ready reference.

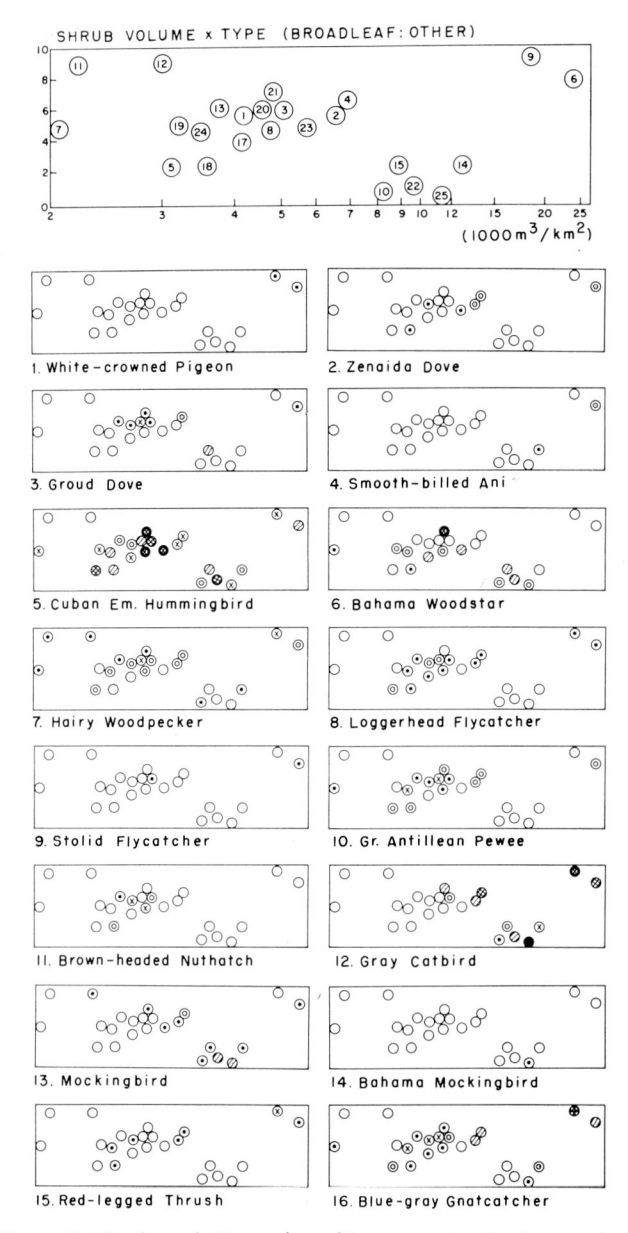

FIGURE 21. Winter distribution of 36 species with respect to shrub type (vertical axis) and volume of shrub and ground vegetation (horizontal axis). For explanation see Figures 11 and 19.

In this table a low coefficient of variation (dispersion) relative to that shown by the other four species on the same dimension suggests that the species is using cues associated with that dimension in selecting its habitat, while a high coefficient suggests that the dimension is relatively inconsequential to the species in making its selection. However, complicated ecological relationships between various parameters of the forest may negate the validity of such interpretations.

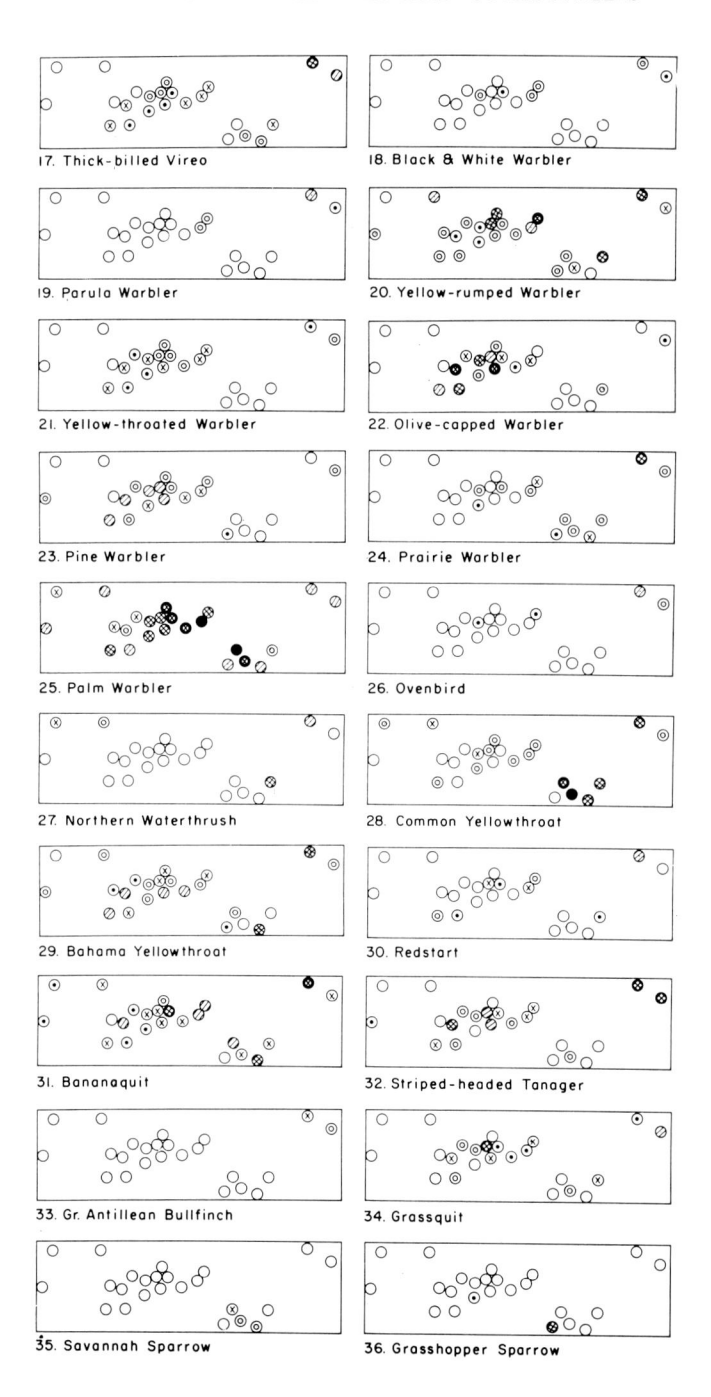

17. Thick-billed Vireo
18. Black & White Warbler
19. Parula Warbler
20. Yellow-rumped Warbler
21. Yellow-throated Warbler
22. Olive-capped Warbler
23. Pine Warbler
24. Prairie Warbler
25. Palm Warbler
26. Ovenbird
27. Northern Waterthrush
28. Common Yellowthroat
29. Bahama Yellowthroat
30. Redstart
31. Bananaquit
32. Striped-headed Tanager
33. Gr. Antillean Bullfinch
34. Grassquit
35. Savannah Sparrow
36. Grasshopper Sparrow

For example, the low C.V. values for the Brown-headed Nuthatch along the pine canopy, tree density, and foliage volume dimensions may indicate a key role for these dimensions for habitat selection in the species, but the equally low coefficients (relative to other species) along the shrub cover and shrub volume dimensions probably should not be interpreted in the same way for this normally aboreal

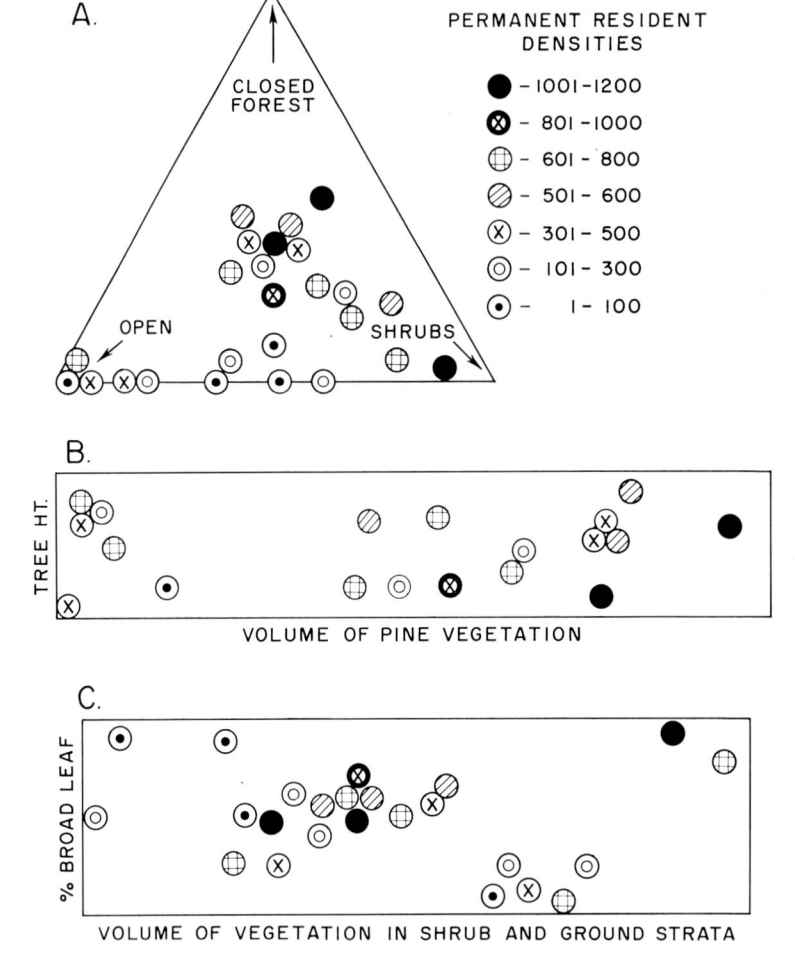

FIGURE 22. Distribution of total population density along habitat gradients for the permanent resident species of the wintering community of Grand Bahama. The points representing the 25 stands are positioned as in Figure 11 where they are identified.

species. They could indicate that when the birds visit the understory they are very selective, but more likely they simply reflect the effect of a dense tree canopy on the growth form of the understory.

For most of the species represented in Figures 19, 20, and 21 I evaluated dispersion or specialization in terms of the proportion of the available range of variation that was occupied along each parameter gradient. A species was classed as a specialist when its distribution along the indicated gradient was restricted to about one-third or less of the range available to it. Species dispersed over about two-thirds of the range were classed as intermediates, and those well dispersed over the entire range, as generalists.

Using these criteria there were more generalists among the winter residents than the permanent residents on all of the dimensions except ground cover exposed to the sky (Table 7, cols. 1 and 2). Further, when the 3 dimensions graphed in

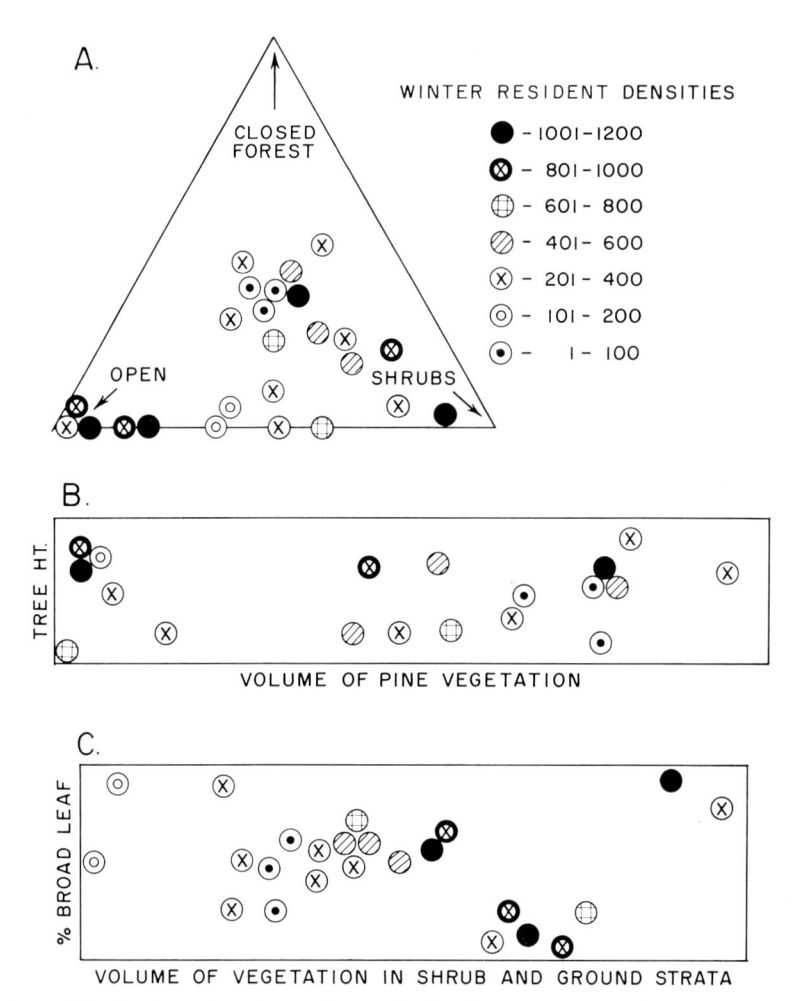

FIGURE 23. Distribution of total population density for the winter resident species.

the triangle diagrams are considered together only 2 of the 12 specialists (17%) were WRs while 15 of the 32 generalists (49%) were WRs. Similarly, when the 2 understory dimensions are combined, only 1 of the 6 specialists (17%) were WRs while 11 of the 30 generalists (37%) were WRs. Generalization is a majority condition in all cases; its higher incidence in winter residents may have evolved as an adaptation for, or arisen as a consequence of the migratory way of life.

Colonizers deriving from island sources might be expected to be less specialized (broader amplitudes) in their habitat responses than those deriving from continental areas where the number of species and community diversity is characteristically greater, and habitats are presumably more finely apportioned among the members of the fauna. The data from Grand Bahama, however, provide little or no support for such an hypothesis. Using the H' measure of diversity across habitat types (Table 5) as the measure of distribution amplitude, and an H' value of 0.90 as the arbitrary threshold of specialization, 7 of the 13 species

TABLE 5a
Distribution of Species Through the Seven Habitat Types on Grand Bahama Island (Permanent Residents)

Perm. res. species	Standard pines	Young pines	Coppets	Mangrove	Marsh	Old fields	Coastal sand	Types (S)	(H') Div.
White-cr. Pigeon	—	—	3.85	—	—	—	—	1	0
Mourning Dove	4.75	—	—	15.00	—	—	—	2	0.551
Zenaida Dove*	4.18	0.93	5.00	—	—	—	—	3	0.932
Ground Dove*	7.60	1.00	1.75	—	—	—	41.50	4	0.650
K. W. Quail Dove	—	—	—	—	—	—	25.50	1	0
Sm.-billed Ani	—	—	10.5	—	5.70	—	—	2	0.650
C. Emerald Hum'bd*	98.50	155.00	90.5	—	12.00	73.80	35.00	6	1.569
Bah. Woodstar*	2.79	72.54	—	—	—	48.00	54.00	4	1.146
Hairy Woodpecker*	14.14	6.61	39.5	3.95	2.50	—	—	5	1.160
Gray Kingbird	—	—	—	0.80	—	—	—	1	0
Logg. Flycatcher*	6.73	3.34	3.85	—	—	—	—	3	1.047
Stolid Flycatcher	0.25	—	3.50	—	—	—	—	2	0.245
Gr. Ant. Pewee*	11.04	9.29	9.00	—	—	—	—	3	1.094
Bahama Swallow*	—	—	—	—	61.00	66.33	4.60	3	9.817
Brown-h. Nuthatch*	16.98	—	—	—	—	—	—	1	0
Mockingbird*	1.50	1.23	1.05	0.75	1.30	44.00	4.60	7	0.795
Bah. Mockingbird	—	—	—	—	—	1.07	—	1	0
Red-leg. Thrush*	1.99	1.19	28.90	—	—	—	—	3	0.389
Bl-gr. Gnatcatcher*	30.96	11.76	153.00	—	10.00	2.57	—	5	0.873
Thk.-billed Vireo*	15.21	18.91	133.50	—	35.00	7.33	—	5	1.112
Yel.-throated Warb.*	30.51	15.90	9.55	—	—	—	—	3	0.890
Olive-cap. Warb.*	113.50	69.46	3.50	—	20.00	—	—	4	0.991
Pine Warbler*	39.75	38.29	9.00	—	—	1.43	—	4	1.023
Bah. Yellowthroat*	28.71	46.36	80.05	7.00	—	53.50	7.00	6	1.517
Bananaquit*	61.66	28.91	159.50	20.85	39.00	65.67	69.50	7	1.752
Str.-headed Tanager*	44.38	24.93	156.50	—	—	3.33	—	4	0.880
Gr. Ant. Bullfinch	—	—	34.00	—	—	—	—	1	0
Grassquit*	37.70	8.53	50.10	3.15	34.00	9.00	—	6	1.488
28 species	21	18	21	7	10	12	8		
Total P.R.	572.8	510.8	986.1	51.5	220.5	376.0	241.7		

(54%) of Antillean derivation were specialists, while 7 of 15 (47%) of the continental species were specialists. In analyses of spread along the 7 habitat dimensions of the habitat diagrams, species of Antillean origin had higher incidences of specialization than continentally derived species in 3, lower in 3, and equal in 1 (Table 7). Looking at recency of colonization (Table 7, last 2 cols.) as indicated by lack of recognized specific or subspecific differentiation, the very small sample showed a higher incidence of specialization among the recent arrivals on 5 of the dimensions, an equal representation on 1 (exposed ground cover), and a lower incidence on 1 (height of pine trees).

Density-Dispersion Relations

The relation between habitat tolerance limits as revealed by dispersion indices (H' values in Table 5a) and density tolerance limits as revealed by densities in the most preferred habitat (maximum densities in Table 5a) were explored

TABLE 5b
Distribution of Species Through the Seven Habitat Types on Grand Bahama Island (Winter Residents)

Winter res. species	Standard pines	Young pines	Coppets	Mangrove	Marsh	Old fields	Coastal sand	Types (S)	Div. (H')
Yel.-bellied Sapsucker	4.29	—	22.00	—	—	—	—	2	0.450
Catbird*	29.25	—	<u>251.00</u>	—	54.00	249.40	14.00	5	1.181
American Robin	—	—	—	—	<u>1.70</u>	—	—	1	0
Bl.-and-Wh. Warb.*	6.25	—	<u>16.05</u>	—	—	—	—	2	0.593
Worm-eating Warb.	<u>0.91</u>	—	—	—	—	—	—	1	0
Orange-crowned Warb.	0.61	—	—	<u>3.65</u>	—	—	—	2	0.409
Parula Warbler*	5.63	1.57	<u>56.90</u>	—	—	—	—	3	0.767
Yellow Warbler	—	—	—	<u>6.50</u>	—	—	—	1	0
Magnolia Warbler	—	—	<u>2.30</u>	—	—	—	—	1	0
Cape May Warbler*	<u>9.75</u>	—	6.00	—	—	—	—	2	0.658
Blk.-thr. Blue Warbler	—	—	<u>48.80</u>	—	—	—	—	1	0
Yel.-rumped Warbler	78.88	43.43	120.50	40.00	<u>146.00</u>	16.67	23.00	7	1.715
Blk.-thr. Green Warb.	0.53	—	<u>7.00</u>	—	—	—	—	2	0.254
Prairie Warbler*	14.63	0.83	<u>87.00</u>	—	17.00	24.90	9.50	6	1.279
Palm Warbler*	255.50	196.71	66.50	71.50	25.00	160.67	<u>558.50</u>	7	1.602
Ovenbird*	1.11	—	<u>63.00</u>	—	—	—	—	2	0.086
N. Waterthrush*	—	—	<u>48.50</u>	27.00	125.00	—	—	3	0.900
Com. Yellowthroat*	13.49	9.80	108.00	43.50	<u>228.00</u>	216.00	341.00	7	1.536
Wilson's Warbler	—	—	<u>6.50</u>	—	—	—	—	1	0
Redstart*	12.69	2.71	<u>48.50</u>	—	5.70	—	—	4	0.894
Red-w. Blackbird*	—	—	—	<u>49.00</u>	31.00	6.67	2.65	4	1.007
Savannah Sparrow	—	—	—	—	—	11.00	<u>34.50</u>	2	0.552
Grasshopper Sparrow*	—	1.04	—	—	—	<u>51.67</u>	—	2	0.098
Lincoln Sparrow	—	—	—	—	—	—	<u>11.50</u>	1	0
24 species	14	7	16	7	9	8	8		
Total W.R.	433.5	256.1	912.7	241.2	633.4	751.3	994.7		
Total P.R. & W.R.	1006.4	766.9	1898.8	292.7	853.9	1127.3	1236.4		

Values are individuals per km² in each type. * = species with total densities greater than 3.0 birds/km².
Values for the preferred habitat(s) of each species are underlined.

by plotting the recorded values for these two parameters for all species in Figure 24. The pattern that emerges shows an overall positive correlation between maximum density and habitat dispersion. But the regression slope obviously changes near midpoint, suggesting that different regulatory factors may be operating under different conditions of density and/or dispersion.

An examination of the overall pattern of points in terms of the models of dynamic density and dispersion regulation depicted in Figure 17 suggests several relationships with heuristic implications. Of special interest is the absence of points in the lower right quadrant. This seems to indicate that no species with a high (> approx. 65 birds/km²) density in its preferred habitat type failed to spill over into secondary types in large numbers. Apparently the density regulating factor(s), whether carrying capacity or social saturation, were functioning and causing overflow in all high density species. In a similar vein the points in the lower left quadrant may represent species that for one reason or another had not reacted to either social saturation or carrying capacity levels in their preferred habitat. Points in the upper left quadrant may by the same token represent

TABLE 6

Position and Disperson of Five Pine Foliage Gleaners Along Nine Gradients of the Pine Forest Habitats[1]

	Brown-headed nuthatch		Blue-gray gnatcatcher		Yellow-throated warbler		Olive-capped warbler		Pine warbler	
	$\bar{x}$[2]	C.V.[3]	$\bar{x}$	C.V.	$\bar{x}$	C.V.	$\bar{x}$	C.V.	$\bar{x}$	C.V.
Pine tree parameters										
Canopy cover	.87	10	.69	23	.72	26	.79	16	.66	28
Tree density	.87	10	.71	24	.73	27	.80	15	.66	29
Tree height	.77	23	.63	33	.60	46	.51	48	.49	57
Foliage volume	.86	10	.69	23	.72	35	.79	15	.58	37
Understory parameters										
Shrub cover	.49	11	.62	33	.60	44	.50	17	.59	26
Shrub height	.24	104	.49	91	.38	86	.09	271	.18	183
Shrub type	.96	23	.94	15	.92	17	.80	26	.69	38
Shrub volume	.61	16	.74	28	.69	27	.54	24	.64	27
Ground cover	.66	26	.68	31	.63	35	.68	26	.63	32
Population density	$\bar{x}$	max	$\bar{x}$	max	$\bar{x}$	max	$\bar{x}$	max	$\bar{x}$	max
Pine forests	10.5	48	25	62	27	56	107	334	44	72
Other habitats	0	0	27	207	3.2	11	2.3	20	3.0	18

[1] Stands with greater than 20% pine cover.
[2] Position of the center (mean) of distribution on the gradient as a percent of the maximum available (x/x max).
[3] Standard deviation expressed as percent of the mean ($\alpha/\bar{x} \times 100$).

species with low social saturation thresholds that had reached those thresholds in the preferred habitats and spilled over extensively, or species whose preferred habitats had low carrying capacities that had been filled and overflowed. And finally, points in the upper right quadrant may represent species that had high maximum density tolerances in habitats capable of supporting dense populations but had nevertheless reached and exceeded those limits in their preferred types and spilled over into secondary types.

The possible role of interspecies competition and other complex factors operating

TABLE 7

Habitat Specialization Along Seven Gradients in Various Elements of the Grand Bahama Land Bird Community[1]

	Community elements[2]						
	Seasonal status		Geographic derivation			Colonization recency	
Habitat parameters	P.R.	W.I.	Cont.	Ant.	C.-A.	Recent	Old
Vegetation layer open to sky							
Pine cover	37	29	67	17	42	50	40
Shrub cover	32	12	17	17	42	50	25
Ground cover	22	35	17	17	33	25	25
Pine vegetation volume	30	24	50	0	42	50	30
Pine tree height	15	6	17	17	17	0	20
Understory volume	42	17	50	33	42	75	35
Understory composition	21	8	17	0	33	50	15
N =	27	17	6	6	12	4	20

[1] Values are incidence (%) of specialized species in the community where specialization is defined as distribution restricted to one-third or less of the range available.
[2] Community elements analyzed are: seasonal status (permanent residents and winter residents), geographic derivation (continental, Antillean, and continent via Antilles), and recency of colonization (recent or old as suggested by degree of taxonomic differentiation). For definitions of terms see text.

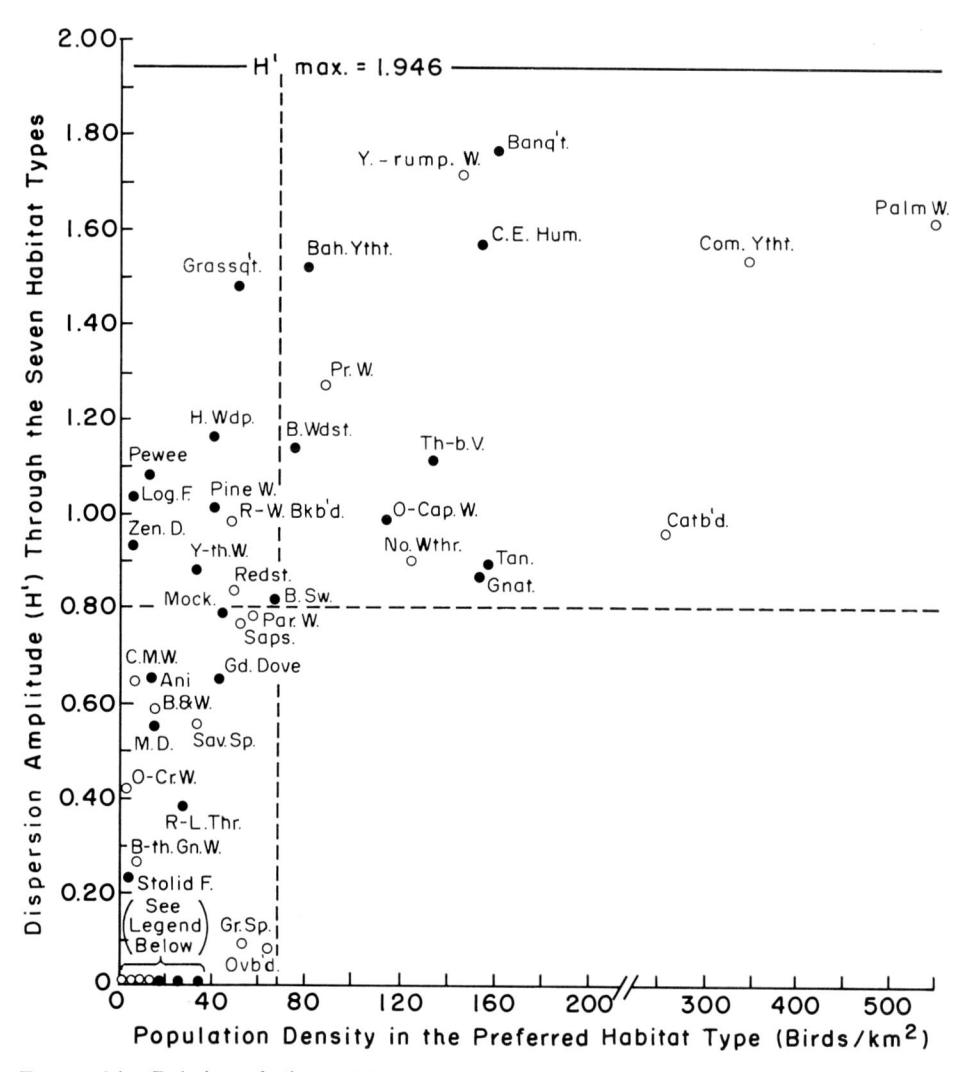

FIGURE 24. Relation of dispersal into secondary habitats (ecological amplitudes) to population density in the preferred habitat. Solid circles indicate permanent resident species; open circles indicate winter residents. The three permanent residents and four winter resident species grouped near the lower left corner are, reading from the left: Magnolia Warbler, Yellow Warbler, Wilson's Warbler, Lincoln's Sparrow, Brown-headed Nuthatch, Key West Quail Dove, and Greater Antillean Bullfinch. Symbols for species can be identified by referring to the list of species in the Appendix or in Table 2.

within habitats is of course bypassed in these analyses. The omission is unfortunate, but until methods for evaluating these factors as separate entities and applying them as modifiers are developed, they must be treated simply as aspects of the habitats affecting both density and dispersion in as yet unmeasured ways.

OVERLAP AND SIMILARITY

Measuring overlaps.—Similar patterns of habitat response in two or more members of a fauna imply a certain amount of cohabitation or distributional overlap, especially when the distributional amplitude of one or both of the species is broad. Furthermore, a high incidence of overlap will tend to increase the frequency of encounters and behavioral interactions between members of the two species and, at least potentially, raise the level of competition for resources in short supply and/or for favorable positions in the vegetation. Habitat overlap or frequency of cooccupation of habitats is thus a critical consideration in the dynamics of a fauna such as that of Grand Bahama Island.

In this analysis we are concerned primarily with the interactions of individuals as representatives of species. The appropriate measure of similarity or overlap between any two species should thus reflect the characteristics of the species regardless of the number of individuals actually involved in the interactions. I have therefore used percent values for the distribution through the seven habitat types and determined the overlap for each species pair by adding the overlaps for all cases where the two occurred together. I then divided the sum by the maximum possible overlap, always 100%, to obtain values suitable for direct comparisons. Such values have little value in themselves but hold considerable heuristic potential for comparisons of phylogenetic, geographic, seasonal, and perhaps other elements in a community.

A tabulation of overlaps between habitat types is presented for all pair combinations among the 34 species with densities greater than 3 birds per km^2 in Table 8.

Overlap and phylogenetic relationships.—Closely related species with their basically similar morphology might be expected to be more similar in habitat distribution and show more habitat overlap than remotely related species, except as competition in sympatry might promote ecological displacement and accelerate evolutionary divergence. Overlap values (Table 8) were very high ($> 80\%$) between the 3 congeneric warblers of the permanent resident element, the Pine Warbler, Olive-capped Warbler, and Yellow-throated Warbler, but aside from this there is no evidence in the data of a positive correlation between phylogenetic relationship and habitat overlap. The incidence of high ($\geq 60\%$) overlap in Table 8 was 4/30 (13.3%) for congeneric pairings, 9/97 (9.3%) for confamilial pairings, and 116/561 (20.7%) for all pairings. The slightly higher incidence for congenerics than confamilials in this series can be accounted for entirely by the high values for the 3 PR warblers mentioned above. The Grand Bahama sample is frustratingly small, but if this apparent negative correlation with phylogenetic relationship is real, the three cases of high overlap in congeneric warblers could reflect unresolved competition following recent colonization, while the low overlap among confamilials reflects relations between species that have been interacting on the Island over longer periods of time.

Overlap and geographic derivation.—Island colonists from the same geographic source, e.g. either the North American continent or the Antilles, were presumably exposed to each other in many cases before they immigrated. As groups they might therefore be predicted to have evolved greater ecological independence and show less overlap than species converging on an island from different sources. The data seem to support this prediction: I compared the incidence of high overlap ($> 80\%$ in Table 8) in pairings where both species were of continental origin

TABLE 8

Overlap in Habitat Selection of the 34 Common Species (Density > 3.0 Birds/km²) in Winter[1]

	[2]Z	G	C	B	H	S	L	G	B	B	C	M	R	G	T	B	P	C	Y	Y	O	P	P	P	O	N	C	B	R	R	B	S	G	G
Zenaida Dove	20																																	
Ground Dove	50	28																																
C. Emerald Hum'bird	11	27	58																															
Bahama Woodstar	80	20	53	12																														
Hairy Woodpecker	33	9	28	2	37																													
Yel.-b. Sapsucker	78	20	65	24	59	33																												
Logg. Flycatcher	78	20	72	32	62	33	89																											
Gr. Antillean Pewee	0	4	22	31	4	46	0	0																										
Bahama Swallow	41	15	21	2	5	48	38	0	0																									
Brown-hd. Nuthatch	52	11	43	31	52	33	36	53	4	5																								
Gray Catbird	5	16	33	40	11	7	5	5	54	3	53																							
No. Mockingbird	59	12	29	5	69	33	38	41	0	6	52	8																						
Red-legged Thrush	70	20	44	8	83	38	49	51	6	15	53	11	83																					
Bl-gr. Gnatcatcher	66	13	42	14	79	49	44	47	20	7	55	13	73	82																				
Thick-billed Vireo	78	18	41	2	87	33	56	59	0	28	52	5	78	87	71																			
Bk.-and-wh. Warbler	61	14	31	4	68	33	39	42	0	9	52	7	95	82	71	81																		
Parula Warbler	79	18	41	2	59	33	76	68	0	62	52	7	44	88	45	66	47																	
Cape May Warbler	53	25	57	20	62	63	54	53	38	17	50	19	37	53	54	44	39	44																
Yel.-rumped Warbler	68	20	67	39	48	22	89	83	0	55	23	7	23	38	43	45	28	72	43															
Yel.-throated Warbler	52	18	59	35	43	17	74	71	10	55	7	9	12	27	28	39	13	19	38	85														
Olive-capped Warbler	61	20	66	44	41	16	79	80	2	45	17	9	20	32	28	38	22	55	38	84	80													
Pine Warbler	60	19	55	25	70	44	38	41	31	10	70	30	63	73	79	66	66	48	56	27	21	22												
Prairie Warbler	33	62	50	59	41	12	39	39	17	19	25	31	15	29	27	24	16	24	27	39	37	40	35											
Palm Warbler	51	7	21	2	61	29	32	0	2	48	5	92	75	65	74	90	40	28	19	3	12	58	7											
Ovenbird	24	3	23	0	34	87	24	24	46	0	24	5	24	29	41	24	24	4	24	11	10	35	11	24										
No. Waterthrush	14	42	40	55	22	37	14	14	50	1	38	41	14	25	13	14	13	51	14	14	47	61	13	40										
Common Yellowthroat	58	21	72	50	62	33	61	64	27	13	68	36	46	55	56	49	47	49	59	51	35	46	68	51	38	27	42							
Bahama Yellowthroat	72	20	45	6	85	41	50	53	8	18	52	9	80	93	88	81	56	39	51	29	71	32	22	53										
Redstart	0	3	13	11	10	35	0	45	0	14	0	14	0	0	0	46	0	0	10	2	30	18	0	35	39	14	8							
Red-w. Blackbird	56	19	65	39	65	44	48	51	27	14	69	34	46	61	62	50	47	38	31	32	76	60	38	57	76	62	24							
Str.-headed Tanager	78	35	51	13	90	33	58	61	1	19	53	8	78	90	81	88	80	58	47	42	71	36	70	24	15	61	90	1	58					
Blk.-faced Grassquit	68	20	56	14	68	39	60	63	30	27	47	17	45	62	69	57	46	62	80	50	44	44	63	41	37	48	46	63	66	32	72	62		
Grasshopper Sparrow	2	2	18	29	2	0	2	2	50	0	46	83	2	2	3	6	0	3	0	6	2	2	4	18	14	0	0	24	26	2	8	17	3	8

[1] Values are percent overlap for each pair combination obtained by summing the overlaps from Table 4 (transformed to percent values) in each of the 7 vegetation types and dividing the total by 100, the values for complete overlap.
[2] Letters at column heads match the initial letters in list of species on left margin.

TABLE 9
Habitat Overlap and Geographic Derivation[1]

Overlaps ≥ 80%	C-A	C-C	A-A	C-C+ A-A
Instances	10	2	2	4
Incidence (%)	71.4	14.3	14.3	28.6
Pairs available	84	21	66	87
Expected incidence	49.1	12.2	38.6	50.8
Actual/expected	1.45	1.17	0.37	0.56

[1] Comparison of the incidence of high (80%) overlap in habitat distribution between pairs of species where the two came from different geographic sources (continent-Antilles) and where both came from the same source (continent-continent, or Antilles-Antilles).

(C-C), or Antillean origin (A-A) with those in which the two came from different sources (C-A) (Table 9). Of the 14 PR species pairs available for the analysis, 4 had common origins and 10 had split origins. Four is only a little more than half that expected for the C-C and A-A categories on the basis of available pairings, while 10 is nearly 50% above that expected for the mixed (C-A) origins category. The data thus appear to support this prediction.

The possibility that some WRs might be dominated by PRs and forced into partial segregation in less favorable habitats, as suggested by Morel (1968) and Moreau (1972), or that WRs might simply avoid established residents, territorial or not, in their preferred habitats by settling elsewhere, was tested by comparing the incidence of habitat overlap in the inter-element pairings, i.e. between PRs and WRs with the intra-element pairing of the PRs (Table 10). Matched against the ratios expected on the basis of available pairings, there is an indication of the predicted lower incidence of overlap in the pairings between PRs and WRs. However, with no controls for such factors as different food habits and distributional amplitudes among WRs, this difference cannot be regarded as more than suggestive of interaction-induced segregation. This question is examined again at the within-habitat level in Chapter 7.

Ecological spacing.—The extent of habitat overlap between two species depends on the similarity as well as the amplitude of habitat responses. Habitat similarity, or the closeness of the centers of ecological distribution of species in multidimensional habitat space may be represented graphically by an ordination procedure developed by Bray and Curtis (1957) and applied to bird communities by Beals (1960, 1973) and Emlen (1972) in which the coordinates represent axes

TABLE 10
Habitat Overlap and Residency Status[1]

Overlaps ≥ 80%	P.R.-W.R.	P.R.-P.R.	W.R.-W.R.
Instances	14	14	5
Incidence (%)	42.4	42.4	15.2
Pairs available	280	190	91
Expected incidence	49.9	32.9	16.2
Actual/expected	0.85	1.29	0.94

[1] Comparison of the incidence of high (≥ 80%) overlap in habitat distribution between (a) permanent residents and winter residents, (b) permanent residents and permanent residents, and (c) winter residents and winter residents. Expected incidence is the percent of high overlaps in the total sample of the indicated category.

of variation in overlap rather than specific variables. The distance between any two points representing species in such an ordination is thus a direct reflection of similarity in habitat responses as determined by the amount of overlap recorded for all species pairs in the community. A two-dimensional ordination of this sort based on the overlaps shown in Table 8 is presented for the seven habitat types of Grand Bahama Island in Figure 25. I used the overlaps between habitat types rather than between stands because of the unequal representation of the major types in the sample of stands available. The distance between any two points in this graph is an objective indication of the similarity in mean habitat responses of the two species they represent, and any grouping of points indicates a cluster of ecologically similar species. These distances are, of course, based entirely on the frequency of habitat overlap or association through the series and, as plotted, are independent of any presumptions of causal factors. Thus the axes in Figure 25 cannot be labelled.

In Figure 25 most of the species are grouped close to one of the terminal species on the x axis (Parula Warbler), indicating minimum overlap with the species at the other terminal (Grasshopper Sparrow). Similarly they are grouped close to the Brown-headed Nuthatch and far from the Red-winged Blackbirds, the two terminal species on the y axis, calculated after and independently of the x ordination. Primarily pineland species are, not surprisingly, grouped near the nuthatch, a pine forest specialist, while open habitat species tend to center near the blackbird. Species related at the family level are well scattered over the grid, but congenerics tend to be clustered. Winter invader species (open circles) seem to be more peripheral than the permanent residents (closed circles) in the overall scatter and show a general concentration near the Parula Warbler at the right end of the x axis. In a similar vein, many of the PRs tend to be clustered near the nuthatch at the top of the y axis. Further analysis of the environmental factors implicated for the two axes in the figure and for additional axes not shown are not attempted in this report.

6—THE PINE FOREST COMMUNITY—SEASONAL CHANGES

Procedures and Definitions

In the rest of this monograph I focus on the bird communities of the submature pine forests, the dominant and most complex of the habitat types on Grand Bahama. Most of the material for these analyses was collected in stands 1, 2, and 3 (Table 1) in 1968, supplemented with data obtained in the across habitat studies of 1969. Details of the within-habitat structure of these forests are presented in Table 11 and summarized graphically in Figure 26. The floristic composition of the tree and shrub strata is summarized in Table 12.

For tracing the seasonal changes in community composition, density and diversity in the forest I use the same basic system employed in the across habitat studies but refine them for more precise analyses. Thus I recognize three seasonal communities and four residency elements: a wintering community with permanent (PR) and winter resident (WR) elements, a breeding season community with permanent (PR) and summer residents (SR), and a transient community in the spring (and fall) when PRs and persisting WRs and/or SRs are temporarily

TABLE 11
Physiognomic Characteristics of the Submature Pine Forests

	Plant dimensions (m)			Foliage type (% of total cover in the class)						Cover surface (%)		Foliage volume[1] (crown depth × area covered)			Number of trees
	Ht.	Crn. dpth.	Crn. diam.	N[2]	P	F	B.l.	B.m.	B.s.	Tot.	Exp. to sky	m³ per ha	%/S[3]	%/T[4]	N
Tree Stratum															
Emergents	17.4	4.3	4.4	100	0	0	0	0	0	1.5	1.5	484	4.0	2.7	10
Canopy trees	11.3	4.2	3.4	99.7	0	0	0	0.1	0.2	35	35	11,025	90.3	61.8	386
Subcanopy trees	7.3	2.9	2.2	99.5	0	0	0	0	0.5	3.2	0	695	5.7	3.9	85
Stumps	4	–	–	–	–	–	–	–	–	tr.[5]	tr.	–	–	–	8.2
All trees	–	–	–	99.7	0	0	0	tr.	0.2	40	37	12,204	100	68.5	488
Shrub Stratum															
High (> 2.0 m)	2.4	1.8	–	–	–	–	–	–	–	7	6	1,260	29.1	7.1	
Medium (1.0–1.9)	1.2	.9	–	–	–	–	–	–	–	23	15	2,070	48.7	11.6	
Low (< 1.0 m)	0.5	0.4	–	–	–	–	–	–	–	23	14	920	21.7	5.2	
All shrubs	–	–	–	0.8	21.6	9.1	33.0	18.5	17.0	53	35	4,250	100	23.8	
Ground Cover				v[6]	g	l	b								
High (> .20 m)	–	–	–	–	–	–	–	–	–	30	8.4	750	55	4.2	
Medium (.08–.20)	–	–	–	–	–	–	–	–	–	40	11.5	480	35	2.7	
Low (< .08 m)	–	–	–	–	–	–	–	–	–	29	8.1	145	10	0.8	
All gnd. cover	–	–	–	20.5	11.9	66.6	1.0	–	–	99	28	1,375	100	7.7	
Totals	–	–	–	–	–	–	–	–	–	192	100	17,829		100.1	

[1] Foliage volume refers to standing foliage, i.e. space occupied by tree crowns, shrub crowns, and ground cover. Data are based on sample sizes of 1,200 for all parameters except the tree height and crown data with 240 measurements.
[2] N = needles, P = palmate, F = fern-like, B.l. = Broadleaf-large, B.m. = Broadleaf-medium, B.s. = Broadleaf-small.
[3] %/S = percent of stratum.
[4] %/T = percent of total.
[5] tr. = trace.
[6] v = vines, g = grass, l = litter, b = bare.

TABLE 12
Dominant and Other Important Tree and Shrub Species in the Submature Pine Forests

Tree stratum		Lysiloma latisiliquum	3.3
Pinus caribaea	99.7	Ernodea littoralis	2.9
Lysiloma latisiliquum	0.3	Tetrazygia bicolor	2.7
		Trema lamarkianum	0.5
Shrub stratum		Ficus aurea	0.6
Metopium toxiferum	23.3	Swietiana mahagoni	0.5
Thrinax morrisii	20.6	Duranta repens	0.9
Pteridium aquilinum	8.3	Solanum erianthum	0.5
Tabebuia bahamensis	4.0	Calliandra haematomma	2.1
Lantana ovatifolia	3.8	Smilax havanensis	1.8
Coccoloba diversifolia	3.7	Myrsine floridana	1.3
Myrica cerifera	3.5	Eugenia axillaris	1.4
		Agave bahamensis	0.6

Values are % representation in their respective strata (based on occurrence at 1200 sample points). Identifications are from Britton and Millspaugh (1920) with revisions by W. Gillis.

supplemented by migrants in transit between northern and southern ranges (Trs). The temporal relations of these three communities and four residency elements on Grand Bahama are diagrammed in Figure 25. March 31 was arbitrarily taken as the termination date for the wintering community, and all WRs after 1 April were grouped with the transient element to constitute the transient community present during April and early May.

Density (individuals per km^2) and biomass (g per km^2) values for each species in a seasonal community were calculated on the basis of the number of equivalent km^2 transected while the particular species was present. For members of the wintering community, this period covered the entire 90 days in January, February, and March (both years). For the breeding season community it included all of April and May for the permanent resident species, but only the period between arrival on the island and the end of May for the summer resident species. Members of the transient community were present for varying periods of time; for the residual winter residents it was from 1 April to their departure; and for in-transit migrants it was from the arrival date to the departure date (period between the earliest and latest records for the species on the island).

Density and biomass values for each of the three seasonal communities are the sums of the values for each member species. Total density, biomass, and diversity for the entire assemblage during any given time interval were obtained by adding the values for the overlapping communities as such overlaps occurred. In this study there was a brief overlap of the wintering and transient communities in late March, and a longer period of overlap of the breeding and transient communities in April and early May (Fig. 27).

Rare species, stragglers, and vagrants create problems in bird community studies, particularly in establishing species lists and richness indices. In this study the problem was handled by operationally defining two classes: members and visitors. Species encountered in the submature forests over periods of more than 15 days and at frequencies greater than 1 in 10 transect counts were designated members. Those that were present for shorter periods or were recorded at lower

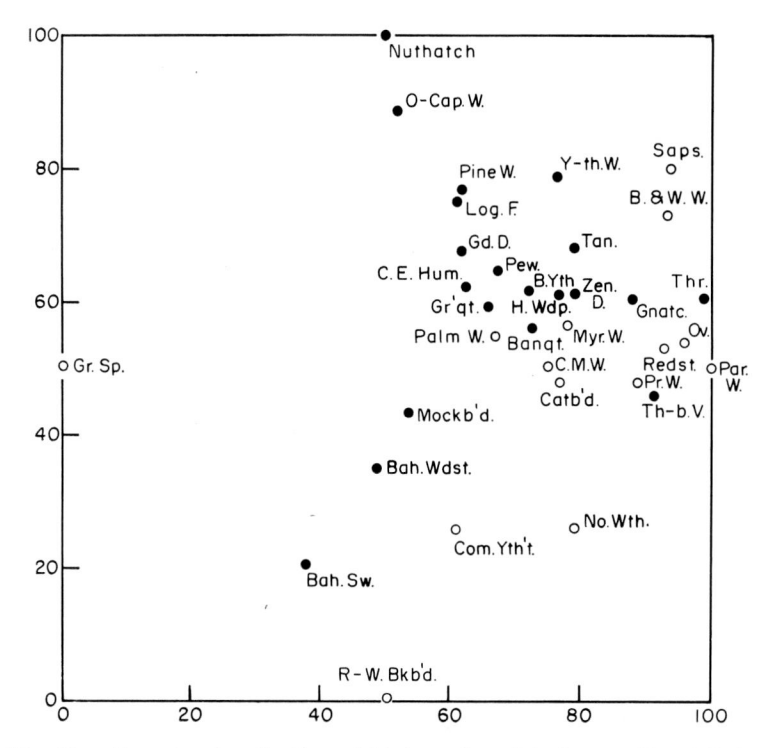

FIGURE 25. Two-dimensional ordination of bird species wintering on Grand Bahama Island showing habitat spacing as revealed by distribution overlaps through the 25 survey stands. Closed circles are permanent resident species; open circles are winter resident species.

frequencies, and those seen only outside the hours scheduled for transects or outside the survey stands were termed visitors.

SEASONAL CHANGES

Progressive monthly changes in the population structure, density, and biomass are shown in Figure 28. The number of species increased with the arrival of in-transit migrants and summer residents to a peak in early May, then dropped abruptly with the departure of the winter residents and in-transit migrants to 62% of the midwinter level at the end of May.

Density values for all species together declined almost linearly from 1,260 per km^2 on 1 January to 648 per km^2 by 1 June (Fig. 28B). The major factor in this reduction was the large difference between the number of winter invaders (3 months mean of 470 per km^2) and summer residents (mean of 18 per km^2). The number of permanent residents in the forests actually increased slightly due to local movements of some Zenaida Doves, Ground Doves, and Bahama Swallows from other habitats on the island, an influx that more than compensated for a partial emigration of Mockingbirds and Cuban Emerald Hummingbirds from the forests. The reduction in winter residents between January and March is attributable largely to a progressive decline in Palm Warblers, particularly in 1968.

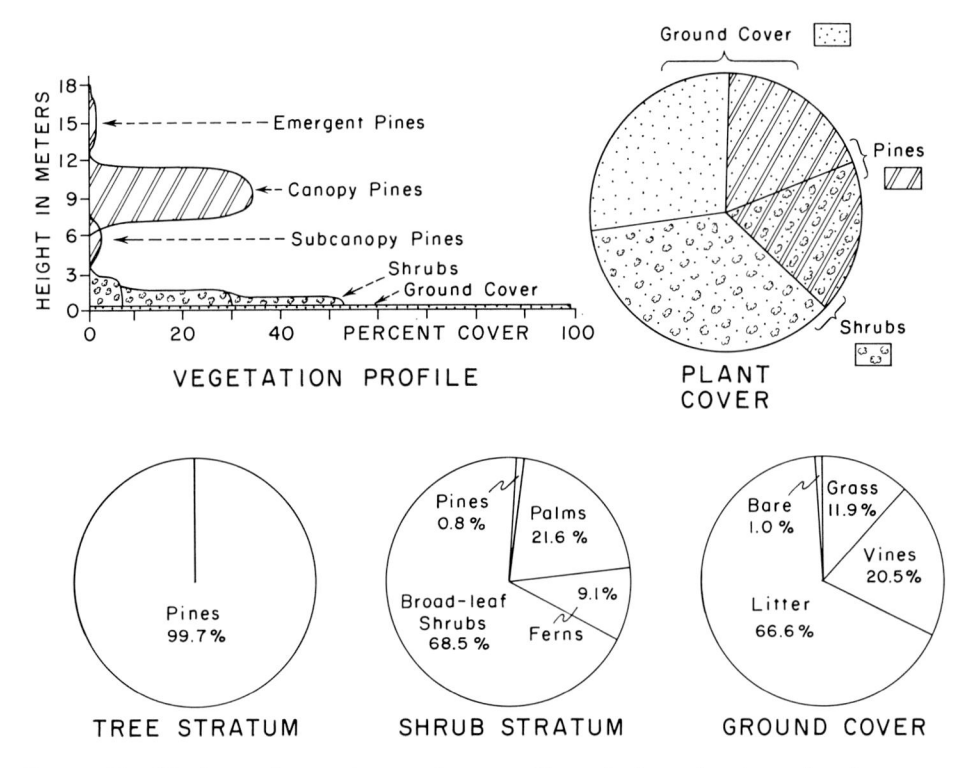

FIGURE 26. Physiognomic structure and composition of the submature pine forests on Grand Bahama Island. Values are means for the three survey stands.

Whether this decline represents an actual departure from the island, a diffusion into other local habitats, or mortality is not known. The remaining winter residents departed during April and early May. In-transit migrants were a minor element, even at the height of migration, and contributed only four individuals per km^2 (< 1%) to the 1 May total. The maximum representation of in-transit birds on any single transect count was on 5 May 1968 when they constituted 11 of the 119 birds recorded (9%).

Biomass values also declined (Fig. 28C) but to a somewhat lesser extent, because of the relatively large body size of the immigrant doves moving in from neighboring habitats.

The breeding season community.—Permanent resident species dominated the breeding season community of the submature pine forests with 19 of the 22 members and 5 of the 6 visitors (Tables 13 and 14). Of the three summer resident members, one, the Bahama Swallow, winters on Grand Bahama in other habitats, moving into the pine forests to nest in early April. The other two, the Gray Kingbird and the Black-whiskered Vireo, are true migrants, moving north from winter homes in the southern Caribbean and South America in early May. A few kingbirds wintered in coastal habitats on Grand Bahama in 1969. The single summer visitor species, the Cuban Nighthawk, migrates in from the south in late April.

TABLE 13
Size, Density, and Biomass[1] of the Residency Elements Composing the Three Seasonal Pine Forest Communities

	Wintering comm.			Breeding comm.			Transient comm.			All comm.
	Specs.	Dens.	Biom.	Specs.	Dens.	Biom.	Specs.	Dens.	Biom.	Specs.
Members										
Permanent res.[2]	19	599	7354	19	630	9000	–	–	–	19
Summer res.	–	–	–	3	18	476	–	–	–	3
Winter res.	13	570	6406	–	–	–	13	107	1167	13
In-transit migr.	–	–	–	–	–	–	–	3	37	1
Total	32	1169	13760	22	648	9476	14	110	1204	36
Visitors										
Permanent res.	5			5			–			5
Summer res.	–			1			–			1
Winter res.	8			–			3			8
In-transit migr.	–			–			6			6
Total	13			6			9			20
Grand Total	45			28			23			56

[1] Size = number of species, density = birds per km², biomass = g per km².
[2] The Yellow-throated Warbler is classified here as a permanent resident species but its population density and biomass are divided according to the relative abundance of the permanent resident and winter resident races.

In terms of density and biomass, the breeding season community was heavily dominated by permanent residents. Summer residents, including the locally migrant swallow, comprised only 3% of the individuals and 5% of the biomass.

The wintering community.—The 24 permanent resident species of the Grand Bahama pineland community (19 members and 5 visitors) were joined during the winter by 21 migrant invaders (WRs) from the north (13 members and 8 visitors) to produce an overall wintering community of 45 species (Tables 13 and 14). One permanent resident, the Yellow-throated Warbler, has a migrant population (race) as well as the resident population, so the total of winter invader species was 22 (14 members plus 8 visitors).

In terms of individuals and avian biomass the winter residents composed almost half (49%) of the wintering community. Without the dominant Palm Warbler, however, they would have constituted less than one fifth (17%) of the total.

These winter migrants came from breeding ranges in North America stretching from the mixed pinelands of the Gulf Coast to the tundra edge in northern Canada (Fig. 29). Seventeen of the species breed in the northern conifer-hardwood life area as mapped by Aldrich (1963), and of these, 11 breed exclusively in that area. Eleven (4 exclusively and 7 partly) make their summer homes in the eastern deciduous forest area between the Piedmont of central Georgia and the Great Lakes, and only 3 (all partly) summer in the mixed pineland of the southern coastal states. MacArthur (1959) has noted that it is the eastern deciduous forests where the migratory habit is most strongly developed; very few southern species are migratory. Although wintering here in a pineland habitat, about a third of the species, including the dominant Palm Warbler, are primarily birds of brushlands or deciduous forests in their northern homes.

TABLE 14
Residency Status, Density, and Biomass of Member and Visitor Species in the Three Seasonal Pine Forest Communities

	Res. status	Wintering community Dens. birds/km²	Wintering community Biom. g/km²	Breeding community Dens. birds/km²	Breeding community Biom. g/km²	Transient[3] community Dens. birds/km²	Transient[3] community Biom. g/km²	Days pres.
Members[1]								
Zenaida Dove	P	4.0	600	8.7	1300	—	—	
Ground Dove	P	3.5	122	9.4	328	—	—	
C. Emerald Hummingbird	P	106.00	318	84.0	252	—	—	
Hairy Woodpecker	P	10.6	530	8.7	435	—	—	
Yellow-bellied Sapsucker	W	3.5	158	—	—	0.5	22	20
Gray Kingbird	S	—	—	4.6	276	—	—	
Loggerhead Flycatcher	P	4.2	202	7.2	345	—	—	
Stolid Flycatcher	P	2.2	49	0.5	11	—	—	
Greater Antillean Pewee	P	17.0	170	21.9	219	—	—	
Bahama Swallow	S[4]	—	—	11.0	165	—	—	
Brown-headed Nuthatch	P	21.0	105	21.5	108	—	—	
Northern Mockingbird	P	3.2	153	0.4	19	—	—	
Catbird	W	7.7	292	—	—	3.9	112	41
Red-legged Thrush	P	3.0	210	7.2	503	—	—	
Blue-gray Gnatcatcher	P	49.0	245	48.6	243	—	—	
Thick-billed Vireo	P	12.6	202	25.2	403	—	—	
Black-whiskered Vireo	S	—	—	2.2	35	—	—	
Bahama Bananaquit	P	87.0	870	61.8	618	—	—	
Black-and-White Warbler	W	11.1	111	—	—	10.7	107	47
Parula Warbler	W	1.2	8	—	—	1.7	12	41
Cape May Warbler	W	1.0	8	—	—	3.3	37	37
Black-throated Blue Warbler	W	0.7	6	—	—	8.2	66	41
Yellow-rumped Warbler	W	13.5	135	—	—	2.2	22	15
Black-thr. Green Warb.	W	4.9	39	—	—	2.2	18	19
Yellow-throated Warbler (res. race)	P[5]	15.0	150	17.1	171	—	—	
Yellow-throated Warbler (migr. race)	W	45.0	405	—	—	5.0	45	10
Olive-capped Warbler	P	95.0	665	121.0	847	—	—	
Pine Warbler	P	40.5	486	42.5	510	—	—	
Black-poll Warbler	Tr	—	—	—	—	3.1	37	44
Prairie Warbler	W	11.4	91	—	—	4.2	34	20
Palm Warbler	W	452.0	4970	—	—	31.0	341	36
Ovenbird	W	1.5	29	—	—	7.0	133	44
Common Yellowthroat	W	9.7	107	—	—	7.3	80	44
Bahama Yellowthroat	P	30.3	485	31.2	500	—	—	
Redstart	W	6.7	47	—	—	19.7	138	55
Striped-headed Tanager	P	62.5	1440	79.4	1820	—	—	
Black-faced Grassquit	P	32.0	352	33.4	368	—	—	
Visitors[2]								
White-crowned Pigeon	P	N[6]		N		—		
Mourning Dove	P	N		N		—		
Yellow-billed Cuckoo	Tr	—		—		N		
Smooth-billed Ani	P	N		N		—		
Chuck-wills-widow	W	N		—		—		
Cuban Nighthawk	S	—		N		—		
Bahama Woodstar	P	N		N		—		
House Wren	Tr	—		—		T		
Ruby-crowned Kinglet	Tr	—		—		N		
Yellow-throated Vireo	Tr	—		—		N		
Blue-headed Vireo	W	N		—		—		
Worm-eating Warbler	W	T[7]		—		T		
Orange-crowned Warbler	W	N		—		—		
Golden-wing Warbler	W	T		—		—		
Magnolia Warbler	W	N		—		T		
Kirtland Warbler	W	N		—		—		

TABLE 14 (CONTINUED)

	Res. status	Wintering community Dens. birds/km²	Wintering community Biom. g/km²	Breeding community Dens. birds/km²	Breeding community Biom. g/km²	Transient[3] community Dens. birds/km²	Transient[3] community Biom. g/km²	Days pres.
Northern Waterthrush	W	N	—	—	—	T		
Hooded Warbler	Tr	—	—	—	—	T		
Indigo Bunting	Tr	—	—	—	—	T		
Greater Antillean Bullfinch	P	N		N		—		

[1] A member is a species that is present over a period of more than 15 days and observed more than once per 10 transect counts.
[2] A visitor is a species that does not meet the member criteria.
[3] The transient community includes all migratory species occurring only in transit plus all winter residents remaining after 31 March. The number of days when each transient species was present is shown in the last column. The density and biomass values for transients are averaged for the entire 60-day transient period.
[4] The Bahama Swallow is a permanent resident on Grand Bahama Island but was absent from the submature forests during the winter.
[5] The Yellow-throated Warbler has a resident, Bahama race and a migrant race invading the same habitat in winter. The two are generally distinguishable in the field.
[6] Indicates that the species was observed nearby, but not in the transect stands.
[7] T (trace) indicates that the species was observed in small numbers (<1 per 10 transects).

The dominance of the northern element among the winter invaders was more pronounced in the measurements of density and biomass than of species (Fig. 28). Approximately 86% of the individuals were from the northern forest area, 13% from the eastern or central area, and only 1% from the southern area. Nine-tenths of the birds in the northern element were Palm Warblers.

The transient community.—All 13 of the winter resident members and 3 of the 8 winter resident visitors remained for varying lengths of time after 1 April (Table 13) and thus became members (or visitors) of the transient community. These 16 species were joined by 7 in-transit species to produce a transient community totaling 23 species, variously present in the stands for from 10–55 days of the artificially delimited 60-day period (see Table 14, last column).

The residual winter invaders accounted for 97% of the individuals and 97% of the biomass in the transient community. Yellow-rumped Warblers and the migrant race of the Yellow-throated Warbler dropped off during the first half of April, and the dominant Palm Warblers between 6 and 16 April. But several of the winter species increased markedly for short periods during April or May as they received reinforcements from in-transit migrants. Waves of migrants, characteristic of migration on the continent, were only weakly developed except on

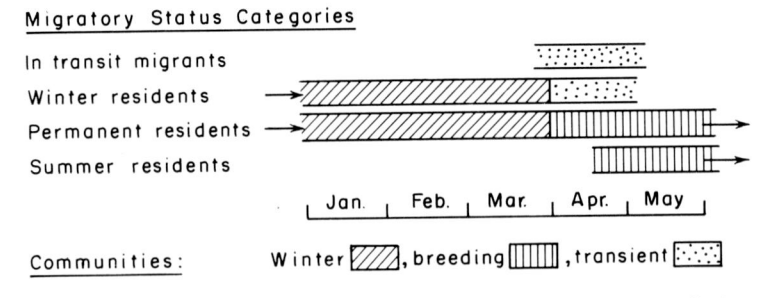

FIGURE 27. Assigned temporal limits and residence category structure of the wintering, breeding, and transient bird communities of the Grand Bahama submature pine forests.

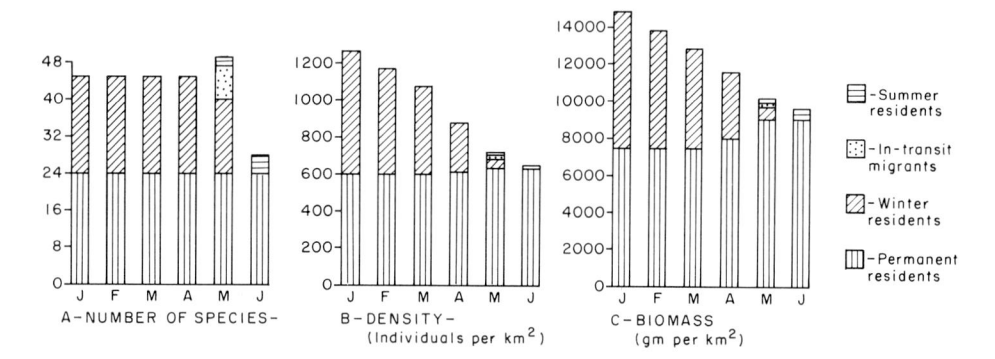

FIGURE 28. Monthly changes in the size and composition (by residence categories) of the bird communities of Grand Bahama submature pinelands, 1968–1969. The number of species present is recorded, and the density and biomass are estimated for the first of each month from January to June. For the permanent residents I used the wintering community 2-year average for density and biomass as given in Table 2 for the 1 January, 1 February and 1 March values, and the breeding community average for the 1 May and 1 June values; the 1 April value was interpolated. For the winter residents I took the density and biomass values for the wintering community and scaled them according to my records of day-to-day changes on the transect routes to give the 1 January to 1 April figures. The 1 May figures reflect the decline from the 1 April figures as indicated on the transect record sheets. For the summer residents, I applied the breeding community values as given in Table 14 directly for the 1 June figures, and scaled these figures down according to my records of arrival dates for the four species to give the 1 May figures. Density and biomass values for the in-transit migrants are those for the Blackpoll Warbler, the only completely in-transit species, plus increments above winter levels in persisting winter resident species.

one occasion, 5 May 1968, when birds belonging to winter resident and in-transit species comprised 63% of the total count.

IMPACT OF THE WINTER MIGRANT INVASION

The impact of a heavy annual invasion of migrants into the domain of a supposedly balanced bird community raises a number of interesting theoretical questions, especially in situations where habitat conditions and food resources are quite stable through the annual cycle. If the number of breeding species present on an island reflects a delicate equilibrium between colonization and extinction rates as proposed by MacArthur and Wilson (1967), what will be the effect of a doubling of the species numbers each fall? And if breeding densities are regulated by available food resources as argued by Lack (1954) and many others, what will be the effect of doubling the overall densities at a time when food supplies have not increased?

My Grand Bahama data provide no answers to the first question, but note that while species richness (members and visitors) in the pine forests increased from 28 in summer to 45 in winter (transients ignored), bird species diversity (H′) was actually slightly lower (2.39 vs. 2.62) in winter. This reduced diversity is clearly attributable to the relatively low equitability of the winter resident element—over 77% of the total population belonging to a single species. I know of no

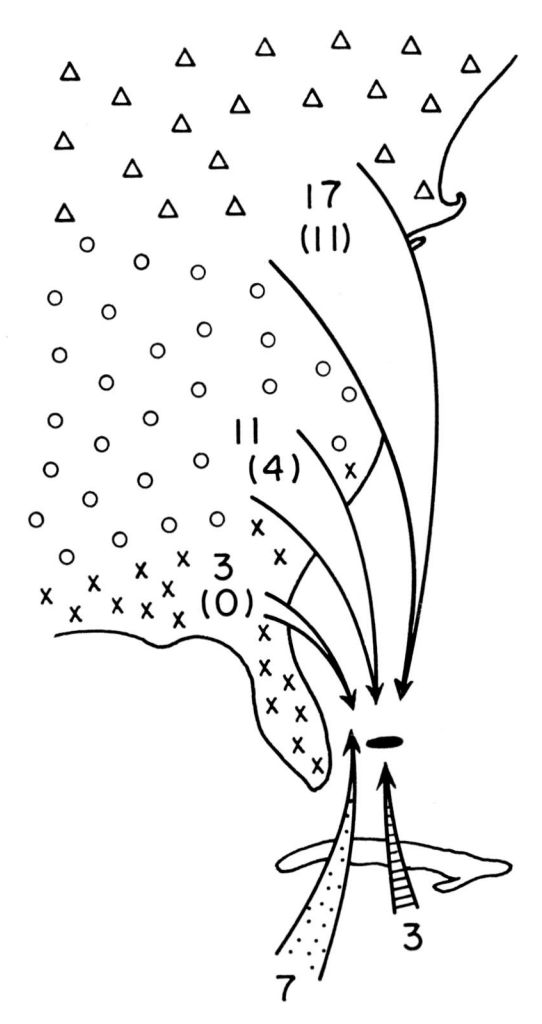

FIGURE 29. Geographic sources of bird species migrating to or through the Grand Bahama pine forests. The width of the arrows at their bases roughly represents the number of species in each regional element. The actual number is given, and, in parentheses, the number that belongs exclusively to the element. Open arrows represent the winter resident species migrating in from (a) the northern coniferous-hardwood forest region, (b) the central deciduous forest region, and (c) the southern mixed pineland region of eastern North America. The cross-hatched arrow represents the summer resident species from Antillean islands to the south. The stippled arrow represents the species recorded only as in-transit spring migrants.

published data on seasonal changes in H′ values for closely delineated (single habitat type) communities elsewhere.

The effect of an annual influx and subsequent withdrawal of hordes of migrant individuals on the stability of southern bird communities has been considered by Moreau (1972), Morel (1968), Fretwell (1972), and others. Winter invaders often form a strong minority element in wintering communities, and on occasion, as in several of the Grand Bahama habitats (see Table 4) may constitute a substantial majority. In the submature pine habitat on Grand Bahama the winter influx

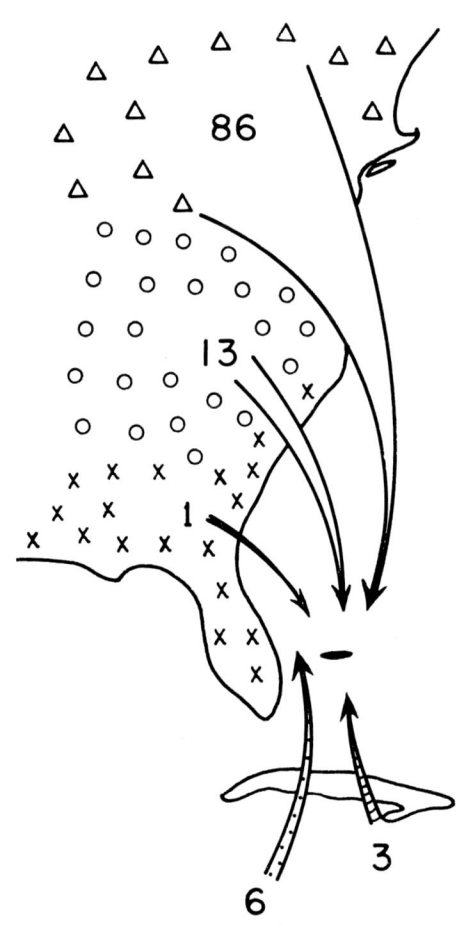

FIGURE 30. Numerical strength (relative population density) of the regional elements of birds migrating to or through the Grand Bahama pinelands. The three winter migrant elements (matching those in Figure 29) are calculated as percentages of the total of winter resident birds. The values for the summer resident and in-transit elements are figures equated against the winter resident percentage values. As in Figure 29, the in-transit element in this calculation excludes residual winter residents, but includes estimates of the in-transit populations of winter resident species (where the migration season level exceeded the winter level).

essentially doubled the overall density (599 to 1,169 birds) and biomass (7,354–13,760 g). The possibility that this seasonal increase was accompanied by a concurrent and comparable increase in food supply was checked by sampling foliage, bark, and ground insect communities at the three study sites in January and May of 1971. The results as presented and discussed in Chapter 8 were negative in all cases (see Fig. 31). Tentatively I conclude that food was not a limiting factor for community population density on Grand Bahama, a proposition I have developed further in a comparison of Florida and Bahama bird communities Emlen (1978, in press) and a comparison of pine tree gleaners on two Bahama islands (Emlen in prep.).

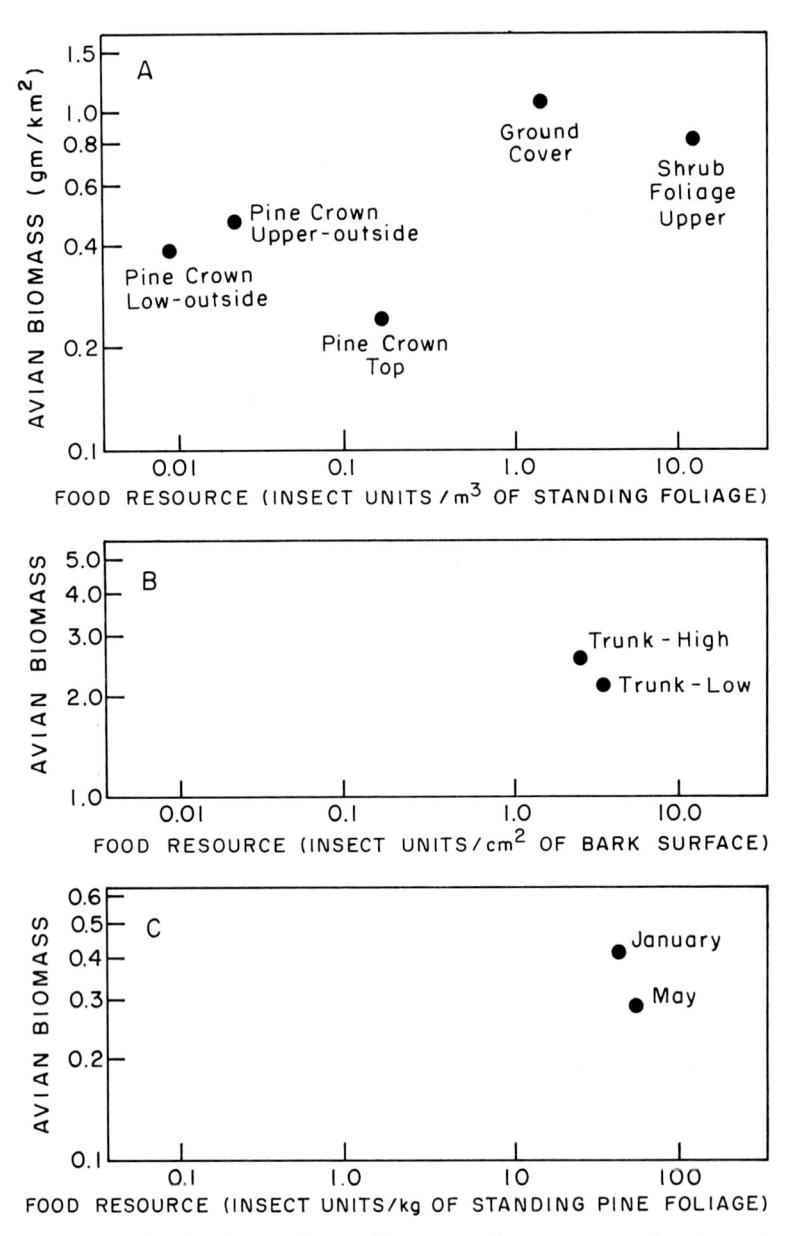

FIGURE 31. Ratio of avian insect gleaner biomass to food resource abundance in selected compartments of the Bahama pineland habitat. A, winter data for five foliage compartments; B, winter data for two tree trunk compartments; C, winter and spring data for one tree foliage compartment (low-outside).

7—SPATIAL DISTRIBUTION WITHIN THE PINE FOREST

Bird species differ in their distribution through the space within a stand of vegetation. As described in Chapter 2, two methods of partitioning this space were used for plotting species distributions within the pine forests of Grand Bahama Island: (1) a series of horizontal layers were defined extending from

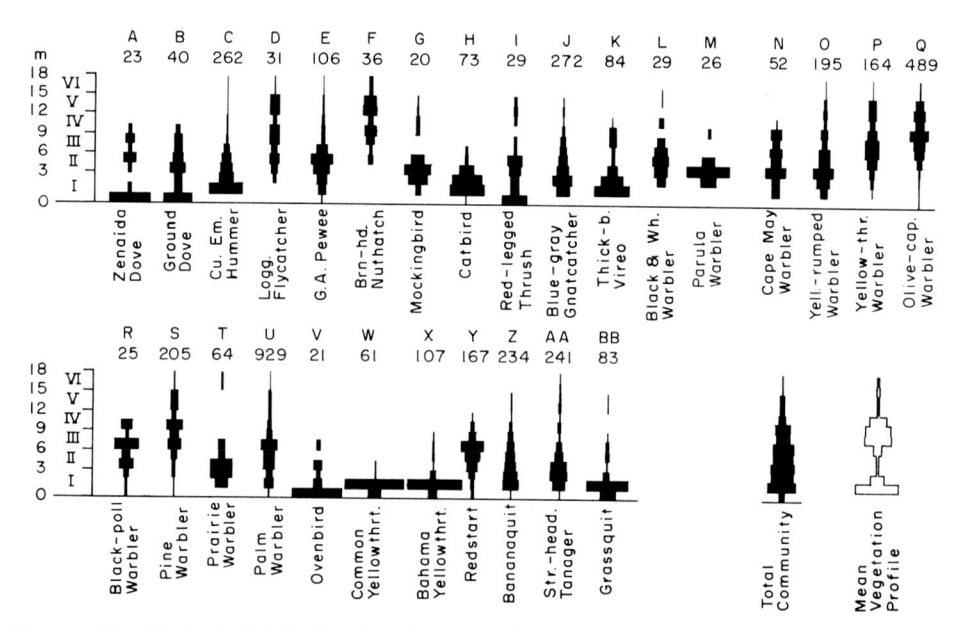

FIGURE 32. Vertical distribution in the vegetation of the 28 species with 20 or more records. Proportional representation in each of six 1.52-m (5-ft.) layers is graphically indicated for each species. The bottom layer is subdivided into a ground level (0–0.3 m) and upper level (0.3–1.52 m) in all except the vegetation profile. Sample sizes are given at the top of each profile diagram. An overall community profile and a vegetation profile are shown at the lower right.

the ground surface to the tops of the trees, and (2) blocks of habitat space or compartments were delineated with reference to prominent recurring features in the forest structure such as individual shrubs, individual trees, etc.

VERTICAL DISTRIBUTION (LAYERS)

Data on height above the ground as estimated at the moment of detection were variously grouped for tabulation and analysis. These vertical distribution records for each of the 28 species with 20 or more data points are graphed as a series of profile diagrams in Figure 32. The profiles at the lower right show the vertical distribution of all bird records (all species pooled), and in the unshaded diagram, the volume of standing vegetation. The step interval used in these diagrams is 1.52 m (5 feet) except at the base where the first step has been subdivided into a 0.3-m (1-ft.) and a 1.2-m (4-ft.) unit; the effect of this subdivision is to produce a stemlike base on several of the diagrams. Species show a wide variety of height distributions and varying degrees of specialization along the gradient. Noteworthy is the strong representation of many species in the sparsely foliaged layer between the shrub tops and the bottoms of the tree crowns. This layer shows as a narrow "waistline" in the profile of standing vegetation volumes.

Vegetative structure and avian utilization at five levels.—Changes in vegetation structure with height are summarized by grouping the data into 5 layers of equal

TABLE 15
Vertical Distribution of Bird Populations in the Wintering Community of the Pine Forest[1]

	\multicolumn{5}{c}{Five Layers (Height in meters)}	
	0–3	3–6	6–9	9–12	12–15	Total
Structural elements						
Needles			++	++	++	
Leaves	++					
Twigs	++		++	++	++	
Branches		+	++	+	+	
Vertical surfaces		+	+	+	+	
Horizontal surfaces	+					
Total space (m³) per ha	30,000	30,000	30,000	30,000	30,000	150,000
Volume of standing vegetation (m³) per ha	5,625	700	5,500	5,500	500	17,825
No. of bird species	36	35	31	24	22	38
Heavily represented species (20%)	11	4	1	0	3	19
Well-represented species (20%)	24	21	11	3	7	38
Total density per km²	369.3 (32%)	286.3 (25%)	248.3 (22%)	134.6 (12%)	113.3 (10%)	1151.8
Total bird density per million m³ of space	123.1	95.3	83.8	44.9	37.8	76.8
Total bird density per million m³ of standing vegetation	657	4090	452	245	2266	646
Bird species diversity (H′)	2.910	2.743	2.571	2.177	2.246	

[1] Characteristics of the vegetation and bird populations as shown for five equally thick (3-m) layers of space between the ground surface and the tree tops.

depth (3 m) between the ground surface and the tree tops in Table 15 and Figure 33. The lowest layer contains essentially all of the ground cover and shrubs. The second encompasses the relatively open space between the shrubs and the tree crowns; the third, the lower half of the pine canopy; the fourth, the upper half of the pine canopy; and the fifth, the tops of the taller crowns of the canopy plus the scattered emergent crowns. Emergent crowns above the 15-m level are omitted in this analysis.

While the amount of space in each of the five layers is equal, the amount and type of substrate available for bird use differs considerably. In the basal layer, 5,625 m³ of the 30,000 m³ of space (19%) was occupied by relatively dense and diverse vegetation, dominated by leaves and twigs over a rather densely matted, heavily pitted ground surface (Table 15). Perches and escape cover were well distributed for small birds, and food was provided by seed-producing grasses and forbs as well as nectar-producing blossoms and many intricately divided insect-supporting foraging surfaces. Seed-eating doves and grassquits, low-foraging insectivorous catbirds, vireos, ovenbirds and yellowthroats, and blossom-frequenting hummingbirds and bananaquits were best represented in this layer, and with others comprised the largest and richest element in the forest. Eleven species, designated "heavily represented" in Table 15, had more than half of their numbers recorded in this layer.

The second layer (3–6 m) contained only about ⅛ as much standing vegetation per unit of space as the basal layer. Large horizontal branches and vertical trunks replaced the leaves and fine twigs with firm lookout perches and

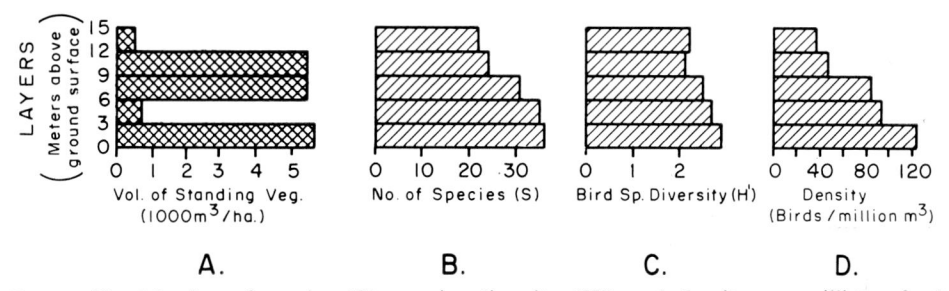

FIGURE 33. Number of species (S), species diversity (H') and density per million m³ of space (D_V) of the winter bird community of submature pine forests compared with the volume of standing vegetation in each of five equal horizontal divisions of space (layers) between the ground surface and the tree tops. (Emergent crowns above 15 m are not included.)

broad foraging surfaces. Visibility was clear over relatively long distances while escape cover was spatially removed. Despite the sparsity and low diversity of the foliage, birds were numerous and varied in this subcanopy layer, which was second only to the basal layer in number of species, bird species diversity, and density (Fig. 33). Prominent among the well-represented species were the insect-chasing Greater Antillean Pewee (51% of all records fall in this layer) and Stolid Flycatcher (34%), the branch-perching Ground Dove (30%), the ground-pouncing Mockingbird (50%) and Red-legged Thrush (31%), the open-trunk-gleaning Black-and-white Warbler (45%), and the subcanopy branch and low pine foliage gleaners: gnatcatcher (32%), Parula Warbler (73%), Cape May Warbler (40%), Yellow-rumped Warbler (39%), Black-throated Green Warbler (72%), Black-throated Blue Warbler (32%), Black-poll Warbler (32%), Prairie Warbler (37%), Palm Warbler (28%), redstart (39%), bananaquit (29%), and Striped-headed Tanager (34%).

The third and fourth layers encompassed the pine crowns of the canopy. Vegetation, occupying about 18% of the total space in each of these layers (Table 15), consisted almost entirely of pine needles and the subhorizontal twigs and branches supporting them. Foliage distribution was patchy, each crown constituting a roughly circular patch with needles dominating peripherally and branches dominating centrally. Of the two layers, the lower had thinner foliage (sparser and more scattered needle clusters) and heavier branches. It thus formed a transition between the open subcanopy of the second layer and the relatively dense foliage of the fourth. The number of species, diversity, and density of birds was less in these than in the lower layers, and appreciably less in the fourth layer (upper half of the crowns) than the third layer (lower half). Two species, the Hairy Woodpecker (50%) and the Yellow-throated Warbler (36%), reached their maximum densities in the third layer, and representation was above average for 7 more: Stolid Flycatcher (33%), Black-and-white Warbler (21%), Olive-capped Warbler (25%), Black-poll Warbler (36%), Pine Warbler (29%), Palm Warbler (27%), and redstart (38%). Only 3 species reached above average densities in the fourth layer; the Brown-headed Nuthatch with 25%, the Olive-capped Warbler with 35%, and the Pine Warbler with 28%.

The fifth and highest layer closely resembled the fourth in structure and texture, except that the patches were more widely scattered and collectively provided less than one-tenth as much standing foliage. Also present were occasional dead branches and stubs providing high lookout perches. Two species, both of them birds that fly out for aerial insects from open perches, reached their highest numbers in the tops of the tall canopy and emergent trees: the Bahama Swallow (100%) and the Gray Kingbird (56%). Also well represented were the Loggerhead Flycatcher (29%) and three high foliage gleaners: the Brown-headed Nuthatch (53%), the Olive-capped Warbler (29%), and the Pine Warbler (22%).

The overall picture of bird distribution was one of gradual and fairly even decline in species number, species diversity, and total population density upward through the five layers (Fig. 33). Vegetation density per cubic unit of space, representing the quantity of substrate in a layer for perching, foraging, etc., varied considerably and irregularly however, with highs in the first and fourth layers 8–10 times those in the second and fifth. Reflecting these irregularities bird-substrate ratios varied greatly through the layers (Table 15) leaving the impression that, in this context at least, bird numbers and densities are much more closely related to space *per se* than to the amount of substrate available for perching and foraging.

Population structure in the five layers.—Because of great differences between species in overall population density, species with a low percentage representation in a given layer often outnumbered well-represented species in that layer. For example, the dominant (most numerous) member of the wintering community in the basal layer was the Palm Warbler with 241 individuals recorded per hectare, yet this constituted only 25% of its numbers, a lower basal layer representation than that shown by 20 less abundant species. The numerical dominance structure of the wintering community of the pinelands in each of the five 3-m layers is presented in Figure 34. The height of each segment in the columns shows the relative frequency of occurrence of each species in the layer.

The distributions of abundance follow expected logarithmic declines. Of the total bird population in each layer, 80% belongs to between 25 and 29% of the species present. The Palm Warbler is the dominant species in the first three layers and is in second position in the other two where it falls behind the Olive-capped Warbler.

The division of habitat space into 5 layers also provides a means for analyzing the distribution of the impact of seasonal immigration within the community (Figure 35). The influx of migrants was heaviest in the lower tree canopy and subcanopy layers (3–9 m) where winter residents outnumbered permanent residents about 4:3 during the winter months; it was lightest in the high tree layer where WRs were only half as numerous as PRs. Summer residents constituted a very minor element in all layers except the upper canopy where they were 5.4% as numerous as the permanent residents.

COMPARTMENT DISTRIBUTION

The vegetation compartments used in this study (see Fig. 1) provide a series of divisions and subdivisions of the habitat space, unequal in volume but directly

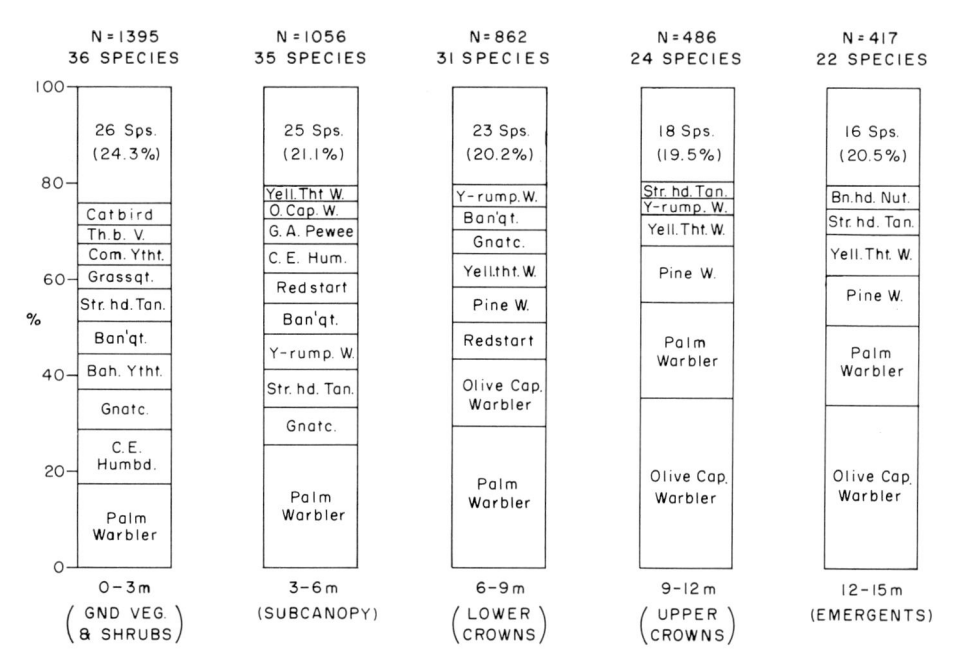

FIGURE 34. Relative abundance (numerical dominance) of the bird species comprising the wintering community in each of five equal (3-m) layers between the ground surface and the tree tops.

comparable as units of living space for bird populations. As units they are more natural than the equal horizontal layers examined in the preceding pages and combine aspects of substrate use and preference not possible with the heterogenously structured, horizontal layers. The compartments, on the other hand, are not amenable to the serial arrangement that made it possible to trace within-habitat trends in species distribution and community structure. Some of the analyses that

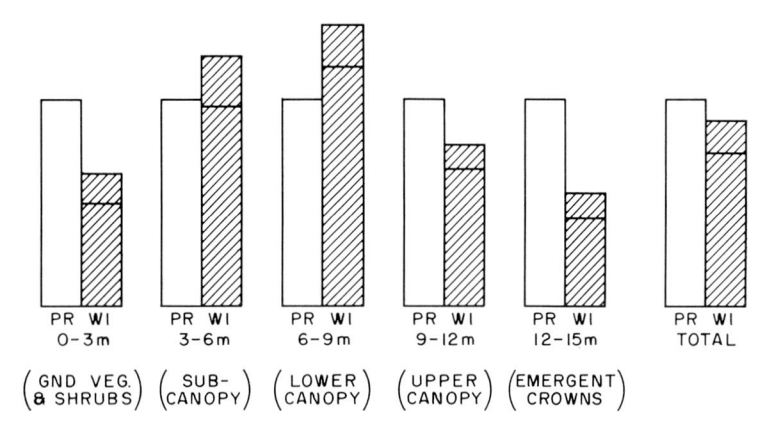

FIGURE 35. Numbers of winter residents compared with permanent residents in the five horizontal layers of the standard pineland habitat in winter. Lower portions of shaded columns show numbers of Palm Warblers.

TABLE 16
Volume and Structural Characteristics of the Major Habitat Compartments in the Pine Forests[1]

	Trunk space[2]	Tree crowns Shell	Tree crowns Core	Shrubs Shell	Shrubs Core	Ground cover	Air space	Total
Total space								
(1000 m³/ha)	0.39	8.20	4.00	2.83	1.42	1.38	152	170
(%)	(0.2)	(4.8)	(2.4)	(1.7)	(0.8)	(0.8)	(89.4)	–
Structural elements								
Needles	0	+++	+	0	0	0	0	
Leaves	0	0	0	+++	+	++	0	
Twigs	0	+++	+	+++	++	++	0	
Branches	+	+	+++	0	++	+	0	
Vertical surfaces	+++	0	0	0	±	0	0	
Horizontal surfaces	0	0	0	0	0	+	0	

[1] Plus signs give a rough appraisal of the representation of each structural element from light(+) to heavy(+++).
[2] Volume of cylinders 0.30 m in diameter incorporating each trunk.

follow resemble those used in the discussion of the layers, others will explore aspects of the dynamics and regulation of habitat distribution.

Physical characteristics of the compartments.—The amount of space included within each major habitat compartment is presented in Table 16 together with an appraisal of the structural elements or perching substrates in each.

The trunk compartment, divided at the base of the crown into upper and lower subcompartments for some analyses, comprises the composite of spaces around each of the tree trunks and stumps in the forest. Arbitrarily defined as the space within imaginary cylinders 0.30 m in diameter surrounding each trunk, the total volume is only 390 m³ per ha[2], or 0.2% of the 170,000 m³ of space present between the ground surface and the canopy top. Vertical wood and bark surfaces are the dominant structural elements in this compartment, but the basal few centimeters of branches also contribute an important perching and foraging substrate for certain species.

Pine tree crowns, potentially divisible from the field data into 12 subcompartments, comprise the second major compartment. The upper and outer portions or shells of the crowns contain a rather dense matrix of needles and twigs; the inner portions or cores are dominated by horizontal and subhorizontal branches with smaller quantities of needles and twigs (Table 16). The volume of space occupied by crown shells and cores is 8,200 m² and 4,000 m³ per ha² respectively, or 4.8 and 2.3% of the total habitat space.

Broadleafed trees, as already noted, were small and comprised only 0.1% of the tree stratum in the standard forests. Because of their low representation and small size, they are incorporated into the shrub compartment in the present analysis.

Shrubs, potentially divisible into 15 subcompartments on the basis of field data, constitute the third major compartment. The upper and outer portions of shrubs are characterized by many leaves and twigs and collectively occupy 2,830 m³ per ha. The lower or basal portions are dominated by branches and heavy twigs and occupy 1,420 m³ per ha. Shrubs are, of course, close to the ground surface and therefore more available than trees as escape and perching cover for ground-foraging birds.

The thin layer of space over the ground surface occupied by trailing vines and herbaceous foliage comprises the ground cover compartment. Varying in depth, it is considered to incorporate a total of 1,380 m^3 per ha, thus being the smallest compartment except for the tree trunks. The structure is characterized by a reticulum of subhorizontal twigs and slender stems interspersed with small leaves and grass blades over a highly irregular, deeply pitted limestone base.

The airspace between and surrounding these 6 vegetation-filled compartments occupied 152,000 m^3 per ha or 89.4% of the total space below the tree tops. Being without resting surfaces, the utility of this space is limited to passage between perches and brief sallies for capturing flying insects. Bahama Swallows and Nighthawks, the only aerial screeners in the pinelands community, do nearly all of their foraging above the tree tops and hence outside any of the compartments in this system. Because of its generally transitory significance as substrate, and particularly because of the biases introduced by the high detectability of birds when in it, the airspace is ignored in most of the compartment distribution analyses in this study.

Bird species distribution through the compartments.—Distribution through the compartments of the submature pinelands is shown for the 30 species with 20 or more records in Figure 36. From the plethora of positional data on the field record sheets, 10 compartments were selected for these representations, the 7 structurally characterized in Table 16 with the first 3 further subdivided on the basis of position. Diagrams in the top row of the figure identify the compartments and give the pooled data for species groups, including one for all species combined and one for foliage volumes in each compartment. The figures in each box are frequency values, expressed as percents of the total sample available for the species or group. Sample sizes are given to the right of each diagram, followed by an index of distributional amplitude (H') and an index of compartment preference (observed frequency in the favored compartment divided by expected frequency, assuming equal distribution through the four major compartment categories, tree crowns, shrubs, trunks, and ground cover). With 4 major compartments this latter index will range from 1.0 for a species not deviating from an even distribution to 4.0 for a species found entirely in a single compartment.

Among these 30 species the Mockingbird showed the most diverse compartment distribution (H' = 0.91) and the Olive-capped Warbler the least (H' = 0.07). Of the 30 species 4 favored the trunk compartment, 12 the tree crowns, 11 the shrubs, and 3 the ground cover. The 4 trunk specialists with their index of preference were the Yellow-bellied Sapsucker (3.4), Hairy Woodpecker (3.0), Black-and-white Warbler (2.7), and Brown-headed Nuthatch (2.1). Tree crown specialists included the Olive-capped Warbler (3.8), Loggerhead Flycatcher (3.7), Pine Warbler (3.4), and pewee (3.2). The principal shrub species in order of specialization were the Common Yellowthroat (3.4), catbird (3.1), Bahama Yellowthroat (3.0), and Greater Antillean Bullfinch (3.0), and the principal ground compartment specialists were the grassquit (3.4) and Ovenbird (3.2).

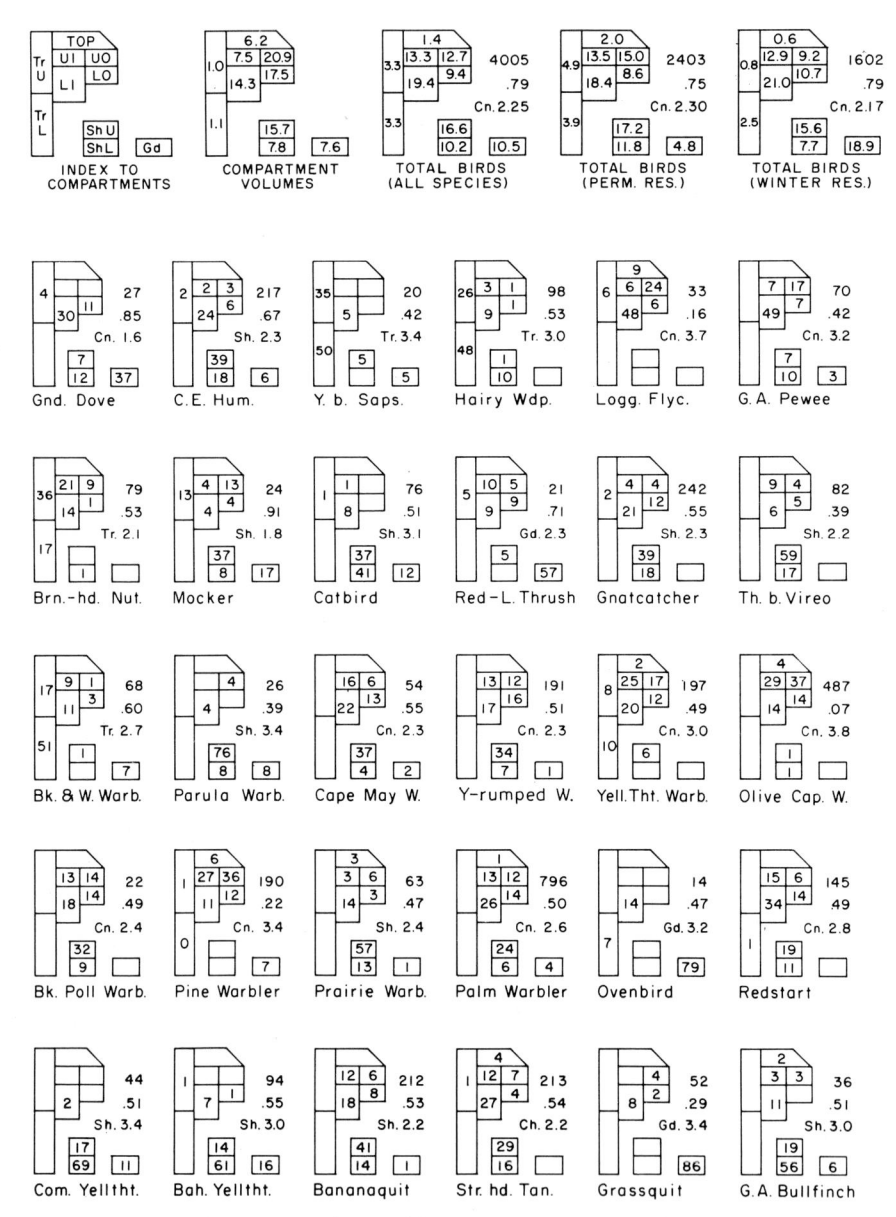

FIGURE 36. Distribution of detection positions through ten vegetation compartments for the 30 species with 20 or more position records. All routes and seasons are pooled. Figures in the diagrams are percent values. Sample size, an index of distributional amplitude (H'/H' max.), and an index of compartment preference (4d/D) among the four major compartment categories are shown at the right of each diagram (see text for further explanation). Compartment abbreviations: TrU = upper trunk, TrL = lower trunk, Top = crown top, UI = upper inside, UO = upper outside, LI = lower inside, LO = lower outside, ShU = upper shrub, ShL = lower shrub, Gd = ground surface, Cn = crown.

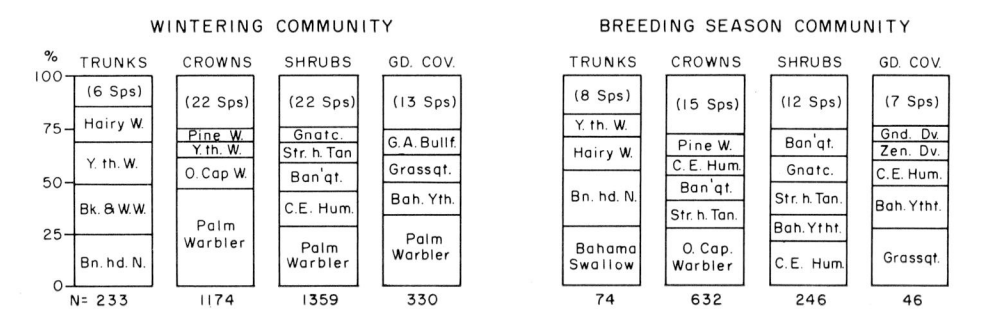

	WINTERING COMMUNITY				BREEDING SEASON COMMUNITY			
%	TRUNKS	CROWNS	SHRUBS	GD. COV.	TRUNKS	CROWNS	SHRUBS	GD. COV.
100	(6 Sps)	(22 Sps)	(22 Sps)	(13 Sps)	(8 Sps)	(15 Sps)	(12 Sps)	(7 Sps)
75	Hairy W.	Pine W.	Gnatc.	G.A. Bullf.	Y. th. W.	Pine W.	Ban'qt.	Gnd. Dv. Zen. Dv.
50	Y. th. W.	Y. th. W. O. Cap W.	Str. h. Tan Ban'qt.	Grassqt.	Hairy W.	C.E. Hum. Ban'qt.	Gnatc. Str. h. Tan.	C.E. Hum.
25	Bk. & W.W.	Palm Warbler	C.E. Hum. Palm Warbler	Bah. Yth. Palm Warbler	Bn. hd. N.	Str. h. Tan. O. Cap. Warbler	Bah. Ytht. C.E. Hum.	Bah. Ytht. Grassqt.
0	Bn. hd. N.				Bahama Swallow			
	N= 233	1174	1359	330	74	632	246	46

FIGURE 37. Relative abundance (dominance) of the bird species of the wintering and breeding season communities in the four major habitat compartments of the standard forests.

Winter resident species as a group were less well represented than permanent resident birds in the trunk (3.3% vs. 8.8%) and shrub (23.3% vs. 29.0%) compartments, and better represented in the ground cover (18.9% vs. 4.8%). These differences were largely due to the tree and ground-foraging proclivities of the strongly dominant Palm Warblers among the winter invaders.

Distribution within the tree crowns varied greatly from species to species. Among the 18 species with 10 or more records in the crowns, 16 were more frequently encountered in the core compartments than in the outer shell, even though the core contained less than half as much space. Of the 16 core species, 4, the nuthatch, thrush, vireo, and Yellow-throated Warbler were most numerous in the upper portion and 12, the Hairy Woodpecker, Loggerhead Flycatcher, pewee, Black-and-white Warbler, Yellow-rumped Warbler, Cape May Warbler, Palm Warbler, Prairie Warbler, Black-poll Warbler, redstart, bananaquit, and tanager in the lower portion. The two species best represented in the shell space were the Olive-capped and Pine Warblers, both concentrating in the upper-outer subcompartment.

Population structure in the compartments.—The numerically dominant species of the breeding season and winter communities and their percent representation in each of the four major compartments are shown in Figure 37. These dominance rankings differ considerably from the specialization rankings in the same compartments (see Figure 36) because of great differences in the overall densities of the species. In the wintering community, Palm Warblers dominated in the crown, shrub, and ground cover compartments, and the Brown-headed Nuthatch in the trunk compartment. Among the four dominant species in each compartment three were permanent residents. In the breeding season community, there was less overlap between compartments, each of the four having different prime dominants.

Demographic data for the four major compartments are presented in Table 17. In the breeding season community, the tree crowns had the largest number of species, the highest diversity value (H'), and the highest bird density per areal unit. Winter residents included 11 species using the shrub compartment against nine in the crowns, and these, superimposed on the permanent residents, shifted the balance of species number and diversity from the crown to the shrub compartment during the winter months. The number of individuals (density) among the winter residents, however, was strongest in the tree-crown compartment where they roughly equalled the resident population. In the shrubs, the winter residents nearly equalled the number of permanent resident shrub birds persisting from the summer, but a seasonal movement by certain permanent resident species down from the tree crowns raised the total winter density in the shrubs to more than double that of the breeding season.

Densities expressed as birds per m^3 of compartment space were highest in the trunk compartment and lowest in the ground cover (last rows in Table 17). The reversal of relative rank between trunk and crown compartments from that recorded for the areal density measurement is, of course, due to the much smaller space occupied by the trunk compartment. These volumetric density values will be used in considerations of substrate selection and crowding dynamics in the next chapter.

Seasonal changes in spatial distributions.—Quantitative distributional analyses such as those presented above have limited utility beyond pure description except as they can be used to measure differences between localities, habitats, years, or seasons. In this section I attempt a comparison of the compartment distributions of the permanent resident species of the Grand Bahama pine forests before and after the winter migrants departed for their northern homes. The pertinent data for each species in the four major compartments are presented in Table 18.

In the trunk compartment the departure of three migrant species, the Yellow-bellied Sapsucker, Black-and-white Warbler, and Yellow-throated Warbler (migrant race) with a combined density equal to about 41% of the wintering compartment total, triggered no major shifts among the remaining permanent residents. There was, however, a slight increase in trunk foraging by several primarily foliage-related species to effect a small rise in the total number of species and species diversity (Table 17). Two summer immigrants, the Gray Kingbird and the Bahama Swallow spent much time perched high on stubs near the top of the tree canopy; although assigned to the trunk compartment, these birds had little or no interaction with other trunk compartment species.

Among the permanent residents frequenting the tree trunk compartment, the two dominant species, the Hairy Woodpecker and the Brown-headed Nuthatch, showed no appreciable change in their preference for trunks between winter and summer (Pref. 2.92–2.94 and 2.11–2.20 respectively). I have no good data on changes in the compartment distribution of the third permanent resident species of the trunk compartment, the Yellow-throated Warbler, since, as already noted, the permanent resident population was supplemented in winter by an invasion of migrants not always distinguishable in the field from birds of the resident race. My notes on positively identified birds indicate that the resident birds were more strongly oriented to the trunk compartment than the migrants. This impression is supported by the higher preference for trunks (1.01) shown by the breeding community birds (all PRs) than the mixed wintering community (0.61).

In the tree crown compartment the departure of 10 species (1, an interhabitat shift on the island), and the arrival of 1 summer resident produced a net decrease in species number from 29 to 20, a decrease in individuals per km^2 from 644 to 395, and, because of a more equitable distribution of numbers, an increase in

TABLE 17
DEMOGRAPHIC CHARACTERISTICS OF THE BIRD POPULATIONS IN THE 4 MAJOR COMPARTMENTS OF THE PINE FOREST

	Wintering community				
	Trunks	Crowns	Shrubs	Ground cover	Total
Number of species[1]	10	26	27	17	31
Permanent residents	8	18	17	12	20
Winter residents	3	9	11	5	12
Summer residents	—	—	—	—	—
Strongly represented species ($\geq 50\%$)	4	9	14	2	29
Permanent residents	2	6	8	2	—
Winter residents	2	3	6	0	—
Summer residents	—	—	—	—	—
Well-represented species ($\geq 20\%$)	4	18	22	7	31
Permanent residents	2	13	12	6	—
Winter residents	2	5	10	1	—
Summer residents	—	—	—	—	—
Bird Diversity (H′)	1.767	1.931	2.285	2.093	2.389
Permanent residents	1.458	2.193	2.034	1.972	2.404
Winter residents	.473	.278	.952	.645	.998
Summer residents	—	—	—	—	—
Density-1 (#/km^2)	45.1	644.3	402.1	51.6	1143.1
Permanent residents	31.5	324.1	245.3	29.5	630.4
Winter residents	13.6	320.2	156.8	22.1	512.7
Summer residents	—	—	—	—	—
Density-2 (#/million m^3)	117.1	52.8	94.6	37.5	302.0
Permanent residents	81.9	26.6	57.7	22.3	188.5
Winter residents	35.2	26.2	36.9	15.2	113.5
Summer residents	—	—	—	—	—

	Breeding season community				
	Trunks	Crowns	Shrubs	Ground cover	Total
Number of species[1]	13	20	17	12	23
Permanent residents	12	19	15	12	21
Winter residents	—	—	—	—	—
Summer residents	1	1	2	0	2
Strongly represented species ($\geq 50\%$)	4	9	3	0	16
Permanent residents	4	8	2	0	—
Winter residents	—	—	—	—	—
Summer residents	0	1	1	0	—
Well-represented species ($\geq 20\%$)	6	19	10	6	23
Permanent residents	5	18	9	6	—
Winter residents	—	—	—	—	—
Summer residents	1	1	1	0	—
Bird diversity (H′)	1.900	2.479	2.299	2.110	2.617
Permanent residents	1.827	2.312	2.141	2.110	2.596
Winter residents	—	—	—	—	—
Summer residents	—	—	—	—	.507
Density 1 (#/km^2)	43.7	395.2	169.5	39.5	647.9
Permanent residents	42.7	392.6	166.8	39.5	641.6
Winter residents	—	—	—	—	—
Summer residents	1.0	2.6	2.7	0	6.3
Density-2 (#/million m^3)	114.5	32.4	39.9	30.5	217.3
Permanent residents	111.9	32.3	39.2	30.5	194.9
Winter residents	—	—	—	—	—
Summer residents	2.6	0.2	0.7	0.0	22.4

[1] Species recorded on more than 5 occasions.

TABLE 18
COMPARTMENT DISTRIBUTIONS AND PREFERENCES (UNDERLINED) OF MEMBERS OF THE WINTERING AND BREEDING COMMUNITIES[1]

	Winter community (before migrant exodus)						
	Trunks	Crowns	Shrubs	Gd. Cover	N	Preference	Amplitude
Permanent residents							
Zenaida Dove	–	1.3	–	2.7	6	2.70	.46
Ground Dove	–	0.4	1.4	1.8	10	2.00	.69
Cuban Emerald Hummingbird	2.1	32.9	62.5	5.3	165	2.43	.64
Hairy Woodpecker	7.8	1.4	1.5	–	73	2.92	.56
Stolid Flycatcher	–	1.3	0.9	–	5	2.36	.49
Loggerhead Flycatcher	0.4	3.8	–	–	24	3.62	.22
Greater Antillean Pewee	–	15.0	1.2	0.5	40	3.59	.28
Brown-headed Nuthatch	11.1	9.9	–	–	40	2.11	.50
Bahama Mockingbird	0.3	0.9	1.3	0.6	26	1.68	.91
Red-legged Thrush	–	0.4	1.3	1.3	7	1.73	.72
Blue-gray Gnatcatcher	0.4	17.6	30.4	0.5	130	2.49	.58
Thick-billed Vireo	–	1.4	11.2	–	37	3.56	.25
Yellow-throated Warbler[2]	4.3	12.5	0.3	–	52	3.07	.50
Olive-capped Warbler	–	94.1	1.0	–	293	3.96	.04
Pine Warbler	–	37.3	2.0	0.4	132	3.76	.18
Bahama Yellowthroat	0.3	2.1	20.0	7.6	71	2.67	.61
Bananaquit	–	30.5	53.9	1.7	146	2.50	.53
Stripe-headed Tanager	–	25.6	36.9	–	103	2.36	.49
Grassquit	–	2.5	15.0	7.1	41	2.44	.64
Greater Antillean Bullfinch	–	2.1	8.0	5.9	16	2.00	.70
Total	26.7	293.0	249.3	35.4	1510	2.06	.73
Winter Residents							
Yellow-bellied Sapsucker	2.5	0.4	0.7	–	20	2.78	.59
Gray Catbird	–	0.7	5.9	1.2	75	3.03	.52
Black-and-White Warbler	11.1	–	–	–	11	4.00	.00
Yellow-throated Warbler	4.9	33.3	4.5	–	93	3.12	.49
Prairie Warbler	–	4.5	6.8	0.2	52	2.37	.54
Palm Warbler	–	302.8	122.0	18.1	815	2.73	.54
Yellow-rumped Warbler	–	7.7	5.7	0.1	185	2.28	.52
Other foliage warblers	–	1.9	4.9	0	29	2.88	.50
Common Yellowthroat	–	0.3	6.9	2.5	31	2.85	.50
Redstart	–	3.8	2.8	–	36	2.30	.49
Total	18.5	355.4	153.6	22.1	1347	2.50	.64
Grand Total	45.1	648.4	402.9	57.5	2587	2.25	.69

	Breeding season community (after migrant exodus)						
	Trunks	Crowns	Shrubs	Gd. Cover	N	Preference	Amplitude
Permanent residents							
Zenaida Dove	–	3.8	.9	3.9	9	1.81	.69
Ground Dove	0.5	5.5	.5	3.0	20	2.32	.70
Cuban Emerald Hummingbird	0.8	39.5	36.1	5.0	66	1.94	.66
Hairy Woodpecker	6.4	2.3	–	–	26	2.94	.42
Stolid Flycatcher	0.1	0.4	–	–	8	3.20	.36
Loggerhead Flycatcher	–	7.2	–	–	7	4.00	.00
Greater Antillean Pewee	–	11.0	5.7	1.5	46	2.42	.63

TABLE 18 (CONTINUED)

| | Breeding season community (after migrant exodus) ||||| ||
	Trunks	Crowns	Shrubs	Gd. Cover	N	Preference	Amplitude
Brown-headed Nuthatch	11.8	9.7	–	–	38	2.20	.50
Bahama Mockingbird	–	–	–	–	0	–	.00
Red-legged Thrush	–	4.0	0.9	2.2	16	2.25	.68
Blue-gray Gnatcatcher	1.0	24.8	22.4	0.5	122	2.04	.60
Thick-billed Vireo	–	9.1	16.1	–	45	2.56	.47
Yellow-throated Warbler[2]	4.3	12.5	0.3	–	52	2.92	.47
Olive-capped Warbler	1.2	115.0	1.2	2.4	196	3.84	.15
Pine Warbler	1.3	37.8	1.3	1.3	75	3.63	.22
Bahama Yellowthroat	–	6.6	24.2	8.2	24	2.48	.66
Bananaquit	–	41.4	19.8	–	74	2.71	.45
Stripe-headed Tanager	2.4	52.4	23.8	0.8	112	2.64	.57
Grassquit	–	9.0	12.0	12.0	22	1.45	.79
Greater Antillean Bullfinch	–	0.5	0.9	1.1	19	1.76	.76
Total	29.8	392.5	166.1	41.9	977	2.48	.70
Summer residents							
Gray Kingbird	1.0	2.6	0.5	–		2.54	.64
Bahama Swallow[3]	12.9	–	–	–		4.00	–
Black-whiskered Swallow	–	–	2.2	–		4.00	–
Total	13.9	2.6	2.7	–		2.90	.56
Grand Total	43.7	395.1	168.8	41.9		2.43	.73

[1] Values are birds per km². Sample sizes, compartment preference (4d/D) and indices of distributional amplitude (H'/H' max.) are shown in the last three columns.
[2] The winter community values for the permanent resident Yellow-throated Warbler are arbitrarily treated here as direct repetitions of the breeding season community values and added to the winter resident values.
[3] The Bahama Swallow is considered a summer invader for this tabulation.

bird species diversity from 1.93 to 2.48 (Table 17). With these changes in community structure the amount of permanent resident activity in the crowns apparently increased appreciably in 9 species, decreased appreciably in 3, dropped out in 1, and held fairly constant in 6. The basis for these changes could have been intercompartment shifts, interhabitat shifts, movements to or from the island, mortality, or errors in the census operations. Unfortunately my data are inadequate to provide more than crude guesses on what was involved in the individual cases. In species where increases or decreases in activity in the crown department are clearly matched by reciprocal changes in other compartments in Table 18 I interpret the record as indicating an intercompartment shift. Where informal spring observations in other habitats suggest reciprocal seasonal changes with those recorded in the pine forests I suspect an interhabitat shift. On this basis I suspect that there was a partial shift up from the shrub and ground cover compartment of the pine forest in the Cuban Emerald Hummingbird, Red-legged Thrush, Blue-gray Gnatcatcher, Bahama Yellowthroat, bananaquit, Striped-headed Tanager, and grassquit, and a partial shift down into the shrub compartment by the Greater Antillean Pewee. I also suspect a movement into the pine habitat from more open situations by the Ground Dove and Bahama Swallow and a movement out to the dense coppets by the Greater Antillean Bullfinch.

In the shrub compartment the spring exodus involved 157 birds of 11 species from a winter community of 402 birds and 27 species; 2.7 birds of 2 species entered as summer immigrants. Concurrent with this reduction in overall density, the activity of permanent residents in the compartment declined from 245 to 167. Largest decreases were by the Cuban Emerald Hummingbird, bananaquit, Striped-headed Tanager, and Greater Antillean Bullfinch, attributed primarily to shifts of activity up into the tree crown compartment.

In the ground cover compartment the departure of 5 species with 22 individuals per km^2 left a community of 12 permanent resident species with 30 individuals. These permanent residents increased to 40 birds largely as a result of increased ground activity by several arboreal warblers and shrub-inhabiting grassquits.

These data are based on a single season's observations and in many cases on small samples. Insofar as they are representative, however, they indicate trends of considerable interest to students of community dynamics, trends that may be summarized by reducing the confusing array of values to a common denominator. Starting with 100 birds in the wintering community of the pine forests, spring migration removed about 45 winter residents and added one summer resident for a net reduction to 56 birds. This breeding community consisted of 29 crown-frequenting birds reduced 50% from 57, 22 shrub birds reduced 39% from 35, 2.8 trunk birds reduced 41% from 4.7, and 2.7 ground birds reduced 43% from 4.5. This precipitous decline in overall density was accompanied by a shift in the distribution of activity by the permanent resident species among the four habitat compartments. The principal net movement was away from the shrubs (a decrease of 32%) up into the crowns (an increase of 21%) and down to the ground compartment (an increase of 42%). This response is opposite to what would be predicted from a model based on compensatory adjustments to migrant departures. Again, the expectations of traditional competition theory are not supported.

8—GUILD DISTRIBUTION WITHIN THE PINE FOREST

Concepts and Definitions

The segregation of species within a habitat may be based on functional as well as physical criteria. Thus, species that feed, sing, nest, or seek shelter on different substrates of the vegetation, or that use the substrates and their resources in different ways, are buffered against (functionally segregated from) potential competitors even when they are occupying the same habitats and the same compartments within those habitats. In this study I recognized four functional systems: foraging, nesting, singing, and resting, corresponding to the four major activities recorded in my field notes. For each of these systems I delineated a series of functional "provinces" or departments, and the birds that were found foraging, singing, etc., within a province were collectively termed a "guild" (Root 1967) with a name corresponding to the province. These provinces and the guilds of species that occupy or exploit them combine both functional position (the resource or substrate selected and the way it is used) and spatial position (compartment). They may thus be used as comprehensive units for analyzing ecological distribution and the dynamics of interactions between species within a habitat such as the submature pine forests under discussion.

The number of guilds to be recognized in a system depends on the analysis to be undertaken and the degree of refinement desired for that analysis. Something between a lumping of all variations into two or three broad categories and a splitting to the level where each species fits a separate guild can provide a useful basis for studying functional relationships between species. At these intermediate levels, a species will, as a result of its behavioral variability and flexibility, characteristically hold membership in several guilds concurrently. Empirically based assignments of fractional memberships for each species in the community can then be made and used to provide a comprehensive empirical record of the species' foraging behavior, a record that is roughly equivalent to the realized niche (trophic aspects) of the species as conceived by Hutchinson (1957). Such analyses with fractional guild assignments are possible, of course, only when data are collected concurrently on all the species in the community and through all compartments of the habitat. A list of the guilds recognized in this study is presented in Table 19.

Semi-independent conditions of competition and behavioral exclusion presumably exist in each of the four functional systems. However, my data are adequate to quantitatively analyze segregation and overlap in only one, the foraging guild system.

Procedures

Delineation of the foraging guilds of the Grand Bahama submature forests and assignments of species in the system were based on the position in which birds were observed in the field with respect to three ecological criteria: compartment position, food type, and foraging method. Recognizing 10 compartments (as defined in the last chapter), 10 food types (seeds, fruits, buds, leaves, nectar, sap, and flying, crawling, hiding, and burrowing animals) and 7 major foraging methods (gleaning, plucking, probing, drilling, pouncing, sallying, and screening), there could theoretically be 700 foraging guilds among which to distribute the species. In actuality the three criteria are not independent, and most of the potential combinations do not exist. Edible fruits and buds, for instance, are found in the Bahama pinelands only in shrub and ground cover compartments and taken only by plucking methods. The 18 foraging provinces and their guilds listed in Table 18 thus represent essentially all of the natural combinations of compartments, food types, and foraging methods to be found in the pine forest habitat of the Island.

Since members of most of the bird species in the forest foraged in several vegetation compartments and used several types of food and feeding methods, each was regarded as holding membership in several of the 18 foraging guilds. The fraction of a species' foraging activity assignable to each guild was determined by reference to all available data on food habits, foraging behavior, and compartment distribution. Food habits data were obtained from a few freshly killed specimens found in the course of the study, but primarily from the published records of stomach contents summarized in Martin *et al.* (1951), Bent (1939, 1940, 1942, 1948, 1953, 1968), and Wetmore (1916). The principal datum taken from these works was the ratio of plant and animal material in specimens collected as close as possible to the locality (i.e. Puerto Rico and/or Southeastern U.S.). Compromises were necessary where data were few, and in several cases

TABLE 19
Guilds and Guild Provinces Recognized in the Submature Pine Forests of Grand Bahama Island

Foraging guilds	Nesting guilds
1. Herbivores	1. In cavities
a. Ground seed gleaners	a. In prepared excavations
b. Stem seed pluckers	b. In natural crevices
c. Fruit and bud harvesters	2. On horizontal substrates
d. Nectar sippers	a. On ground in open
e. Sap and cambium eaters	b. On ground in dense cover
f. Foliage eaters	c. On branch
2. Carnivores	d. On twig spray—tree
a. Ground insect gleaners	e. On twig spray—shrub
b. Ground insect pouncers	3. In subvertical crotches
c. Flower insect probers	a. In tree branches
d. Shrub foliage gleaners	b. In tree twigs
e. Shrub stem drillers	c. In shrub twigs
f. Tree bark and wood drillers	
g. Tree bark gleaners	Resting guilds
h. Tree twig gleaners	1. On exposed perches
i. Cone probers	a. Above the dominant canopy
j. Needle gleaners	b. Within the tree canopy
k. Air sallyers	c. Below the canopy
l. Air screeners	d. On shrubs
	e. On the ground
Singing guilds	2. In dense foliage
1. From exposed (open) perches	a. In needles
a. Above tree canopy	b. In leaves
b. Below tree canopy	c. In ground cover
2. From foliage	3. On vertical trunks
a. In trees	
b. In shrubs	
3. From the air	
(Flight songs)	

it was necessary to make best guesses on the basis of available information for other species known to have similar feeding habits.

More detailed information on the type of plant or animal material taken by the birds could generally be determined with considerable confidence from observations on feeding location and foraging method. A total of 1,912 special observations of feeding activity (independent of the census operations) provided most of this information, but a few subjective adjustments of these records were necessary because of differential observability in certain situations. Most of the foraging observations on Palm Warblers, for instance, were made of birds in tree crowns, yet data on first detections indicated that these birds foraged more in the shrub and ground vegetation than in trees. For most situations, the tallies of compartment distribution in the census transect records could not be used in making foraging guild assignments because time could not be taken then to observe special activities and examine foraging substrates.

In the absence of a single direct method for assigning guild memberships, I used all data available for each species, relying most heavily on my special foraging observations. I then subjectively divided the total foraging activity of each species into tenths and indicated further instances of unusual behavior as "traces" (T).

For the analyses that follow, I have multiplied the pine forest density and biomass values for each species (see Table 2) by the bird's relative representation in each guild. This provides absolute values of guild roles and a basis for determining the overall density and biomass of each guild as well as the contribution of each species to it.

Table 20 shows the foraging guild distribution in tenths of total foraging activity for each of the 33 species occurring as regular members of the avian communities of the submature pine forest habitat. A "T" in the table refers to observations of occasional activity in a guild by species concentrating their foraging in other guilds. In the descriptions and discussions that follow I will use the following terms to reflect the distribution of specialization of species in the foraging guild system. A "primary member" of a guild is one that does half or more of its feeding in that guild; a "secondary member" is one that feeds from two- to four-tenths of the time in the guild, and a tertiary member is one that does only one-tenth of its feeding in the guild. The Cuban Emerald Hummingbird is thus a primary member of the nectar-sipping guild, a secondary member of the flower-probing insectivore guild, a tertiary member of the needle insect-gleaning guild and shows a trace of activity in the pine twig insect-gleaning guild.

THE FORAGING GUILDS OF THE GRAND BAHAMA PINE FOREST

The memberships and relative strengths of dominant species in each of the 16 occupied foraging guilds of the wintering community are graphically portrayed in Figure 38. The calculated number of individuals per km^2 is given for each species in Table 21, and the biomass in grams per km^2 in Table 22. Tables 23 and 24 present these density and biomass values as the percentage contribution of each species to the guild composition.

In the descriptions of guild structure that follow, relative abundance or numerical ranking of the species in a guild is expressed in terms of dominance. The dominant and subdominant members are the species with 40% or more, and between 15 and 39% representation in the guild respectively; subordinate species are those furnishing between 5 and 15% of the guild membership. Species contributing from 1 to 4% are classed as incidental members, and those with only traces of activity in the guild are regarded as visitors rather than members. In this system a species of small body size may, of course, be dominant in the density ranking, yet subordinate or even incidental in the biomass ranking.

Ground-gleaning herbivores.—It is generally impossible to determine just what a ground-gleaning bird is ingesting, and thus to separate seed-eating from insect-eating. Published accounts of food habits for each species and considerations of feeding equipment, particularly the bill, were used in combination with personal observations to delineate the ground-gleaning herbivores of the Grand Bahama pinelands.

Two permanent resident species, the Zenaida Dove and the Ground Dove, apparently limit their foraging almost entirely to this guild (Table 20, column 1); two others, the Red-legged Thrush and the grassquit are secondary members. In the winter these four are joined to a limited extent by the primarily insectivorous catbirds and Mockingbirds.

The doves comprised 45% of the individuals in the guild in winter (Table 23a, column 1) but 79% of the biomass (Table 24a, column 1). After the winter

TABLE 20
FORAGING GUILD DISTRIBUTION OF MEMBERS OF THE PINE FOREST BIRD COMMUNITY ON GRAND BAHAMA ISLAND[1]

Foraging guilds[2]	Herbivores a	b	c	d	e	f	Carnivores (mainly insects) a	b	c	d	e	f	g	h	i	j	k	l	N[3]	Ampl.[4]
Zenaida Dove	9	–	1	–	–	–	–	–	–	–	–	–	–	–	–	–	–	–	7	.11
Ground Dove	10	–	–	–	–	–	–	–	–	–	–	–	–	–	–	–	–	–	21	.00
C. Emerald Hum'bird	–	–	–	6	–	–	–	–	3	–	–	–	–	T	–	1	–	–	23	.35
Hairy Woodpecker	–	–	2	–	–	–	–	–	–	–	1	2	4	1	–	–	–	–	85	.51
Yel.-bellied Sapsucker	–	–	1	–	5	–	–	–	–	–	–	1	3	–	–	–	–	–	6	.41
Gray Kingbird	–	–	–	–	–	–	–	2	–	–	–	–	–	–	–	–	8	–	6	.17
Loggerhead Flycatcher	–	–	–	–	–	–	–	4	–	–	–	–	T	–	–	–	6	–	14	.27
Stolid Flycatcher	–	–	–	–	–	–	–	1	–	–	–	–	–	–	–	1	8	–	15	.22
Gr. Antillean Pewee	–	–	–	–	–	–	–	2	–	1	–	–	T	T	–	–	7	–	33	.31
Bahama Swallow	–	–	–	–	–	–	–	–	–	–	–	–	–	–	–	–	–	10	17	.00
Brown-hd. Nuthatch	–	–	–	–	–	–	–	–	–	–	–	1	4	3	1	1	–	–	97	.49
Bahama Mockingbird	1	–	6	–	–	–	1	2	–	T	–	–	–	–	–	–	T	–	14	.45
Gray Catbird	1	–	5	–	–	–	3	T	–	1	–	–	–	–	–	–	–	–	13	.44
Red-legged Thrush	3	–	3	–	–	–	4	–	–	–	–	–	–	–	–	–	–	–	17	.38
Bl.-gray Gnatcatcher	–	–	–	–	–	–	T	–	–	3	–	–	2	1	–	4	T	–	169	.51
Thick-billed Vireo	–	–	1	–	–	–	–	1	–	7	–	–	–	–	–	1	–	–	50	.33
Blk.-whiskered Vireo	–	–	1	–	–	–	–	–	–	8	–	–	–	1	–	–	–	–	3	.22
Blk.-and-Wh. Warbler	–	–	–	–	–	–	–	–	–	–	–	–	10	T	T	–	–	–	50	.07
Parula Warbler	–	–	1	–	–	–	–	–	–	9	–	–	–	–	–	T	–	–	19	.15
Cape May Warbler	–	–	1	2	–	–	–	–	T	2	–	–	–	T	–	4	1	–	38	.58
Blk.-thr. Blue Warbler	–	–	–	–	–	–	–	–	1	8	–	–	–	1	–	–	–	–	2	.22
Yellow-rumped Warbler	–	–	4	–	–	–	T	–	–	–	–	–	T	3	–	1	2	–	36	.51
Blk.-thr. Green Warbler	–	–	–	–	–	–	–	–	–	6	–	–	–	1	–	3	–	–	7	.31
Yel.-throated W. (migr.)	–	–	T	–	–	–	–	–	–	–	–	–	1	2	1	6	T	–	104	.45
Yel.-throated W. (res.)	–	–	–	–	–	–	–	–	–	–	–	–	7	2	T	1	T	–	48	.35
Olive-capped Warbler	–	–	–	–	–	–	–	–	–	–	–	–	T	1	T	9	T	–	351	.22
Pine Warbler	–	–	–	–	–	–	–	–	–	–	–	–	1	T	T	9	T	–	89	.22
Prairie Warbler	–	–	–	–	–	–	–	–	–	5	–	–	–	T	–	5	–	–	51	.28
Palm Warbler	–	–	1	1	–	–	3	–	T	1	–	T	T	–	3	1	–	–	226	.80
Ovenbird	–	–	–	–	–	–	10	–	–	T	–	–	–	–	–	–	–	–	14	.04
Common Yellowthroat	–	–	–	–	–	–	8	–	–	2	–	–	–	–	–	–	–	–	5	.17

TABLE 20 (CONTINUED)

Foraging guilds[2]	Herbivores						Carnivores (mainly insects)												N[3]	Ampl.[4]
	a	b	c	d	e	f	a	b	c	d	e	f	g	h	i	j	k	l		
Bahama Yellowthroat	–	–	–	2	–	–	6	–	1	1	–	–	–	–	–	–	–	–	57	.38
Redstart	–	–	–	–	–	–	–	–	–	4	–	–	T	–	–	1	5	–	69	.36
Bananaquit	–	–	T	4	–	–	–	–	2	2	–	–	–	–	–	2	–	–	81	.50
Str.-headed Tanager	T	–	9	–	–	T	–	–	–	1	–	–	–	–	–	–	–	–	32	.18
Black-f. Grassquit	2	5	1	–	–	–	1	–	–	–	–	–	–	–	–	1	–	–	43	.47
Number of species with 1/10 or more	6	1	14	5	1	0	8	6	4	16	1	3	7	9	2	17	8	1		
Total number of species	7	1	16	5	1	1	10	7	6	18	1	3	13	17	6	18	14	1	(1912)	

[1] Estimated to nearest tenth from observations of foraging activity in 1968, 1969, and 1971 and from published information on food habitats.
[2] For identity of foraging guilds see Table 19.
[3] N = sample size of foraging activity observations.
[4] Amplitude = guild dispersion amplitude (H'/H' max.).

residents had gone, i.e. the breeding season, these 2 species comprised 66% of the individuals and 87% of the biomass (Tables 23b and 24b).

I have very little information on the food items taken, but doves, particularly the Zenaida Dove, clearly concentrated on relatively large seeds. They fed while

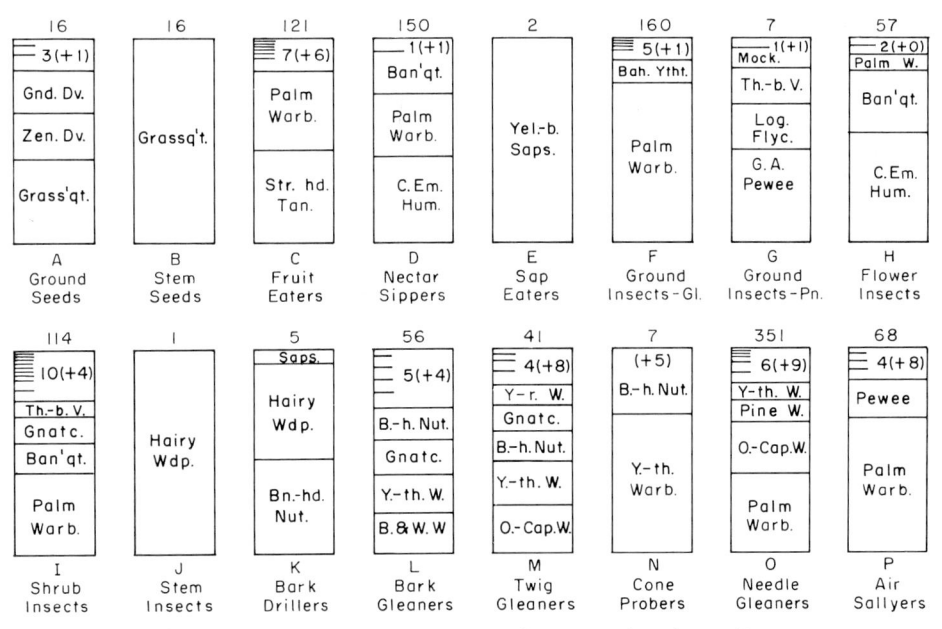

FIGURE 38. Membership and dominance structure in the 16 foraging guilds of the wintering community of the standard forests. The figure above each column is the total density (birds per km²) in the guild. The dominant and subdominant members are named in order from the bottom up; the figures inside each column at the top give the number of additional species with 1% or more representation and, in parentheses, the number of visitors, i.e. species with less than 1% representation.

TABLE 21a
Species Densities (Birds/km^2) in the Foraging Guilds—Wintering Community

	Herbivores							Carnivores (insects, etc.)										
	a[1]	b	c	d	e	f		a	b	c	d	e	f	g	h	i	j	k	l[1]
Permanent residents																			
Zenaida Dove	3.6	—	0.4	—	—	—		—	—	—	—	—	—	—	—	—	—	—	—
Ground Dove	3.5	—	—	63.5	—	—		—	—	—	—	—	—	—	—	—	—	—	—
Cuban Emerald Hummingbird	—	—	—	—	—	—		—	—	31.8	—	—	—	—	—	—	10.6	—	—
Hairy Woodpecker	—	—	2.1	—	—	—		—	—	—	—	1.1	2.1	4.2	T	—	—	—	—
Loggerhead Flycatcher	—	—	—	—	—	—		—	1.6	—	—	—	—	T	1.1	—	—	2.6	—
Stolid Flycatcher	—	—	—	—	—	—		—	0.2	—	—	—	—	—	—	—	—	1.7	—
Greater Antillean Pewee	—	—	—	—	—	—		—	3.4	—	1.7	—	—	—	T	—	0.2	—	—
Brown-headed Nuthatch	—	—	—	—	—	—		—	—	—	—	—	—	—	6.3	2.1	—	11.9	—
Red-legged Thrush	0.9	—	0.9	—	—	—		1.2	—	—	—	—	2.1	8.4	—	—	2.1	—	—
Blue-gray Gnatcatcher	—	—	—	—	—	—		T	—	—	14.7	—	—	9.8	4.9	—	19.6	T	—
Thick-billed Vireo	—	—	1.3	—	—	—		—	1.3	—	8.8	—	—	—	—	—	1.3	—	—
Yellow-throated Warbler	—	—	—	—	—	—		—	—	—	—	—	—	10.5	3.0	T	1.5	T	—
Olive-capped Warbler	—	—	—	—	—	—		—	—	—	—	—	—	T	9.5	T	85.5	T	—
Pine Warbler	—	—	—	—	—	—		T	—	—	—	—	—	4.1	T	T	36.5	T	—
Bahama Yellowthroat	—	—	—	6.1	—	—		18.2	—	—	—	—	—	—	—	—	—	—	—
Bananaquit	T	—	T	34.8	—	—		—	—	3.0	3.0	—	—	—	—	—	17.4	—	—
Stripe-headed Tanager	—	—	56.2	—	—	T		—	—	17.4	17.4	—	—	—	—	—	—	—	—
Grassquit	6.4	16.0	3.2	—	—	T		3.2	—	—	6.3	—	—	—	—	—	3.2	—	—
Total permanent residents	14.4	16.0	64.1	104.0	0	0		22.6	6.5	52.2	51.9	1.1	4.2	37.0	24.8	2.1	178	16.2	0
Bird species diversity	1.23	0	0.55	0.83				0.60	1.11	0.83	1.56	0	0.69	1.53	1.43	0	1.53	0.76	
Winter residents																			
Yellow-bellied Sapsucker	—	—	.4	—	1.8	—		—	—	—	—	—	0.3	1.1	—	—	—	—	—
Mockingbird	0.3	—	1.9	—	—	—		0.3	0.7	—	T	—	—	—	—	—	—	T	—
Catbird	0.8	—	3.9	—	—	—		2.3	T	—	0.8	—	—	—	—	—	—	—	—
Ruby-crowned Kinglet	—	—	—	—	—	—		—	—	—	1.4	—	—	—	T	T	0.4	0.2	—
Black-and-White Warbler	—	—	—	—	—	—		—	—	—	—	—	—	11.0	T	—	—	—	—
Parula Warbler	—	—	0.1	—	—	—		—	—	—	1.1	—	—	—	T	—	T	—	—
Cape May Warbler	—	—	0.1	0.2	—	—		—	—	T	0.2	—	—	—	0.1	—	0.4	0.1	—
Black-throated Blue Warbler	—	—	—	—	—	—		—	—	0.1	0.5	—	—	—	4.0	—	—	—	—
Yellow-rumped Warbler	—	—	5.4	—	—	—		T	—	—	—	—	—	—	0.5	—	1.3	2.7	—
Black-throated Green Warbler	—	—	—	—	—	—		—	—	—	3.0	—	—	—	9.0	4.5	1.5	T	—
Yellow-throated Warbler	—	—	T	—	—	—		—	—	—	—	—	—	4.5	T	T	27.0	T	—
Prairie Warbler	—	—	—	—	—	—		—	—	—	5.6	—	—	—	T	—	5.7	—	—
Palm Warbler	—	—	45.2	45.2	—	—		126	—	5.0	45.2	—	—	2	3	T	136	45.2	—
Ovenbird	—	—	—	—	—	—		1.5	—	—	T	—	—	—	—	—	—	—	—
Common Yellowthroat	—	—	—	—	—	—		7.8	—	—	1.9	—	—	—	—	—	—	—	—
Redstart	—	—	—	—	—	—		—	—	—	2.6	—	—	T	T	—	0.7	3.4	—
Total winter residents	1.1	0	57.0	45.4	1.8	0		138	0.7	5.1	62.3	1.1	0.3	18.6	16.6	4.5	173	51.6	0
Total	15.5	16.0	121	150	1.8	0		160	7.2	57.3	114	0	4.5	55.6	41.4	6.6	351	67.8	0
Bird species diversity	1.43	0	1.33	1.39				0.79	1.33	1.12	2.00		0.87	2.00	1.97	0.63	1.74	1.08	

[1] For identity of foraging guilds see Table 19.

TABLE 21b
SPECIES DENSITIES (BIRDS/KM²) IN THE FORAGING GUILDS—BREEDING SEASON COMMUNITY

	Herbivores						Carnivores (insects, etc.)									
	a[1]	b	c	d	e	f	a	b	c	d	e	f	g	h	i	j	k	l[1]
Permanent residents																		
Zenaida Dove	7.8	—	0.9	—	—	—	—	—	—	—	—	—	—	—	—	—	—	—
Ground Dove	9.4	—	—	—	—	—	—	—	—	—	—	—	—	—	—	—	—	—
Cuban Emerald Hummingbird	—	—	—	50.4	—	—	—	—	25.2	—	—	—	—	—	—	8.4	—	—
Hairy Woodpecker	—	—	1.7	—	—	—	—	—	—	—	0.9	1.7	3.4	0.9	—	—	—	—
Loggerhead Flycatcher	—	—	—	—	—	—	—	2.9	—	—	—	—	T	—	—	—	4.3	—
Stolid Flycatcher	—	—	—	—	—	—	—	0.1	—	—	—	—	—	—	—	0.1	0.4	—
Greater Antillean Pewee	—	—	—	—	—	—	—	4.4	—	—	—	—	—	T	—	—	15.3	—
Brown-headed Nuthatch	—	—	—	—	—	—	—	—	—	2.2	—	2.1	8.6	6.5	2.1	2.1	—	—
Red-legged Thrush	2.2	—	2.2	—	—	—	2.9	—	—	—	—	—	—	—	—	—	—	—
Blue-gray Gnatcatcher	—	—	—	—	—	—	T	—	—	14.6	—	—	9.8	4.9	—	11.9	T	—
Thick-billed Vireo	—	—	2.6	—	—	—	—	2.6	—	17.6	—	—	—	—	—	2.6	—	—
Yellow-throated Warbler	—	—	—	—	—	—	—	—	—	—	—	—	12.0	3.3	T	1.5	T	—
Olive-capped Warbler	—	—	—	—	—	—	—	—	—	—	—	—	T	12.1	T	109.0	T	—
Pine Warbler	—	—	—	—	—	—	T	—	—	—	—	—	4.3	T	T	38.2	—	—
Bahama Yellowthroat	—	—	—	6.2	—	—	18.8	—	3.1	3.1	—	—	—	—	—	—	—	—
Bananaquit	—	—	T	24.7	—	T	—	—	12.4	12.4	—	—	—	—	—	12.4	—	—
Stripe-headed Tanager	T	—	71.5	—	—	—	—	—	—	7.9	—	—	—	—	—	—	—	—
Grassquit	6.7	16.7	3.3	—	—	—	3.3	—	—	—	—	—	—	—	—	3.3	—	—
Total permanent residents	26.1	16.7	82.2	81.3	0	T	25.0	10.0	40.7	57.8	0.9	3.8	38.1	27.7	2.1	197	20.2	0
Bird species diversity	1.28	0	0.59	0.86	0	0	0.72	1.12	0.85	1.60	0	0.69	1.51	1.38	0	1.42	0.61	0
Summer residents																		
Gray Kingbird	—	—	—	—	—	—	—	0.9	—	—	—	—	—	—	—	—	3.7	—
Bahama Swallow	—	—	—	—	—	—	—	—	—	—	—	—	—	—	—	—	—	11.0
Black-whiskered Vireo	—	—	0.3	—	—	—	—	—	—	1.6	—	—	—	0.3	—	—	—	—
Total summer residents	—	—	0.3	—	0	—	—	0.9	—	1.6	—	—	—	0.3	—	—	3.7	11.0
Total	26.1	16.7	82.5	81.3	0	T	25.0	10.9	40.7	59.4	0.9	3.8	38.1	28.0	2.1	197	23.9	11.0
Bird species diversity	1.28	0	0.60	0.86	0	0	0.72	1.11	0.85	1.68	0	0.69	1.51	1.42	0	1.42	.952	0

[1] For identity of foraging guilds see Table 19.

TABLE 22a
BIOMASS OF EACH SPECIES (G/KM^2) IN THE FORAGING GUILDS—WINTERING COMMUNITY

	Herbivores						Carnivores (insects, etc.)									
	a[1]	b	c	d	e	f	a	b	c	d	e	f	g	h	i	j	k	l[1]
Permanent residents																		
Zenaida Dove	540	—	60	—	—	—	—	—	—	—	—	—	—	—	—	—	—	—
Ground Dove	122	—	—	191	—	—	—	—	—	—	—	—	—	—	—	—	—	—
Cuban Emerald Hummingbird	—	—	106	—	—	—	—	—	95	—	—	—	—	—	—	32	—	—
Hairy Woodpecker	—	—	—	—	—	—	—	—	—	—	53	106	212	T	—	—	121	—
Loggerhead Flycatcher	—	—	—	—	—	—	81	—	—	—	—	—	T	53	—	—	39	—
Stolid Flycatcher	—	—	—	—	—	—	5	—	—	—	—	—	T	T	—	5	—	—
Greater Antillean Pewee	—	—	—	—	—	—	34	—	—	17	—	11	42	32	11	11	119	—
Brown-headed Nuthatch	—	—	—	—	—	—	—	—	—	—	—	—	—	—	—	—	—	—
Red-legged Thrush	63	—	63	—	—	—	84	—	—	—	—	—	—	—	—	—	—	—
Blue-gray Gnatcatcher	—	—	—	—	—	—	T	—	—	74	—	—	49	25	—	99	T	—
Thick-billed Vireo	—	—	20	—	—	—	20	—	—	142	—	—	—	—	—	20	T	—
Yellow-throated Warbler	—	—	—	—	—	—	—	—	—	—	—	—	105	30	T	15	T	—
Olive-capped Warbler	—	—	—	—	—	—	—	—	—	—	—	—	T	67	T	598	T	—
Pine Warbler	—	—	—	97	—	—	T	—	49	49	—	—	49	T	T	438	T	—
Bahama Yellowthroat	—	—	T	349	—	—	291	—	174	174	—	—	—	—	—	—	—	—
Bananaquit	—	—	1296	—	—	T	—	—	—	144	—	—	—	—	—	174	—	—
Stripe-headed Tanager	70	176	35	—	—	T	35	—	—	—	—	—	—	—	—	35	—	—
Grassquit	795	176	1580	637	0	T	410	140	318	600	53	117	457	207	11	1427	279	0
Total permanent residents																		
Winter residents																		
Yellow-bellied Sapsucker	—	—	16	—	79	—	15	31	—	T	—	16	47	—	—	—	—	—
Mockingbird	15	—	92	—	—	—	88	T	—	29	—	—	—	—	—	—	T	—
Catbird	29	—	148	—	—	—	88	—	—	7	—	—	—	—	—	2	1	—
Ruby-crowned Kinglet	—	—	—	—	—	—	—	—	—	—	—	—	—	—	—	—	—	—
Black-and-White Warbler	—	—	—	—	—	—	—	—	—	—	—	—	110	T	T	T	—	—
Parula Warbler	—	—	1	2	—	—	—	—	T	7	—	—	—	T	—	T	T	—
Cape May Warbler	—	—	1	—	—	—	—	—	1	2	—	—	—	1	—	3	1	—
Black-throated Blue Warbler	—	—	54	—	—	—	—	—	—	5	—	—	—	—	—	—	—	—
Yellow-rumped Warbler	—	—	—	—	—	—	T	—	—	24	—	—	T	41	—	14	27	—
Black-throated Green Warbler	—	—	T	—	—	—	T	—	—	—	—	—	—	4	—	12	—	—
Yellow-throated Warbler	—	—	—	—	—	—	—	—	—	—	—	—	41	81	41	243	T	—
Prairie Warbler	—	—	—	—	—	—	—	—	—	46	—	—	—	T	—	46	—	—
Palm Warbler	—	—	497	497	—	—	1380	—	55	497	—	—	22	33	T	1492	497	—
Ovenbird	—	—	—	—	—	—	29	—	—	T	—	—	—	—	—	—	—	—
Common Yellowthroat	—	—	—	—	—	—	86	—	—	21	—	—	—	—	—	—	—	—
Redstart	—	—	—	—	—	—	—	—	—	19	—	—	T	T	—	5	24	—
Total winter residents	44	0	809	499	79	0	1598	31	56	651	0	16	220	160	41	1817	550	0
Total	839	176	2389	1136	79	0	2008	171	374	1251	53	133	677	367	52	3244	829	0

[1] For identity of foraging guilds see Table 19.

TABLE 22b
Biomass of Each Species (g/km²) in the Foraging Guilds—Breeding Season Community

	Herbivores						Carnivores (insects, etc.)								
	a	b	c	d	e	f	a	b	c	d	e	f	g	h	i	j	k	l[1]
Permanent residents																		
Zenaida Dove	1170	—	130	—	—	—	—	—	—	—	—	—	—	—	—	—	—	—
Ground Dove	330	—	—	—	—	—	—	—	—	—	—	—	—	—	—	—	—	—
Cuban Emerald Hummingbird	—	—	—	151	—	—	—	—	76	—	—	—	—	—	—	—	—	—
Hairy Woodpecker	—	—	85	—	—	—	—	—	—	—	45	85	170	T	—	—	—	—
Loggerhead Flycatcher	—	—	—	—	—	—	—	139	—	—	—	—	T	45	—	25	—	—
Stolid Flycatcher	—	—	—	—	—	—	—	1	—	—	—	—	—	—	—	—	206	—
Greater Antillean Pewee	—	—	—	—	—	—	—	44	—	22	—	11	43	T	—	1	9	—
Brown-headed Nuthatch	—	—	—	—	—	—	—	—	—	—	—	—	—	32	11	11	153	—
Red-legged Thrush	152	—	152	—	—	—	200	—	—	—	—	—	—	—	—	—	—	—
Blue-gray Gnatcatcher	—	—	—	—	—	—	T	—	—	73	—	—	49	25	—	97	T	—
Thick-billed Vireo	—	—	42	—	—	—	—	42	—	282	—	—	—	—	—	42	T	—
Yellow-throated Warbler	—	—	—	—	—	—	—	—	—	—	—	—	120	33	T	15	T	—
Olive-capped Warbler	—	—	—	—	—	—	—	—	—	—	—	—	T	85	T	762	T	—
Pine Warbler	—	—	—	—	—	—	T	—	—	—	—	—	52	T	—	458	—	—
Bahama Yellowthroat	—	—	—	9	—	—	301	—	—	—	—	—	—	—	—	—	—	—
Bananaquit	T	—	T	247	—	—	—	—	—	—	—	—	—	—	—	124	—	—
Striped-headed Tanager	—	—	—	—	—	T	—	—	—	—	—	—	—	—	—	—	—	—
Grassquit	74	184	36	—	—	T	36	—	—	—	—	—	—	—	—	36	—	—
Total permanent residents	1726	184	2090	497	0	0	537	225	250	733	45	96	434	220	11	1571	368	0
Summer residents																		
Gray Kingbird	—	—	—	—	—	—	—	54	—	—	—	—	—	—	—	—	222	—
Bahama Swallow	—	—	—	—	—	—	—	—	—	—	—	—	—	—	—	—	—	165
Black-whiskered Vireo	—	—	5	—	—	—	—	—	—	26	—	—	—	5	—	—	—	—
Total summer residents	—	—	5	—	0	0	—	54	—	26	—	—	—	5	—	—	222	165
Total	1726	184	2095	497	0	0	537	279	250	759	45	96	434	225	11	1571	590	165

[1] For identity of foraging guilds see Table 19.

TABLE 23a
SPECIES DENSITY COMPOSITION (PERCENT) OF FORAGING GUILDS—WINTERING COMMUNITY

	Herbivores						Carnivores (insects, etc.)									
	a[1]	b	c	d	e	f	a	b	c	d	e	f	g	h	i	j	k	l[1]
Permanent residents																		
Zenaida Dove	23	—	T	—	—	—	—	—	—	—	—	—	—	—	—	—	—	—
Ground Dove	22	—	—	—	—	—	—	—	—	—	—	—	—	—	—	—	—	—
Cuban Emerald Hummingbird	—	—	—	43	—	—	—	—	55	—	—	—	—	—	—	3	—	—
Hairy Woodpecker	—	—	2	—	—	—	—	22	—	—	100	47	7	T	—	—	4	—
Loggerhead Flycatcher	—	—	—	—	—	—	—	3	—	—	—	—	T	3	—	T	3	—
Stolid Flycatcher	—	—	—	—	—	—	—	47	—	2	—	—	—	—	—	1	17	—
Greater Antillean Pewee	—	—	—	—	—	—	—	—	—	—	—	47	15	15	32	—	—	—
Brown-headed Nuthatch	6	—	1	—	—	—	1	—	—	—	—	—	—	—	—	—	—	—
Red-legged Thrush	—	—	1	—	—	—	T	—	—	13	—	—	17	12	—	6	T	—
Blue-gray Gnatcatcher	—	—	—	—	—	—	—	18	—	7	—	—	—	—	T	T	T	—
Thick-billed Vireo	—	—	—	—	—	—	—	—	—	—	—	—	19	7	T	24	T	—
Yellow-throated Warbler	—	—	—	—	—	—	T	—	—	—	—	—	T	23	T	11	—	—
Olive-capped Warbler	—	—	—	4	—	—	11	—	5	—	—	—	7	T	—	—	—	—
Pine Warbler	T	—	T	23	—	T	—	—	30	3	—	—	—	—	—	5	—	—
Bahama Yellowthroat	—	100	47	—	—	—	—	—	—	15	—	—	—	—	—	—	—	—
Bananaquit	41	100	3	—	—	—	2	—	—	6	—	—	—	—	—	1	—	—
Stripe-headed Tanager	93	100	53	70	0	100	14	90	90	46	100	94	66	60	32	51	24	—
Total permanent residents																		
Winter residents																		
Yellow-bellied Sapsucker	—	—	T	—	100	—	1	10	—	T	—	6	2	—	—	—	—	—
Mockingbird	2	—	2	—	—	—	—	T	—	1	—	—	—	—	—	—	T	—
Catbird	5	—	3	—	—	—	—	—	—	1	—	—	—	—	—	—	T	—
Ruby-crowned Kinglet	—	—	—	—	—	—	—	—	—	—	—	—	—	—	—	—	—	—
Black-and-White Warbler	—	—	T	—	—	—	—	—	2	1	—	—	20	T	T	T	T	—
Parula Warbler	—	—	T	T	—	—	T	—	—	T	—	—	—	T	—	T	T	—
Cape May Warbler	—	—	—	—	—	—	—	—	2	T	—	—	—	T	—	T	—	—
Black-throated Blue Warbler	—	—	5	—	—	—	—	—	—	—	—	—	T	10	—	T	4	—
Yellow-rumped Warbler	—	—	—	—	—	—	—	—	—	3	—	—	—	1	—	T	T	—
Black-throated Green Warbler	—	—	T	—	—	—	—	—	—	—	—	—	8	22	68	8	T	—
Yellow-throated Warbler	—	—	—	—	—	—	—	—	—	5	—	—	—	T	T	2	—	—
Prairie Warbler	—	—	37	30	—	—	79	—	8	40	—	—	4	7	T	39	67	—
Palm Warbler	—	—	—	—	—	—	1	—	—	T	—	—	—	—	—	—	—	—
Ovenbird	—	—	—	—	—	—	5	—	—	2	—	—	—	—	—	—	—	—
Common Yellowthroat	—	—	—	—	—	—	—	—	—	2	—	—	—	—	—	T	5	—
Redstart	7	0	47	30	100	0	86	10	10	55	0	6	34	40	68	49	76	0
Total winter residents	15.5	16.0	121	150	1.8	T	160	7.2	57.3	114	1.1	4.5	55.6	41.4	6.6	351	67.8	
N (wintering community)																		

[1] For identity of foraging guilds see Table 19.

TABLE 23b
SPECIES DENSITY COMPOSITION (PERCENT) OF FORAGING GUILDS—BREEDING SEASON COMMUNITY

	Herbivores						Carnivores (insects, etc.)									
	a	b	c	d	e	f	a	b	c	d	e	f	g	h	i	j	k	l[1]
Permanent residents																		
Zenaida Dove	30	—	1	—	—	—	—	—	—	—	—	—	—	—	—	—	—	—
Ground Dove	36	—	—	—	—	—	—	—	—	—	—	—	—	—	—	—	—	—
Cuban Emerald Hummingbird	—	—	2	62	—	—	—	—	62	—	—	—	—	—	—	—	—	—
Hairy Woodpecker	—	—	—	—	—	—	—	—	—	—	100	45	9	T	—	4	—	—
Loggerhead Flycatcher	—	—	—	—	—	—	—	27	—	—	—	—	T	3	—	—	17	—
Stolid Flycatcher	—	—	—	—	—	—	—	1	—	—	—	—	—	—	—	T	2	—
Greater Antillean Pewee	—	—	—	—	—	—	—	40	—	4	—	55	23	T	—	1	65	—
Brown-headed Nuthatch	—	—	—	—	—	—	—	—	—	—	—	—	—	23	100	—	—	—
Red-legged Thrush	8	—	2	—	—	—	11	—	—	—	—	—	—	—	—	—	—	—
Blue-gray Gnatcatcher	—	—	—	—	—	—	T	—	—	—	—	—	26	18	—	10	T	—
Thick-billed Vireo	—	—	3	—	—	—	—	24	—	25	—	—	—	—	—	2	T	—
Yellow-throated Warbler	—	—	—	—	—	—	—	—	—	29	—	—	31	12	T	1	T	—
Olive-capped Warbler	—	—	—	—	—	—	—	—	—	—	—	—	T	43	T	55	T	—
Pine Warbler	—	—	—	—	—	—	T	—	—	—	—	—	11	T	—	19	—	—
Bahama Yellowthroat	—	—	—	8	—	—	76	—	8	5	—	—	—	—	—	—	—	—
Bananaquit	—	—	T	30	—	T	—	—	30	21	—	—	—	—	—	6	—	—
Stripe-headed Tanager	—	—	87	—	—	—	—	—	—	13	—	—	—	—	—	—	—	—
Grassquit	T	—	4	—	—	—	13	—	—	—	—	—	—	—	—	2	—	—
Total permanent residents	100	100	99	100	—	100	100	92	100	97	100	100	100	99	100	100	84	0
Summer residents																		
Gray Kingbird	—	—	—	—	—	—	—	8	—	—	—	—	—	—	—	—	16	—
Bahama Swallow	—	—	—	—	—	—	—	—	—	—	—	—	—	—	—	—	—	100
Black-whiskered Vireo	—	—	1	—	—	—	—	—	—	3	—	—	—	1	—	—	—	—
Total summer residents	0	0	1	0	0	0	0	8	0	3	0	0	0	1	0	0	16	100
N (breeding community)	26.1	16.7	82.5	81.3	0	T	25.0	10.9	40.7	59.4	0.9	3.8	35.6	27.1	2.1	197	23.7	11.0

[1] For identity of foraging guilds see Table 19.

TABLE 24a
Percent Biomass Composition of Foraging Guilds—Wintering Community

	Herbivores						Carnivores (insects, etc.)											
	a[1]	b	c	d	e	f	a	b	c	d	e	f	g	h	i	j	k	l[1]
Permanent residents																		
Zenaida Dove	64	—	3	—	—	—	—	—	—	—	—	—	—	—	—	—	—	—
Ground Dove	15	—	—	—	—	—	—	—	—	—	—	—	—	—	—	—	—	—
Cuban Emerald Hummingbird	—	—	—	16	—	—	—	—	25	—	—	—	—	—	—	—	—	—
Hairy Woodpecker	—	—	4	—	—	—	—	—	—	—	100	80	31	14	—	—	—	—
Loggerhead Flycatcher	—	—	—	—	—	—	47	—	—	—	—	—	T	—	—	T	15	—
Stolid Flycatcher	—	—	—	—	—	—	3	—	—	—	—	—	—	—	—	T	5	—
Greater Antillean Pewee	—	—	—	—	—	—	20	—	—	—	—	—	—	—	—	—	14	—
Brown-headed Nuthatch	—	—	—	—	—	—	—	—	—	—	—	8	6	9	21	—	—	—
Red-legged Thrush	8	—	3	—	—	—	4	—	—	1	—	—	—	—	—	3	—	—
Blue-gray Gnatcatcher	—	—	—	—	—	—	T	—	—	—	—	—	7	7	—	1	T	—
Thick-billed Vireo	—	—	1	—	—	—	—	12	—	6	—	—	—	—	—	T	T	—
Yellow-throated Warbler	—	—	—	—	—	—	—	—	—	11	—	—	16	8	T	18	T	—
Olive-capped Warbler	—	—	—	—	—	—	—	—	—	—	—	—	T	18	T	14	T	—
Pine Warbler	—	—	—	—	—	—	T	—	—	—	—	—	T	T	—	—	—	—
Bahama Yellowthroat	—	—	—	9	—	—	14	—	13	4	—	—	—	—	—	5	—	—
Bananaquit	—	—	T	31	—	T	—	—	47	14	—	—	—	—	—	—	—	—
Stripe-headed Tanager	—	—	54	—	—	—	—	—	—	12	—	—	—	—	—	1	—	—
Grassquit	8	100	1	—	—	—	2	—	—	—	—	—	—	—	—	—	T	—
Total permanent residents	95	100	66	56	0	100	20	82	85	48	100	88	67	56	21	43	34	—
Winter residents																		
Yellow-bellied Sapsucker	—	—	1	—	100	—	1	—	—	T	—	12	7	—	—	—	—	—
Mockingbird	2	—	4	—	—	—	18	—	2	—	—	—	—	T	—	T	—
Catbird	3	—	6	—	—	—	4	T	—	T	—	—	—	T	—	T	T	—
Ruby-crowned Kinglet	—	—	—	—	—	—	—	—	—	T	—	—	—	T	T	T	—	—
Black-and-White Warbler	—	—	—	—	—	—	—	—	T	T	—	—	16	T	T	T	T	—
Parula Warbler	—	—	T	T	—	—	—	—	T	T	—	—	—	T	—	—	—	—
Cape May Warbler	—	—	T	—	—	—	T	—	—	—	—	—	T	T	—	T	—	—
Black-throated Blue Warbler	—	—	2	—	—	—	—	—	—	2	—	—	T	11	—	T	3	—
Yellow-rumped Warbler	—	—	—	—	—	—	T	—	—	—	—	—	—	1	—	T	—	—
Black-throated Green Warbler	—	—	T	—	—	—	—	—	—	4	—	—	6	22	79	8	T	—
Yellow-throated Warbler	—	—	—	—	—	—	—	—	—	40	—	—	—	T	—	2	—	—
Prairie Warbler	—	—	21	44	—	—	69	—	15	T	—	—	3	9	T	46	60	—
Palm Warbler	—	—	—	—	—	—	1	—	—	2	—	—	—	—	—	—	—	—
Ovenbird	—	—	—	—	—	—	4	—	—	2	—	—	—	—	—	—	—	—
Common Yellowthroat	—	—	—	—	—	—	—	—	—	—	—	—	T	T	—	T	3	—
Redstart	5	0	34	44	100	0	79	18	15	52	0	12	33	43	79	56	66	—
Total winter residents	839	176	2389	1136	79	0	2008	171	374	1251	53	133	677	367	52	3249	829	0
N (wintering community)																		

[1] For identity of foraging guilds see Table 19.

TABLE 24b
PERCENT BIOMASS COMPOSITION OF FORAGING GUILDS—BREEDING SEASON COMMUNITY

	Herbivores						Carnivores (insects, etc.)										
	a	b	c	d	e	f	a	b	c	d	e	f	g	h	i	j	k	l[1]
Permanent residents																		
Zenaida Dove	68	—	6	—	—	—	—	—	—	—	—	—	—	—	—	—	—	—
Ground Dove	19	—	—	—	—	—	—	—	—	—	—	—	—	—	—	—	—	—
Cuban Emerald Hummingbird	—	—	—	30	—	—	—	—	30	—	—	—	—	—	—	—	—	—
Hairy Woodpecker	—	—	4	—	—	—	—	—	—	—	100	88	39	T	20	—	—	—
Loggerhead Flycatcher	—	—	—	—	—	—	—	50	—	—	—	—	T	—	—	2	35	—
Stolid Flycatcher	—	—	—	—	—	—	—	T	—	—	—	—	—	—	—	—	2	—
Greater Antillean Pewee	—	—	—	—	—	—	—	16	—	3	—	—	—	T	—	T	26	—
Brown-headed Nuthatch	—	—	—	—	—	—	—	—	—	—	—	12	10	14	11	1	—	—
Red-legged Thrush	9	—	7	—	—	—	37	—	—	—	—	—	—	—	—	—	—	—
Blue-gray Gnatcatcher	—	—	—	—	—	—	T	—	—	10	—	—	12	11	—	6	T	—
Thick-billed Vireo	—	—	2	—	—	—	—	15	—	37	—	—	—	—	—	3	—	—
Yellow-throated Warbler	—	—	—	—	—	—	—	—	—	—	—	—	28	14	T	1	T	—
Olive-capped Warbler	—	—	—	—	—	—	—	—	—	—	—	—	T	38	T	49	T	—
Pine Warbler	—	—	—	—	—	—	T	—	—	—	—	—	12	T	—	29	—	—
Bahama Yellowthroat	—	—	—	20	—	—	56	—	20	7	—	—	—	—	—	—	—	—
Bananaquit	—	—	T	50	—	—	—	—	50	16	—	—	—	—	—	8	—	—
Stripe-headed Tanager	T	100	79	—	—	T	—	—	—	24	—	—	—	—	—	—	—	—
Grassquit	4	—	2	—	—	—	7	—	—	—	—	—	—	—	—	2	—	—
Total permanent residents	100	100	100	100	—	100	100	81	100	97	100	100	101	97	100	101	63	0
Summer residents																		
Gray Kingbird	—	—	—	—	—	—	—	19	—	—	—	—	—	—	—	—	38	—
Bahama Swallow	—	—	—	—	—	—	—	—	—	—	—	—	—	—	—	—	—	100
Black-whiskered Vireo	—	0	T	0	—	0	0	19	0	3	0	0	0	2	0	0	38	100
Total summer residents	—	0	T	0	—	0	0	19	0	3	0	0	0	2	0	0	38	100
N (breeding community)	1726	184	2095	497	—	—	537	279	76	577	401	96	434	225	11	1571	590	165

[1] For identity of foraging guilds see Table 19.

walking rapidly on fairly open ground, primarily roadbeds and road shoulders, turning and jabbing at surface objects at the rate of 20–30 pecks per min. Grassquits, although primarily stem seed pluckers, were often observed biting and hulling small grass seeds on the ground. The other three species are assigned membership in this guild only because they are known to eat fallen fruit and small amounts of seed. Their foraging methods suggest that seeds are generally ignored.

This summary suggests that each member of the guild occupies a relatively separate subprovince and that interspecies overlap of food resources is slight. Ground Doves, aside from their assumed selection of smaller seeds than Zenaida Doves, tend to forage in more open sections of the forest.

Stem seed-pluckers.—This guild is distinctive and readily delineated. It has only one member in the Grand Bahama pinelands, the grassquit, and this member does about half of its foraging in the guild. The birds generally work from the ground, reaching up to nibble at the tiny seeds in the grass heads, or leaping up to bite off a seed or to pull the whole head down within reach. Seeds are apparently bitten off the heads and hulled on the spot with rapid mandibular movements. A grassquit was once seen perched on and feeding on the seeds of a thistle, an uncommon plant on the study areas.

Fruit and bud harvesters.—Berries of many varieties were common and widespread in the shrub stratum of the Bahama pinelands through both the winter and spring months, and new buds were numerous, particularly in the early months of the year. Seven species of permanent resident birds and 8 of winter residents were observed feeding on fruits and/or buds, but only 3 of these, one permanent resident and 2 winter invaders, were primary members of the guild.

The Striped-headed Tanager, the fourth most common bird of the breeding season community, specialized on fruits and buds and constituted 87% of the individuals (Table 23b) and 79% of the biomass (Table 24b) of this guild at that time. Secondary and tertiary fruit-bud eaters of the breeding season community were the Hairy Woodpecker (a pine trunk driller), the Red-legged Thrush (a ground-gleaning insectivore), the Thick-billed Vireo (a shrub foliage gleaner), and the grassquit (an herb and grass plucker). Bananaquits were seen on fruit once.

The Striped-headed Tanager also dominated the fruit-bud eating guild in the wintering community, with 47% of the individuals and 54% of the biomass. It was closely followed by the abundant Palm Warbler with 37% and 21%. Because of their low densities, the two primary fruit eaters among the winter residents, the catbird and Mockingbird, were incidental members of the guild with only 3% and 2% of the membership and 6% and 4% of the biomass, respectively. The Yellow-rumped Warbler contributed an additional 5% of the membership and 2% of the biomass. Lesser members were the Yellow-bellied Sapsucker, the Parula Warbler, Cape May Warbler, and the migratory race of the Yellow-throated Warbler.

Striped-headed Tanagers perched quietly in small groups near the berries on which they fed, reaching out to bite then mandibulate the pulp and allowing the peels and husks, when present, to fall to the ground. Feeding apparently occupied only a small fraction of the daylight hours, and much time was spent by the tanagers quietly perching high in the pines. Other fruit eaters of the breeding season were specialists in other guilds and apparently encountered little or no competition for fruits or buds.

The two dominants of the wintering community guild fed on different items. The Palm Warbler, a highly eurytrophic bird at this season, took nine-tenths of its food in other guilds and assumed importance in the fruit-eating guild only because of its very large numbers. Like the less common Yellow-rumped Warbler, it focused largely on the Wax Myrtle berry, a fruit of secondary importance to the tanager. Catbirds and Mockingbirds fed mainly on fleshy berries such as those of *Smilax* and *Lantana,* fruits also harvested by the tanagers. In view of the leisurely feeding habits of all these species and the continuous abundance of fruits, significant competition probably did not occur during the periods of this study.

Nectar sippers.—Blossoms of many types were abundant on Grand Bahama Island through all the winter and spring months. No measurements were attempted, but the successive blossoming of various species of *Ernodea, Calliandra, Agava, Lysiloma, Tetrazygia, Tabebouia,* and *Acacia* appeared to offer an abundant supply of nectar for the members of this guild. Of special interest were the spectacular blooms of *Agave braceana* in the pine forests in February and March. The huge heads of showy yellow flowers, literally dripping with nectar, attracted many winter residents as well as permanent residents and created many "food territory" situations with intensive fighting and chasing (Kale 1967, Emlen 1973).

It was generally impossible to determine when a flower-probing bird was sipping nectar and when it was taking small insects. A crude decision on this matter was made on the basis of published data on stomach contents of related species. The error in this decision may be considerable.

Three species constituted the nectar-sipping guild in the breeding season. The only primary member was the Cuban Emerald Hummingbird which, with an overall density of 106 birds per km^2, contributed 62% of the guild membership and 30% of the biomass. A strong secondary member was the bananaquit, with 30% of the membership and 50% of the biomass. The third member, the ground-skulking Bahama Yellowthroat, commonly probed the small tubular flowers of *Ernodea* and contributed the remaining 8% of the individuals and 20% of the biomass.

Two species were added to this guild during the winter months, the abundant Palm Warbler and the relative scarce Cape May Warbler. Palm Warblers, although only tertiary nectar sippers, added 45 members per km^2 to constitute 30% of the winter guild membership and 44% of the biomass, while the Cuban Emerald Hummingbird held its dominant numerical position with 43% of the membership, but had only 16% of the biomass. These wintering warblers concentrated their nectar sipping on the Agave blossoms where they came into close contact and frequent aggressive encounters with the hummingbirds and bananaquits.

The irregular changing of floral distribution in the forest had an obvious effect on the distribution of nectar sippers. This, and the frequent aggressive encounters particularly on the Agave heads, indicated interference within and between the species belonging to the guild. The Bahama Yellowthroat, concentrating on the low-lying and widely scattered *Ernodea* blossoms, was essentially independent, but the other four species of the wintering community clearly competed for this particular resource at times.

Sap and cambium eaters.—Apparently only one species, the winter resident Yellow-bellied Sapsucker, exploits this food resource. In my limited observations I saw sapsuckers feeding on berries once, and assume, on the basis of published accounts of food habits in North America, that the birds take considerable insect food from the trunk and bark of pine trees. In my best estimate this species is a primary member of the sap and cambium-eating guild and comprises a density in the guild of about 1.8 birds and 79 g per km^2 (Tables 21 and 22).

Foliage browsers.—Except that this guild has importance in certain avian communities elsewhere, I would merge it with the fruit and bud harvesters, for my only evidence of foliage browsing is one case in the Striped-headed Tanager. A bird was watched as it nibbled for several seconds at the succulent tip of a growing Smilax stem.

Ground-gleaning carnivores.—As already noted it is often impossible to tell the nature of a ground gleaner's prey. On the basis of published records on stomach contents in related species, the Bahamian doves are assumed to be primarily herbivorous, and the mimids, thrushes, and warblers primarily insectivorous when ground gleaning. Birds that pounce on ground-inhabiting insects are treated in another guild.

The ground-gleaning carnivore guild apparently has three members on Grand Bahama during the breeding season and seven during the winter. In the breeding season the Bahama Yellowthroat is the only primary ground gleaner. The Red-legged Thrush takes slightly less than half of its food in this guild, and the grassquit a smaller amount. Several others, including the Pine Warbler and Blue-gray Gnatcatcher, obtained some insect food by ground gleaning. The dominant member of the guild is the Bahama Yellowthroat, with 76% of the membership and 56% of the biomass. The rather scarce Red-legged Thrush contributes 11% of the guild's population and 37% of its biomass, while the grassquit contributes 13% and 7%.

In the winter the guild, with 7 members, is dominated by winter residents to the extent of 86%. The principal member of this invading force is the Palm Warbler which, with 25 – 30% of its feeding in this guild constitutes 79% of the individuals and 69% of the biomass of the guild. Much less important as members are the Mockingbird (< 1% and 1%), the Common Yellowthroat (5% and 4%), and the Ovenbird, a primary member (1% and 1%).

Two distinct size classes characterize the ground-gleaning carnivores, and the larger mimids and thrushes presumably take different (larger) prey than the warblers. Among the larger members, the Red-legged Thrush and the Mockingbird forage in open situations, the thrush along roadways and the mockingbirds primarily in clearing at the forest edge. Among the warblers the same variety of feeding situations may be recognized, leading to segregation of the potentially competing guild members. Bahama Yellowthroats frequent the deep litter under shrubs, actually tunnelling under vines and leaves. Ovenbirds feed primarily on the litter surface as do Palm Warblers, but the latter tend to select more open situations in the forest. Finally, the grassquits, Pine Warblers and other incidental members of this guild are found mostly on nearly barren ground as along roadways or in recent burns.

Because of this diversity of feeding situations and the related variations in foraging behavior, there appears to be very little direct overlap in the foraging niches of the various guild members.

Ground pouncers.—A second method of foraging on terrestrial arthropods is to pounce on them from an elevated perch. This method, referred to as "drop to ground" by Orians (1969), is effective on a somewhat different prey fauna than ground gleaning and is generally practiced by a different group of birds. For these reasons I have recognized its practitioners as a distinct guild in this analysis.

Four permanent residents, one summer resident, and one winter resident practiced ground-pouncing in the Grand Bahama pinelands. None of these, however, used pouncing as their principal method of foraging, and the total guild membership was very small. In the breeding season community all four members of the flycatcher family, the Gray Kingbird, Loggerhead Flycatcher, Stolid Flycatcher, and Greater Antillean Pewee, occasionally dropped to the ground to capture insects, and the Thick-billed Vireo was observed to do it several times. Mockingbirds commonly fed in this way in the open terrain of their summer habitat and were observed doing it in the pine forest in winter on one occasion.

Flower probers.—It is well known that many, perhaps all, flower-probing birds take a certain number of insects as well as nectar; in some cases their principal food source is apparently insects. It is therefore appropriate to recognize a flower-probing carnivore guild, although I have insufficient data to quantify its membership and its overall significance in the Bahama pineland community.

In the absence of information on food habits I will guess that three prominent flower probers of the breeding season community are secondary or tertiary members of this guild. These are the Cuban Emerald Hummingbird, the Bahama Yellowthroat, and the bananaquit. The abundance of these species suggests that the total membership of the guild is quite large, perhaps about 50 individuals per km^2. This group is apparently supplemented in winter by 3 migrant species, the Palm Warbler, Cape May Warbler, and Black-throated Blue Warbler, and I will guess that this supplement amounts to 10% or less of the total.

Shrub foliage gleaners.—After an unsuccessful attempt to differentiate stem and leaf insect gleaners in the shrub stratum I lumped all such birds and added those that foraged in the occasional Lysiloma or Gumbo Limbo (*Bursera simarouba*) tree (rarely more than 5 m tall) into a single guild of shrub foliage gleaners. Insect and spider foraging usually could be separated from berry-eating without difficulty.

No less than 7 species in the breeding season community and 15 in the wintering community did some shrub-foliage gleaning. Two members of the breeding season community, the Thick-billed Vireo and Black-whiskered Vireo, were primary members of the guild. The Thick-billed Vireo contributed 37% of the membership and biomass respectively. Bananaquits with two-tenths of their activity in the guild and Striped-headed Tanagers with one-tenth were subdominants in terms of both numbers and biomass. The gnatcatcher, a subdominant numerically, was a subordinate in biomass. Greater Antillean Pewees and Bahama Yellowthroats did a small amount of foraging in this guild.

Catbirds and 8 of the 11 species of migrant warblers joined the guild of shrub foliage gleaners in winter. With them the total membership and biomass more than doubled. As in 6 other guilds, the principal member of this invading contingent, constituting nearly three-quarters of its total, was the Palm Warbler, which dominated the wintering guild with 40% of its total membership and 40% of its biomass.

Two major foraging methods were noted among the shrub foliage gleaners. The two vireos advanced slowly through the foliage, perching on a twig or branch and peering about for 5 or more sec before leaping or fluttering a half meter or more to snatch an insect from a twig or leaf surface. Warblers and Gnatcatchers moved more rapidly, generally making their final jump from a distance of only a few centimeters. The differences in these two foraging procedures and in the many variations of them probably function variously for different types of insect prey. Combined with differences in compartment distribution and in body size, they presumably spread the pressures of bird predation on shrub foliage insects over many behavioral and morphological types.

Shrub stem drillers.—Shrub stems constitute a minor segment of the vegetation of a pine stand, and the guild which exploits the insect populations on Grand Bahama Island is apparently limited to one species, the permanent resident Hairy Woodpecker. Of the 85 observed feedings of this bird 17% were on shrub stems. No consistent difference between the sexes was noted in this sample.

Pine bark and wood drillers.—The excavating and extracting of insects from within or beneath bark appears to warrant the recognition of a special guild, distinct from that encompassing the gleaners, which cover the bark surface or probe under the edges of bark flakes (next section).

Membership in the bark- and wood-drilling guild on Grand Bahama includes only the Hairy Woodpecker and the Brown-headed Nuthatch in the breeding season. The Woodpecker does about two-tenths of its foraging in the guild but constitutes 45% of the membership and 88% of the biomass of the guild. The Brown-headed Nuthatch, a much smaller bird with limited capacities in wood drilling, allotted about one-tenth of its foraging to this guild and contributed 55% of the guild's membership and 12% of its biomass.

In the winter the guild is joined by the Yellow-bellied Sapsucker, a sap and cambium eater, which contributes less than one-tenth of the guild's winter membership.

Bark gleaners.—The bark-gleaning guild is quite clearly delineated in its spatial distribution, the bark surfaces of pine trunks and branches, and in its food composition, which is almost entirely anthropods. The feeding behavior dimension is less clearly defined in that the distinction between pecking and drilling is sometimes difficult to make.

The composition of this guild is surprisingly complex on Grand Bahama Island. In the breeding season community there is one primary member, the resident Bahama race of the Yellow-throated Warbler, three secondary members— the Hairy Woodpecker, Brown-headed Nuthatch, and Blue-gray Gnatcatcher, and one tertiary—the Pine Warbler. Loggerhead Flycatchers, Greater Antillean Pewees, and Olive-capped Warblers were also seen foraging on bark surfaces on a few occasions. The most numerous bark gleaner in the submature forests was the Yellow-throated Warbler, with 31% of the membership and 28% of the guild biomass; the gnatcatcher and Brown-headed Nuthatch were close behind with 26% and 23% of the membership, and 12% and 10% of the biomass respectively. Hairy Woodpeckers contributed only 9% of the membership but a significant 39% of the biomass, while the Pine Warbler was represented with 11% of the membership and 12% of the biomass.

In the wintering community, migrants made up 34% of the individuals and 33% of the biomass of the 9-member guild. The most important member of this contingent was the Black-and-white Warbler (20% and 16%). The migrant race of the Yellow-throated Warbler, identified under favorable circumstances by the contrasting white of its underparts, was three times as numerous as the resident race in the winter community but, in marked contrast to the latter, fed only occasionally in the bark-gleaning guild. The redstart, an uncommon member of the wintering community, fed only occasionally on bark in 1968 and 1969, but as an abundant transient briefly dominated that guild in May of 1971.

Three major methods of foraging were used by bark-gleaners in the Grand Bahama pinelands: pecking or probing into cracks or under the edges of bark flakes, flushing the prey and chasing it, and pouncing on the bark surface. The first was the commonest and was used most often by the dominant and subdominant Yellow-throated Warbler, Nuthatch, Hairy Woodpecker, and Black-and-white Warbler. The flushing method was commonly used by gnatcatchers and was the principal method of the redstart. Both of these species spread and flash strikingly marked tail patterns toward the surface as they hitch along. Actual captures were not often seen, but a tumbling chase was obviously a response to the flushing of an insect. Yellow-throated Warblers also used this method on occasion. The third method, pouncing on the trunk, was used by kingbirds and pewees and occasionally by gnatcatchers, redstarts, and others.

While the identity of the prey was not determined in my observations, I suspect that the three methods tend to function for different types of prey and that these differences, together with prey size selection by large and small bird species, result in a dispersion of predator pressures and a reduction in potential competition for any specific insect type.

Pine twig gleaners.—For the purposes of this study pine twigs are defined as branches less than 2 cm in diameter with few or no green needles. Such twigs are generally 2–3 years old and up to 1 m long. The surface is gray and scrofulous with old needle scars, in contrast to the large brown plates and flakes (bark) on the surfaces of older and larger branches. Many birds, particularly needle-gleaners, use both live and dead twigs for perching, but guild membership as here defined is limited to the relatively few birds that actually forage on the twig surfaces or drill into them. Examination of several hundred twig samples revealed a very sparse population of spiders and small insects among the old needle scars.

The twig-gleaning guild in the Grand Bahama pinelands contained 6 primary and secondary plus 3 incidental members in the breeding season, and 9 members plus 7 incidentals in the winter. No species spent more than 30% of its foraging activity in the guild, and only 2 permanent residents, the Brown-headed Nuthatch and the Yellow-throated Warbler, and 1 winter resident the Yellow-rumped Warbler, took as much as 20% of their food from twigs.

The 3 dominant and subdominant members of the guild during the breeding season were the Olive-capped Warbler, the Brown-headed Nuthatch, and the Blue-gray Gnatcatcher with about 43%, 23%, and 18% of the membership respectively, and 38%, 14%, and 11% of the biomass. The Hairy Woodpecker (3% and 20%), the resident race of the Yellow-throated Warbler (12% and 14%), and the summering Black-whiskered Vireo (1% and 2%) had minor representation in the guild, while hummingbirds, pewees, and Pine Warblers were each recorded foraging on twigs on a few occasions.

Winter residents raised the total membership from 28 to 41 birds per km^2 and the biomass from 220 to 367. Prominent among this winter contingent were the Yellow-rumped and migrant Yellow-throated Warblers (19% and 22% of the members and 11% and 22% of the biomass respectively) and the ubiquitous Palm Warbler, which though feeding only incidentally on twigs contributed 8% of the winter membership and 9% of the biomass.

Pine twigs were apparently poor sources of food and served as no more than secondary or incidental foraging sites for any species. They were used extensively as lookout perches for flycatching sallyers, however, and as access routes to the relatively rich foliage and bark substrates by most if not all the arboreal birds of the forest. Their occasional or incidental use as food substrates by many species is, therefore, not surprising. Dead twigs appeared to offer more food than live twigs, but no consistent records were kept to permit quantitative comparisons. Foraging methods included direct searching and pecking by most species, drilling by the nuthatches and woodpeckers, flushing and chasing by redstarts and gnatcatchers, and hovering by hummingbirds, pewees, and several warblers.

Pine cone probers.—The small (5–7 cm) cones of mature Caribbean Pines are retained on the twigs and branches in large numbers for several years, opening their scales after the first year to present large irregular clusters of deeply creviced feeding substrates for insectivorous and pine-seed-eating birds. Cones are reported to be important sources of insects and seeds for titmice in England (Gibb 1960) and for nuthatches, warblers and other species in North America (Morse 1966). The resource was, however, very weakly exploited on Grand Bahama Island during the period of this study. Even the Brown-headed Nuthatch, a habitual exploiter of cones where it has been studied on the continent, was rarely seen foraging on cones.

In the breeding season the only consistent member of the cone-gleaning guild was the Brown-headed Nuthatch, and it did less than 10% of its foraging on cones. All three species of resident arboreal warblers often hopped over cones or paused on them to sing but were observed probing the cone surface or crevices on only a few occasions.

The migrant Yellow-throated Warbler frequented cones during its winter stay in the pine forest and apparently took about a quarter of its food in this guild. It was thus the dominant cone-gleaner during the winter, with the nuthatch a strong subdominant and five warbler species recorded as occasional visitors.

Pine needle gleaners.—I have included all types of foraging in needle clusters in this guild. The dividing line between twig and needle cluster is not always clear to an observer on the ground, but all birds that pecked at the base of or out into the needles of the previous season's growth are included.

About half of the pineland bird species foraged at least occasionally in pine needles. In the breeding season community two species, the Olive-capped and Pine Warblers, were primary needle gleaners; and two, the gnatcatcher and the bananaquit, were secondary members. Cuban Emerald Hummingbirds, Stolid Flycatchers, Brown-headed Nuthatches, Thick-billed Vireos, Yellow-throated Warblers, and grassquits also foraged in needles for minor portions of their food.

The dominant needle gleaner in the breeding season, contributing 55% of the membership and 49% of the biomass, was the Olive-capped Warbler. It was followed by the Pine Warbler (19% and 29%), the Blue-gray Gnatcatcher (10% and 6%), and the bananaquit (6% and 8%).

The invasion of winter migrants doubled the membership of the pine-gleaning guild and more than doubled its biomass. The main contributer to this increase was the Palm Warbler which, with about 30% of its feeding in the needles, introduced 136 individuals and 1,492 g per km^2 to the guild. This constituted 39% of the membership and 46% of the biomass of the wintering guild. Other migrant members of the wintering guild were Cape May Warbler, Yellow-rumped Warbler, Black-throated Green Warbler, Yellow-throated Warbler (migrant race), Prairie Warbler, and redstart. Of these the Yellow-throated Warbler and the Prairie Warbler were primary needle gleaners, but because of their relative scarcity constituted only 8% and 2% of the membership and 8% and 2% of the biomass respectively.

Three foraging methods were employed by needle gleaners: (1) reaching out from the twig base of a cluster, (2) crawling into the needles and pecking either inward toward the shoot or outward, and (3) hovering outside the cluster (Table 25). The first of these is used by nearly all members of the guild and may thus be considered the least specialized. The wintering Palm, Yellow-rumped, and Yellow-throated Warblers, which feed largely in rather different habitats on their breeding ground in the north, fed almost entirely in this way when in the needle compartment on Grand Bahama as did most of the resident species. Crawling or tunnelling into the needle clusters was the dominant foraging method of the Olive-capped Warbler and an important secondary method in the Pine Warbler (Table 25b). These were the two primary needle-gleaners of Grand Bahama Island. The method is apparently rarely used by other species.

Hovering to snatch prey from the distal portions of needle clusters was the principal needle-gleaning method of the Cuban-Emerald Hummingbird and was observed on several occasions in the Thick-billed Vireo and the Cape May Warbler. It was also used on occasion by nearly all of the needle-gleaning species.

Pecking from the basal twig limits a bird to animals in the basal portions of a needle cluster, while hovering makes the outer portions of needles available. The heart of the cluster, particularly the bases of the needle bundles and the central

TABLE 25

FORAGING METHODS OF PROMINENT MEMBERS
OF THE NEEDLE-GLEANING GUILD[1]

	A				B	
	Winter[2]		Spring[2]		Peck from base	Crawl[3] in
	Hover	Peck	Hover	Peck		
Permanent residents						
Olive-capped Warbler	0	95	2	101	14	53
Pine Warbler	0	37	0	32	25	7
Yellow-throated Warbler (PR)	0	2	0	3	3	0
Other permanent residents	4	18	0	11	11	0
Total permanent residents	4	152	2	147	53	60
Winter residents						
Palm Warbler	8	48	–	–	48	0
Yellow-throated Warbler (WR)	0	25	–	–	25	0
Other winter residents	12	34	–	–	34	0
Total winter residents	20	107	–	–	107	0

[1] 1968 and 1971 data pooled.
[2] Incidence of hovering and pecking from a perch before *vs* after the winter migrants departed.
[3] Incidence of reaching into a cluster from the base *vs* crawling into the cluster. (Unfortunately this division was not incorporated onto my field tally sheets until May of 1971, but incidental entries in my notebooks in both 1968 and 1971 indicate that I never saw the "crawling in" foraging method in the migrant species.)

part of the shoot, are perhaps most readily reached by the needle crawlers. The food supply is thus parcelled out to a variety of species according to the foraging methods employed. The small size of the Olive-capped Warbler may be an asset in its exploitation of the heart of needle clusters, but the Pine Warbler, a large species, has adopted the method to at least a limited degree on Grand Bahama. No birds on Grand Bahama were seen to forage while hanging beneath the twigs like titmice.

Air sallyers.—The term air sallyer is applied to birds that prey on flying insects by sallying out from fixed perches to snatch their prey in midair. The guild is distinguished by the vegetation compartment occupied (between trees) and the foraging method. The food items tend to be adult stages of Diptera Hymenoptera, Lepidoptera, and other free-flying insects. The flushers and chasers of the foliage- and bark-gleaning guilds might be classified here, but the food resource exploited in these cases seems to justify the assignment given them in this report.

Most tyrant Flycatchers are primary air sallyers, and the guild is often closely associated with them. Many other species sally for flying insects at times, however, and no fewer than 15 species were recorded doing so in this study.

The three permanent resident and one summer resident Tyrannid of the Grand Bahama breeding community were all primary air sallyers. They also dominated the guild during the winter, with three resident warblers and the Gnatcatcher contributing minor supplements.

In winter the guild was trebled in both membership and biomass by invading species. The Palm Warblers did much sallying, especially toward evening, and because of their large numbers came to dominate the guild with 67% of the membership and 60% of the biomass during the winter months. Redstarts and

Yellow-rumped Warblers contributed an additional 5% and 4% to the winter membership and 3% and 3% to its biomass. Mockingbirds and several other warblers made lesser contributions.

During the breeding season the Gray Kingbird captured large insects along roadways in the more open areas. Loggerhead Flycatchers apparently took similar prey but tended to forage in the denser areas of the forest. Stolid Flycatchers and pewees took smaller prey, capturing them at lower levels and on shorter sallying flights than the two large species. Insufficient observations (15 records) were obtained on the Stolid Flycatcher to permit a meaningful comparison of its foraging behavior with that of the Pewee.

Air sallying by warblers in the wintering community was, as noted above, largely restricted to special times and special situations. The swarming of small dipterans at dusk was responsible for a large part of their air sallying. On several occasions Palm Warblers seemed to drop all other foraging, gliding out in innumerable sallies to snap up small insects above the shrubs or between the tree crowns. With this concentration of feeding in briefly favorable situations, it is doubtful that they seriously interfered with the foraging of the primary members of the guild.

Air screeners.—The term air screeners is applied to birds that beat back and forth capturing flying insects on the wing. Swifts, swallows, and nightjars are the usual members of this guild, and three of these, the Chuck-wills Widow, the Cuban Nighthawk, and the Bahama Swallow, were observed at one time or another in the Grand Bahama pineland.

Bahama Swallows, the only regular air screener of the standard pineland community, foraged in more open situations and especially along the south coastal beaches during the winter, but they entered the pine forests to nest in cavities in high dead pine stumps and to forage above the tree tops or at lower elevations along roadways and forest edges in April and May. These birds with over 11 individuals and 165 g per km^2 probably did not compete significantly with any of the other regular community members.

Guild Biomass and Food Abundance

A guild analysis based on the sums of fractional guild memberships of all species in a community has a number of useful applications for community and population ecology. First, it provides a new and promising quantitative approach to the elusive problem of consumer-resource relationships, relationships that underlie many basic and popular hypotheses of competition and population regulation but remain essentially untested in natural situations. Measurements of the food supply available to a selected species are rarely attempted in nature because of the near impossibility of identifying and quantifying all the prey organisms under the highly complex and seasonally changing conditions of natural environments. The foraging guild/guild province approach bypasses these difficulties by transferring the analysis to a level where the resource component is a single integrated unit, a prey community, delineated by natural and readily traced spatial boundaries, and the consumer component is identified by definition in terms of those resource boundaries.

The invertebrate populations, i.e. prey communities for insectivorous guilds, were censused in the Grand Bahama pine forests by sampling the foraging substrate in seven spatially defined crown, trunk, shrub, and ground compartments in January of 1969 and in one crown compartment in January and May of 1971. The 1969 data were used for between-compartment comparisons in a single season, and the 1971 data for between-season comparisons in a single compartment.

For the 1969 data Dr. Norman Sloan and I cut and gently lowered three typical pine trees of the canopy stratum. All needles and twigs were then clipped and transferred with a minimum of disturbance to a series of plastic bags, one for each of the recognized crown compartments. Representative segments of the trunks and branches were similarly cut and bagged. Shrub foliage and ground cover materials were clipped directly from the standing vegetation. All materials were fumigated and shipped to Dr. Sloan's laboratory in Michigan where all edible organisms were removed, identified to genus or family, and counted.

Since our objective was to obtain comparable estimates of the standing food supplies in these compartments, and since time was a practical consideration, we did not attempt to weigh the collections but simply categorized the specimens in each compartment sample into four size classes (>8 mm, 4–8 mm, 2–4 mm, <2 mm) and multiplied the number of specimens in each class by 4, 3, 2, and 1 respectively. The sum of the four products, while in no way representing prey biomass, gives a single value in "insect units" suitable for cross-guild comparisons. I also assigned specimens to one of six general morphological types designated "moths," "flies" (both Hymenopterans and Dipterans), "bugs" (including Coleopterans, Orthopterans, etc.), "spiders" (including centipedes and pseudoscorpions), "ants," and "larvae" (including pupae and eggs).

Although extremely crude from the point of view of an insect taxonomist, I considered these categories, based on general form, activity, and approachability by birds, more appropriate for the objectives of the analysis than the usually cited phyletic taxa. One of the morphological types, "ants," was omitted from the tabulations on the premise that ants are largely unacceptable as food by the foliage- and bark-gleaning birds under consideration.

For the between-seasons pine foliage comparison of 1971 Virginia Emlen and I collected samples of foliage directly from the lower outer crown compartment of 20 canopy stratum pines. A metal hoop 50 cm in diameter backed by a large plastic garbage bag and mounted at the end of a 4-m pole was quietly slipped over the end of each selected branch. The branch was then clipped by cord-operated pruning shears and the foliage sample in the bag lowered and tied off for temporary storage without fumigation. From 5 to 10 branches were taken from each of 20 trees in 2 stands. We examined all foliage samples within three hours after collecting, vigorously shaking the branches and needle clusters over a large white tub into which most of the organisms of edible size fell and from which they were removed and stored in specimen vials for subsequent classification and identification. Twigs and needles were also examined closely after the shaking procedure for persisting specimens. The same system of classification into four size classes and six morphological categories was used as that applied in the between-compartment study.

Avian biomass in g per km^2 is plotted against prey density in insect units per m^3 (between-compartment foliage comparisons), cm^2 (between-compartment bark comparisons), or kg of foliage (between-seasons foliage comparisons) in Figure 31 (p. 66). The trend of increasing avian biomass with increasing food supply predicted by the traditional consumer-resource model was not found in these comparisons. Among the three pine canopy compartments, avian biomass was lowest in the crown tops where insect populations reached their highest densities (Fig. 31A). The upper portions of tree trunks had fewer insects but supported more birds than the lower portions (Fig. 31B). In the interseason comparison where the collections were most extensive and the sampling was best distributed, the wintering community had nearly 50% more avian insectivore biomass at the time when the resource base was lowest (Fig. 31C).

Food supply is generally regarded as a key factor in prevailing theories of population regulation and related concepts of intraspecies competition and carrying capacity (Lack 1954, Wynne-Edwards 1962). It also plays a central role in modern theories of interspecies competition, ecological segregation, ecological release, character displacement, and evolutionary divergence. The failure of the observations described above to support the predictions of competition theory therefore demands critical attention.

There are, of course, factors other than food to be considered, and the foraging guilds of the Bahamian pine forests may be atypical or otherwise inappropriate for testing consumer-resource models. Also, at a more specific level, factors other than food supply may have affected the attractiveness of some of the compartments or substrates used in the between-compartment comparisons. For instance, the failure to conform to the predictions of prevailing theory in Figure 31A and B could be attributed to structural or positional factors such as foliage density, foliage type, or proximity of escape cover on the trunks or ground. The comparison in Figure 31C between winter and summer ratios in a single tree crown subcompartment appears to avoid these complicating factors. With substrate accessibility and exposure to predation equated by identical conditions of foliage and position, a seasonal influx of invaders theoretically could not occur on an equal or reduced resource base unless the initial (breeding season) populations were below capacity.

Although my data are admittedly sketchy, and all variables are obviously not accounted for, I consider that the failure of the data to support the predictions of popular competition theories suggests that factors other than food levels are importantly involved in population regulation in at least some of the guilds of the Grand Bahama pine forests. This view is also supported by observations made in 1971 comparing consumer-food supply ratios in the Grand Bahama pine forests with those in closely similar pine stands in Florida where population densities were much lower (Emlen in press) and by observations made in 1976 comparing compartment distributions of the pine tree insectivores on Grand Bahama with those on neighboring Andros Island (Emlen MS).

GUILD STRUCTURE AND COMMUNITY DYNAMICS

A second application of the summed fractions approach to foraging guilds is to trace the ecological distributions of each species within a community and quantify the areas and extent of ecological overlap between species. Extensive overlap in the exploitation of food resources, foraging substrates, and foraging behavior implies more frequent interactions between species and, at least potentially, increased competition for resources, a factor that is traditionally of central concern in considerations of community dynamics. Guild data from the Grand Bahama pine forest communities were analyzed for information on guild structure and diversity, species distributions, and species overlap.

Guild structure and diversity.—The guilds of a bird community may differ in the number of species they contain, the equitability or evenness of representation of these species, and bird species diversity, a combination of species richness and equitability. These indices, especially equitability, are potentially useful as indicators of the amount of resource sharing and of species interaction rates in the various guilds. Values are given in Table 26 for each of the 18 foraging guilds of the Grand Bahama pine forest. These values have little biological usefulness for direct, between-guild comparisons since their resource bases or provinces vary in size and richness and cannot be equated. They may be useful, however, in between-element comparisons. They reveal, for instance, that PRs as a group were more evenly distributed (higher equitability) than WRs in 9 of the 10 guilds with multiple membership. The equitability index could also have some practical utility in revealing where my system of local guild categorization could profitably be refined. For instance, the high equitability value in the bark-gleaning insectivore guild of the wintering community in Table 26 ($J' = 0.91$) suggests that two rather distinct foraging categories were present that could usefully be recognized as separate guilds (also see Fig. 38). No such splitting is indicated for the ground insect gleaners where $J' = 0.38$.

Dispersion of species through the guilds.—As already noted, most bird species in the Grand Bahama submature forests distributed their foraging activities over several guild provinces. The extent of dispersion through the system is shown for each species in an index of amplitude in the last column of Table 20. These indices show the proportion of the maximum possible diversity of distribution that a species achieves ($J' = H'/H'$ max.), i.e. it is a measure of the evenness or equitability of distribution through the 18 guilds where the maximum number of guilds for a species is limited to 10 by the system of allotting representation in tenths. Trace representations were not considered in these calculations. Low values, such as those for the two doves (0.00 and 0.11), the Bahama Swallow (0.00), or the Black-and-white Warbler (0.07) indicate high specialization in one or a few of the guilds; high values such as those for the gnatcatcher (0.51), the Palm Warbler (0.80), or the bananaquit (0.50) indicate wide dispersal of activity through many guild provinces.

The dispersion of a species through the system of guilds (high amplitude) is attributed primarily to ecological and trophic plasticity. A population saturation-overflow model such as that applied to the between habitat analyses in chapter 5 does not seem appropriate at the guild level, but guild dispersion may be facilitated by population pressures in some situations. It might well have been operating, for instance, in the Palm Warblers that assumed the dominant position in no less than

TABLE 26
COMPOSITION AND STRUCTURE OF THE 18 FORAGING GUILDS OF THE GRAND BAHAMA FOREST COMMUNITIES

	Permanent residents							Winter residents							Total community					
	S_R[1]	S_T	Div.	Eq.	Dens.	Biom.	S_R	S_T	Div.	Eq.	Dens.	Biom.	S_R	S_T	Div.	Eq.	Dens.	Biom.
a. Wintering Community
Ground seed gleaners	4	1	1.23	.89	14.4	795	2	0	.58	.84	1.1	44	6	1	1.43	.80	15.5	839
Stem seed pluckers	1	0	.00	—	16.0	176	0	0	.00	—	0	0	1	0	.00	—	16.0	176
Fruits and buds	7	1	.55	.31	64.1	1580	7	1	.77	.55	57.0	809	14	2	1.33	.52	121.1	2389
Nectar sippers	3	0	.83	.76	104.4	637	2	0	.06	.08	45.4	499	5	0	1.39	.86	150.0	1136
Sap and cambium eaters	0	0	.00	—	0	0	1	0	.00	—	1.8	79	1	0	.00	—	1.8	79
Foliage eaters	0	1	.00	—	T	T	0	0	.00	—	0	0	0	1	.00	—	0	0
Ground insect gleaners	3	1	.60	.54	22.6	410	5	1	.37	.23	137.5	1598	8	2	.79	.38	160.0	2008
Ground insect pouncers	4	0	1.11	.80	6.5	140	1	1	.00	—	0.7	31	5	1	1.33	.83	7.2	171
Flower probers	3	0	.83	.76	52.2	318	1	1	.10	.14	5.1	56	4	1	1.12	.70	57.3	374
Shrub foliage gleaners	6	0	1.56	.87	51.9	600	9	2	1.09	.47	62.3	651	15	2	2.00	.72	114.0	1251
Shrub stem drillers	1	0	.00	—	1.1	53	0	0	.00	—	0	0	1	0	.00	—	1.1	53
Bark drillers	2	0	.69	1.00	4.2	117	1	0	.00	—	0.3	16	3	0	.87	.79	4.5	133
Bark gleaners	4	2	1.53	.95	37.0	457	4	3	1.06	.76	18.6	220	8	5	2.00	.91	55.6	677
Twig gleaners	5	3	1.43	.89	24.8	207	4	4	1.12	.69	16.6	160	9	7	1.97	.85	41.4	367
Cone probers	1	3	.00	—	2.1	11	1	1	.00	—	4.5	41	2	4	.63	.91	6.6	52
Needle gleaners	10	0	1.53	.66	177.9	1427	7	1	.75	.36	172.6	1817	17	1	1.74	.60	351.0	3244
Air sallyers	3	4	.76	.69	16.2	279	4	2	.49	.30	51.6	550	7	6	1.08	.52	67.8	829
Air screeners	0	0	.00	—	0	0	0	0	.00	—	0	—	0	0	.00	—	0	0
b. Breeding Season Community
Ground seed gleaners	4	1	1.28	.92	26.1	1726	0	0	.00	—	0	0	4	1	1.28	.92	26.1	1726
Stem seed pluckers	1	0	.00	—	16.7	184	0	0	.00	—	0	0	1	0	.00	—	16.7	184
Fruits and buds	7	1	.59	.33	82.2	2090	1	0	—	—	0.3	5	8	1	.60	.31	82.5	2095
Nectar sippers	3	0	.86	.78	81.3	497	0	0	.00	—	0	0	3	0	.86	.78	81.3	497
Sap and cambium eaters	0	0	.00	—	0	0	0	0	.00	—	0	0	0	0	.00	—	0	0
Foliage eater	0	1	.00	—	T	T	0	0	.00	—	0	0	0	1	.00	—	T	0
Ground insect gleaners	3	1	.72	.66	25.0	537	0	0	.00	—	0	0	3	1	.72	.66	25.0	537
Ground insect pouncers	4	0	1.07	.77	10.0	225	1	0	.00	—	0.9	54	5	0	1.11	.69	10.9	279
Flower probers	3	0	.85	.77	40.7	250	0	0	.00	—	0	0	3	0	.85	.77	40.7	250
Shrub foliage gleaners	6	0	1.60	.89	57.8	733	1	0	.00	—	1.6	26	7	0	1.68	.86	59.4	759
Shrub stem drillers	1	0	.00	—	0.9	45	0	0	.00	—	0	0	1	0	.00	—	0.9	45
Bark drillers	2	0	.69	1.00	3.8	96	0	0	.00	—	0	0	2	0	.69	.99	3.8	96
Bark gleaners	4	2	1.51	.94	38.1	434	0	0	.00	—	0	0	4	2	1.51	.94	38.1	434
Twig gleaners	5	3	1.37	.85	27.7	320	1	0	.00	—	0.3	5	6	3	1.42	.79	28.0	225
Cone probers	0	3	.00	—	2.1	11	0	0	.00	—	0	0	1	3	.00	—	2.1	11
Needle gleaners	10	0	1.42	.61	196.9	1571	0	0	.00	—	0	0	10	0	1.42	.61	197.0	1571
Air sallyers	3	4	.68	.62	20.2	368	1	0	—	—	3.7	222	4	4	.95	.68	23.9	590
Air screeners	0	0	.00	—	0	0	1	0	.00	—	11.0	165	1	0	.00	—	11.0	165

[1] S_R = number of regular species, S_T = number of trace species, Div. = bird species diversity (H′), Eq. = equitability (H′/H′ max), Dens. = density (individuals/km²), Biom. = biomass (grams/km²).

four of the guilds of the wintering community (Fig. 38 and Table 23A). Spatial and/or functional proximity of the foraging substrates were probably key factors in this case and in four instances of double dominance in the breeding season community (Table 23B), the Cuban Emerald Hummingbird (nectar-sipping and flower insect probing), the Greater Antillean Pewee (air sallying and ground pouncing), the Brown-headed Nuthatch (bark gleaning and cone probing), and the Olive-capped Warbler (needle gleaning and pine twig gleaning).

Specialization and generalization (low and high dispersion amplitudes) were widely and rather evenly distributed through the guilds, with specialists and generalists often occurring together in the same guild. Defining a specialist as a species with a guild distribution amplitude of less than 0.23 and a generalist as one with an amplitude value of more than 0.43, winter residents had about the same number of specialists (6) as permanent residents (5) and similar mean amplitudes (0.35 and 0.32). Summer residents were apparently more specialized, with a mean amplitude of 0.13, but in view of the small number of species in the element (3), no significance should be attached to the difference at this time.

Another comparison of interest is that between species of continental and Antillean origin. Species that colonize islands, i.e. the Antillean element in the Grand Bahama avifauna, are theoretically more likely to be generalists because of greater adaptability to novel conditions (MacArthur and Wilson 1967) and a tendency to expand in ecological amplitude when released from the pressures of high continental bird species diversity (Grant 1966, Lack 1970). On Grand Bahama one might thus expect relatively more generalists and fewer specialists among the species of Antillean origin vis-à-vis continental origin. The data do not support this prediction. Among the 7 species classed as recently derived from continental stock (Fig. 3), 3 were generalists and 2 were specialists; among the 8 from Antillean stock 2 were generalists and 2 were specialists. The group of 7 species classed as coming to Grand Bahama from the continent by way of the Antilles contained 1 generalist and 4 specialists.

The top choice of a species among the foraging provinces of a habitat (the guild of primary membership for the species) should be a good place to look for evidence of segregation arising from interspecies competition for food resources. I would predict that the species most successful in establishing themselves in a community would be those that were preadapted or that quickly became adapted to available foraging provinces not already preempted or heavily exploited. This selection of uncrowded provinces should, all else being equal, lead to a rather even dispersion of primary memberships through the local guild system. In contrast to this prediction, the 35 primary guild memberships in the Grand Bahama pine forests were concentrated in 6 of the 18 guilds, and 7 guilds had no primary members at all. Of the primary memberships 25 fell in 5 of the guilds, 5 in each; 1 guild had 4, 2 had 2, and 2 had 1 (Table 19). Specialist species as defined above were dispersed a little more widely than generalists (through 8 vs. 6 guilds), but 3 specialist species had their primary memberships superimposed in one guild (shrub foliage gleaners), and there were 2 double occupancies in each of 4 other guilds. Admittedly, the large amount of cohabitation revealed by these data may reflect gross inequalities in my partitioning of the functional space, but even allowing generously for this, the predictions of the hypothesis of segregation and dispersion of primary memberships in functional space do not seem to be met.

Predictions of general competition theory also failed to find support from observations of distribution adjustments by permanent resident species as winter migrants withdrew from foraging provinces they had dominated. Permanent resident compensatory responses to the exodus of winter residents exceeded 10% of the loss in only one guild; permanent residents actually declined by 22% as the migrants left in one guild (Table 26).

SPECIES OVERLAP AND COMPETITION

Insofar as the guild provinces adopted for this analysis approximate natural subdivisions of the forest's available food resources, the extent of overlap in guild membership between two species reflects the extent of joint use of a common food supply by those species. Similarly, the sum of the overlaps between a species and all the other members of the community indicates the extent to which that species shares its food resources with the rest of the community. Such joint use of common resources may be equated with potential competition, theoretically becoming real competition when and where supplies are limited with respect to total demand.

Indices of guild overlap for all of the 526 two-species combinations of the wintering community and the 211 combinations of the breeding season community are presented in Tables 27 and 28. The values were obtained by summing the tenths of overlap in each column of Table 20 and dividing the total by the maximum score possible for all overlaps—always ten. For example, the Cuban Emerald Hummingbird and the Bananaquit in the wintering community are recorded as overlapping to the extent of 0.4 in the nectar-sipping guild, 0.2 in the flower-probing guild, and 0.1 in the needle-gleaning guild. With 10 tenths possible in cases of complete overlap (perfect coincidence), the index of overlap for these two species is 7 tenths, as shown at the proper coordinate point in Table 27.

Theoretically competition will tend to suppress overlap and prevent the occurrence of high overlap. The data do not support this prediction. Mean overlap for all species pairs in the wintering community was 1.58, appreciably higher than the 1.06 overlap expected by chance. The comparable values for the breeding season were 1.20 and 0.69.

The concentration of relatively high overlap values along the diagonal margin of the triangle of values in Tables 27 and 28 reflects a similarity of foraging behavior in related species which, because of the roughly phylogenetic arrangement of the list of species tend to have their coordinate points grouped in this zone. Within this zone, particularly high values are clustered where the sequentially listed members of natural taxonomic units (e.g. the flycatchers or the *Dendroica* warblers) form associated blocks of coordinate points. This distribution supports the traditional view that species with similar foraging structures, particularly the bill, tend to have similar feeding habits. Data are insufficient to test the prediction of competition theory that closely related congenerics tend to segregate ecologically.

TABLE 27
Overlap in Guild Membership in the 33 Members of the Wintering Bird Community of the Pine Forests (Data from Table 21)[1]

		Z	G	C	H	Y	L	S	G	B	M	C	R	G	T	B	P	C	B	M	B	Y	Y	O	P	P	P	O	C	B	R	B	S	G[1]
P	Zenaida Dove	9																																
P	Ground Dove	0	0																															
P	Cuban Emerald Hummingbird	0	0	0																														
P	Hairy Woodpecker	1	0	0	5																													
W	Yellow-bellied Sapsucker	1	0	0	0	0																												
P	Loggerhead Flycatcher	0	0	0	0	0	7																											
P	Stolid Flycatcher	0	0	1	0	0	8	8																										
P	Greater Antillean Pewee	0	0	0	0	0	4	0	1																									
P	Brown-headed Nuthatch	0	0	0	6	0	1	1	2	0																								
W	Mockingbird	2	1	0	2	1	2	2	0	1	7																							
W	Gray Catbird	2	0	0	1	1	0	0	0	0	5	7																						
P	Red-legged Thrush	4	3	0	2	1	0	0	1	1	4	7	1																					
P	Blue-gray Gnatcatcher	0	0	1	3	2	1	1	0	1	0	5	0	0																				
P	Thick-billed Vireo	1	0	0	0	1	1	1	0	0	1	2	1	2	4																			
W	Black and White Warbler	0	0	0	4	3	0	0	0	0	4	0	0	1	2	0																		
W	Parula Warbler	1	0	0	0	1	0	0	0	1	0	2	1	1	3	6	3																	
W	Cape May Warbler	1	0	3	1	1	1	1	0	2	1	1	2	2	1	6	4	8																
W	Black-throated Blue Warbler	0	0	0	1	0	2	2	1	0	0	4	1	2	0	4	7	0	3															
W	Yellow-rumped Warbler	1	0	1	3	1	2	4	0	2	4	4	4	4	0	4	7	0	8	1	1													
W	Black-throated Green Warbler	0	0	1	1	0	1	1	0	1	2	0	1	3	0	7	7	3	6	2	5	7	2											
W	Yellow-throated Warbler (WR)	0	0	1	2	1	0	1	0	0	5	0	0	0	6	1	1	0	4	1	1	3	4											
P	Yellow-throated Warbler (PR)	0	0	0	0	0	1	0	0	0	7	1	0	0	4	1	7	0	0	4	1	1	3	2										
P	Olive-capped Warbler	0	0	0	0	1	1	1	0	0	2	0	0	0	5	1	0	0	4	4	1	2	4	7	5									
P	Pine Warbler	0	0	0	1	1	0	0	0	0	0	0	0	0	5	1	0	0	4	0	5	7	3	1	3	9								
W	Prairie Warbler	0	0	0	1	1	1	1	0	0	1	1	0	0	7	1	1	0	6	5	1	8	5	1	4	5	5							
W	Palm Warbler	1	0	0	2	1	1	1	0	2	2	2	0	0	6	0	0	0	5	3	3	5	3	1	3	5	3	5						
W	Ovenbird	0	0	0	0	0	0	1	1	0	0	0	0	0	4	3	0	0	2	4	0	3	4	0	0	0	0	0	0					
W	Common Yellowthroat	0	0	0	0	0	0	0	1	0	1	3	0	0	0	0	2	0	2	0	0	0	0	0	0	2	0	0	0	3				
W	Bahama Yellowthroat	0	0	3	0	0	0	0	1	0	0	4	0	0	2	0	0	0	1	2	2	0	0	0	0	2	1	0	1	4	8			
W	Redstart	0	0	0	5	0	0	0	0	0	1	1	0	0	1	1	1	0	5	3	1	3	5	0	1	5	2	1	5	0	5	6		
P	Bananaquit	0	0	0	6	0	0	0	0	0	0	6	2	1	4	5	3	2	4	2	2	5	4	0	5	4	4	4	3	0	2	2	7	
P	Stripe-headed Tanager	1	0	2	0	0	0	1	0	0	1	6	1	0	3	3	1	1	6	6	3	4	4	2	2	4	4	4	1	0	4	4	1	1
P	Grassquit	0	2	1	1	0	1	0	1	0	1	3	2	1	1	4	2	2	2	0	1	1	1	1	1	1	1	1	0	1	1	1	1	1

Instances of major overlaps between species

Overlap	PR×PR	PR×WI	WI×WI	Tot.
9 (90%)	2	0	0	2
8 (80%)	2	1	3	6
7 (70%)	3	9	3	15
3–6	17	53	30	100
1–2	59	107	34	200
None	69	99	35	203
Mean-Recorded	1.22	1.61	2.02	1.58
Expected	0.61	1.60	1.01	1.06

[1] Letters at column heads match the initial letters in the list of species on left margin.

TABLE 28
OVERLAP IN GUILD MEMBERSHIP DISTRIBUTION IN THE 21 MEMBERS OF THE BREEDING SEASON COMMUNITY OF THE PINE FORESTS[1]

	Z	G	C	H	G	L	S	G	B	B	R	B	T	B	Y	O	P	B	B	S	G
P Zenaida Dove																					
P Ground Dove	9																				
P Cuban Emerald Hummingbird	0	0																			
P Hairy Woodpecker	0	0	0																		
S Gray Kingbird	0	0	0	0																	
P Loggerhead Flycatcher	0	0	0	0	8																
P Stolid Flycatcher	0	0	1	0	9	7															
P Greater Antillean Pewee	0	0	0	0	9	8	8														
S Bahama Swallow	0	0	0	0	0	0	0	0													
P Brown-headed Nuthatch	0	0	1	6	0	0	1	0	0												
P Red-legged Thrush	4	3	0	2	0	0	0	0	0	0											
P Blue-gray Gnatcatcher	0	0	1	3	0	0	1	1	0	4	0										
P Thick-billed Vireo	1	0	1	1	1	1	1	2	0	1	1	4									
P Black-wiskered Vireo	1	0	0	1	0	0	0	1	0	1	1	4	7								
P Yellow-throated Warbler	0	0	1	5	0	0	1	0	0	7	0	4	1	1							
P Olive-capped Warbler	0	0	1	1	0	0	1	0	0	2	0	5	1	1	2						
P Pine Warbler	0	0	1	1	0	0	1	0	0	1	0	5	1	0	2	9					
P Bahama Yellowthroat	0	0	3	0	0	0	0	1	0	0	4	1	1	1	0	0	0				
P Bananaquit	0	0	7	0	0	0	1	1	0	1	0	4	3	2	1	2	2	4			
P Striped-headed Tanager	1	0	0	2	0	0	0	0	0	3	1	2	1	0	0	0	1	1			
P Grassquit	0	2	1	1	0	0	1	0	0	1	4	1	2	0	1	1	1	0	1	1	

Instances of major overlaps between species

Overlap	PR×PR	PR×SI	SI×SI	Tot.
9 (90%)	2	2	0	4
8 (80%)	2	1	0	3
7 (70%)	3	1	0	4
3–6	17	1	0	18
1–2	59	11	0	70
None	87	23	2	112
Mean-				
Recorded	1.14	1.49	0.00	1.20
Expected	0.63	1.07	0.00	0.69

[1] Letters at column heads match the initial letters in the list of species on left margin.

Only one of the 11 cases of high overlap (7–9 tenths) in the breeding community involves two congenerics, however, and here the two (Olive-capped Warbler and Pine Warbler) are not very closely related.

Because of different amounts of exposure to interaction one might predict that pair combinations involving 2 permanent resident species (interacting through the year including the breeding season) would show more divergence (have a lower overlap) than combinations of 2 winter resident species or combinations with one permanent resident and one winter resident species. Data in Table 27, summarized in the box at the upper right, generally support this prediction. The mean overlap value of PR × PR pairings was 1.22, while that for WR × WR pairings was 2.02, and for PR × WR pairings, 1.61.

ACKNOWLEDGMENTS

Most of the work reported in this paper was conducted with support from grants from the University of Wisconsin Graduate School and the National Science Foundation (GB-15304). Transportation and operating expenses were covered primarily by grants from the American Philosophical Society and the Frank M. Chapman Memorial Fund. Facilities and logistic assistance on the Island were provided by the Colonial Research Institute of Freeport, Grand Bahama. I particularly thank Virginia Emlen, William Gillis, Paul Fluck, Dorothy Rand, and Norman Sloan for assistance on various aspects of the field work. Many helpful comments and criticisms on the manuscript were offered by Edward Beals, J. Merritt Emlen, Timothy Moermond, Ronald Pulliam, and William Robertson. Useful suggestions on special topics were offered by James Bond. The patience and artistic skills of Cheryl Hughes and Donald Chandler are gratefully acknowledged.

Summary and Conclusions

Introduction, Methods, and Background.—An intensive study of ecological distribution was conducted on the land bird populations of Grand Bahama Island, a 1200 km^2, low-lying, pine-covered island located 105 km off the east coast of southern Florida. Shrunken by rising sea levels from about 15,000 km^2 during the last pleistocene ice age, the island now contains 33 breeding land birds (excluding birds of prey). About one-half of these derive from the Antilles, one-fourth from Central America via the Antilles, and one-fourth, mostly pine forest species, directly from North America.

Absolute density and biomass data were obtained for across-habitat distribution analyses for all species, residents and migrants, at 25 sites representing the range of habitat conditions on the island. More intensive studies of within-habitat distribution were conducted at three sites in the dominant habitat type, submature pine forest.

The Habitats and Their Bird Communities.—Procedures for delineating, measuring, and analyzing the structure and diversity of habitats are outlined and applied to the 25 stands. Techniques for plotting bird distributions along single and compound habitat gradients are described and applied. Prominent aspects of the composition, structure, diversity, and density of the wintering bird communities in the stands are examined and compared between stands and types and along habitat gradients.

Bird species diversity is shown to be correlated with several graded features of habitat structure and with vegetation diversity as measured by the relative quantity of foliage at 3 levels (foliage height diversity). The best correlation found for bird species diversity was, however, with total vegetation volume, measured as cubic meters of standing foliage per km^2. The logical basis for bird diversity-habitat complexity relationships is discussed and the demonstrated best correlation with vegetation volume attributed to complexity factors associated with vegetation volume as it was measured.

Total community density, the sum of all species densities, showed definite trends along several habitat gradients, particularly those of increasing tree and shrub cover. Community density was, however, only weakly correlated with total vegetation volume. The logical basis for a total bird density-vegetation volume correlation is discussed and the demonstrated poor correlation on Grand Bahama cited as a basis for caution against uncritical acceptance of widely held assumptions concerning consumer-resource relations in nature.

Habitat Distribution.—Concepts of the dynamics of density distribution through a mosaic of habitat patches are reviewed. Models are presented in which as yet unestablished birds are viewed as moving into the physically best patches until (1) factors associated with increasing density reduce the net quality of those patches or (2) aggressive resistance by residents terminates further immigration. Density distribution through a series of habitat patches of decreasing physical quality is visualized as progressively declining in the first instance and holding a constant level until carrying capacity falls below social saturation in the second. The patterns of density distribution through the top ten stands for each Grand Bahama species were compared with these models. Relatively aggressive and localized species showed more evidence of a social saturation plateau in these comparisons than nomadic and passive species, suggesting that the social saturation phenomenon, well known in breeding season territorial behavior, was also operating in some members of this wintering community.

In a plotting of maximum densities against dispersion amplitudes, species with high absolute densities in their preferred habitat types were always dispersed broadly into secondary types. These dispersals are tentatively attributed to overflow from capacity populations. Species with low absolute densities in their preferred habitats and narrow dispersal amplitude are tentatively regarded as species that had not filled their preferred habitat to either social saturation or resource-determined carrying capacity levels. Those with low absolute density and broad dispersal amplitude are regarded as species that had dispersed because of (for them) low density tolerances or low capacity habitats.

Winter densities varied greatly among habitat types. Permanent residents as a group outnumbered winter residents in the forest habitats but were outnumbered by them in the open habitats.

Density distributions for most species were unexpectedly irregular and diffuse along the seven selected parameter gradients. Permanent residents increased relative to winter residents with increasing pine cover, decreasing tree height and increasing vegetation volume, but no evidence of seasonal displacement of one group by the other was detected in any habitat.

Overlap in habitat distribution was no greater in closely related than remotely related species except within one group of congeneric pine habitat warblers. It was no greater in pairings of continental or of Antillean species than in mixed geographic pairings, but was greater in pairings of permanent residents and of winter residents than in mixed PR-WR pairings, supporting a prediction that species in the two seasonal elements would tend to segregate.

A two-dimensional ordination of habitat spacing for all the species of the Bahamas wintering community provides a base for evaluating the similarity of habitat selection responses between the species.

The Pine Forest Community—Seasonal Changes.—The bird fauna occupying the pine forest, the most extensive and most complex of the Grand Bahama habitats, changed markedly in composition, diversity, and biomass between January and June, as winter residents departed, summer residents arrived, and transients passed through. The wintering community, divided almost equally between permanent residents and winter migrants, was nearly twice as large in numbers of species, individuals, and biomass as the breeding season community. Summer residents and transients were minor elements in these seasonal changes.

The great annual increase in number of species each fall occurs in the absence of any obvious change in habitat complexity, and the near doubling of total population density and biomass, in the apparent absence of any increase in basic food resources. The impact of increased species numbers on the permanent resident populations may be dulled by a low equitability in the winter migrant element. The impact of increased density and biomass could be more imagined than real if, as I propose, food supply is less critical as a limiting factor than commonly supposed.

Spatial Distribution Within the Pine Forest.—The space within the pine forest habitat was partitioned into 5 equal layers from the ground surface to the tree tops, and 10 (or 4 for some analyses) unequal compartments delineated with reference to prominent recurring features of the forest vegetation.

Species diversity and total density declined gradually and evenly upward through the five equal layers, while foliage density was high in the first, third, and fourth layers and low in the second and fifth. Bird distribution thus appeared to reflect responses to space *per se* rather than to the quantity of perching and foraging surfaces. Winter resident species were relatively best represented in the subcanopy and lower canopy, the third and fourth layers.

Graphic representations of compartment distributions reveal preference, dispersion, and overlap characteristics of 30 common species and various species groups. A comparison of the compartment distribution of permanent resident species before and after the annual departure of winter migrants (i.e. the winter and breeding season distributions) reveal considerable shuffle between compartments and habitats including a net shift from the shrub compartment into the crowns and down to the ground vegetation. The direction of this movement is opposite to that predicted by models of compensation adjustment and traditional competition theory.

Guild Distribution Within the Pine Forest.—In this chapter the ecological distribution of each pine forest species is delineated in terms of the substrates and resources its members exploit and the way they exploit them. For this purpose the forest habitat of Grand Bahama was divided into 18 functionally defined foraging provinces and the avain community into 18 matching foraging guilds. Local observations of foraging behavior were used to assign each bird species fractionally to as many of these guilds as it was seen to enter. Most of the guilds thus contained one or more primary or specialist members and a number of secondary members and visitors. Areal densities from the transect census were multiplied by membership values in tenths to give directly comparable absolute densities for each guild and each guild member. The structure, diversity, and density characteristics of each of the 18 Grand Bahama pine forest guilds are described.

Invertebrate food resources were sampled quantitatively in five pine foliage compartments, two understory compartments, and two trunk compartments. The prey organism densities calculated from these samples were then matched with the measured biomass of avian consumers in those compartments for an across-province comparison of consumer-resource ratios. Results failed to show the positive correlation predicted by traditional carrying capacity theory. In another test the invertebrate food resources of a single pine foliage compartment were sampled before and after the winter migrants departed from the island, and again there was no positive correlation of avian biomass with food supply.

An H' index of the dispersion amplitude of species through the 18 guild provinces of the forest provided a basis for defining levels of specialization in foraging behavior. The winter resident and permanent resident elements had similar mean specialization values, but the winter resident element was more varied. A prediction of relatively high amplitude in species of Antillean origin based on attributes commonly associated with colonization and low diversity island communities was not supported. A prediction that province preference should be widely distributed among species (to avoid crowding in a few provinces) was not supported. Contrary to the predictions of competition theory no general compensatory shift in province distribution by permanent resident species was detected with the spring departure of winter migrants.

Measures of total guild overlap (reflecting joint resource use) for the members of each species pair combination showed an overall incidence appreciably higher than that expected by chance. This, again, appears to be in opposition to the predictions of traditional competition theory. High overlap was correlated with phylogenetic relationship at the family level. A few instances of very high overlap (70–90%) occurred between congenerics. In line with competition theory predictions, overlap was less in pairings within the permanent resident element than in pairings of permanent residents with winter residents or pairings between two winter resident species.

Literature Cited

Aldrich, J. 1963. Geographic orientation of American Tetraonidae. J. Wildl. Mgmt. 27: 529–545.

Alt, D., and H. K. Brooks. 1965. Age of the Florida marine terraces. J. Geol. 73: 406–411.

American Ornithologists' Union. 1957. Check-list of North American birds, fifth ed. Baltimore, Amer. Ornithol. Union.

———. 1973. Thirty-second supplement to the American Ornithologists' Union check-list of North American birds. Auk 90: 411–419.

Beals, E. W. 1960. Forest bird communities in the Apostle Islands of Wisconsin. Wilson Bull. 72: 156–181.

———. 1973. Ordination: mathematical elegance and ecological naiveté. J. Ecol. 61: 23–35.

Bent, A. C. 1939. Life histories of North American woodpeckers. U.S. Natl. Mus. Bull. No. 174.

———. 1940. Life histories of North American cuckoos, goatsuckers, hummingbirds and their allies. U.S. Natl. Mus. Bull. No. 176.

———. 1942. Life histories of North American flycatchers, larks, swallows and their allies. U.S. Natl. Mus. Bull. No. 179.

———. 1948. Life histories of North American nuthatches, wrens, thrashers and their allies. U.S. Natl. Mus. Bull. No. 195.

———. 1953. Life histories of North American wood warblers. U.S. Natl. Mus. Bull. No. 203.

———. 1968. Life histories of North American cardinals, grosbeaks, buntings, towhees, finches, sparrows and their allies. U.S. Natl. Mus. Bull. No. 237.

Bond, J. 1963. Derivation of the Antillean avifauna. Proc. Acad. Nat. Sci. Philadelphia 115: 79–98.

———. 1971. Birds of the West Indies. Boston, Houghton-Mifflin Co.

BRAY, J. R., AND J. T. CURTIS. 1957. An ordination of the upland forest communities of southern Wisconsin. Ecol. Monogr. 27: 325–349.

BRITTON, N. L., AND C. F. MILLSPAUGH. 1920. The Bahama flora. New York, Hafner Publ. Co.

BRODKORB, P. 1959. Pleistocene birds from New Providence Island, Bahamas. Bull. Florida State Mus. 4: 349–371.

BROWN, J. L. 1969. Territorial behavior and population regulation in birds. Wilson Bull. 81: 293–329.

CHAPMAN, F. M. 1891. The origin of the avifaunas of the Bahamas. Amer. Naturalist 25: 528–539.

CODY, M. L. 1968. On the methods of resource division in grassland bird communities. Amer. Naturalist 102: 107–147.

CRITCHFIELD, W. B. 1966. Geographic distribution of the pines of the world. U.S. Dept. Agr. Misc. Publ. 991.

DIAMOND, J. M. 1969. Avifaunal equilibria and species turnover rates on the channel islands of California. Proc. Natl. Acad. Sci. 64: 57–63.

———. 1970. Ecological consequences of island colonization by southwest Pacific birds. Part 2, The effect of species diversity on total population density. Proc. Natl. Acad. Sci. 67: 1715–1721.

EMLEN, J. T. 1956. A method for describing and comparing avian habitats. Ibis 98: 565–576.

———. 1967. A rapid method for measuring arboreal canopy cover. Ecol. 48: 158–160.

———. 1971. Population densities of birds derived from transect counts. Auk 88: 323–342.

———. 1972. Size and structure of a wintering avian community in southern Texas. Ecology 53: 317–329.

———. 1973. Territorial aggression in wintering warblers at Bahama agave blossoms. Wilson Bull. 85: 71–74.

———. 1978. Density anomalies and regulation mechanisms in land bird populations on the Florida peninsula. Amer. Nat. 112: in press.

———. in preparation. Densities and foraging distributions of birds on two Bahama islands.

FRETWELL, S. D. 1972. Populations in a seasonal environment. Princeton, New Jersey, Princeton Univ. Press.

———, AND H. L. LUCAS, JR. 1970. On territorial behavior and other factors influencing habitat distribution in birds. Part 1, Theoretical development. Acta Biotheoretica 19: 16–36.

GIBB, J. A. 1960. Populations of tits and goldcrests and their food supplies in pine plantations. Ibis 102: 163–208.

GILLIS, W. T., R. BYRNE, AND W. HARRISON. 1975. Bibliography of the natural history of the Bahama Islands. Atoll Res. Bull. 191.

GRANT, P. R. 1966. The density of land birds on Tres Marias Islands in Mexico. Part 1, Numbers and biomass. Canadian J. Zool. 44: 805–815.

HILDEN, O. 1965. Habitat selection in birds. Ann. Zoologici Fennici 2: 53–75.

HOWELL, T. R. 1972. Birds of the lowland pine savanna of northeastern Nicaragua. Condor 74: 316–340.

HUTCHINSON, G. E. 1957. Concluding remarks. Cold Spring Harbor Symp. Quant. Biol. 22: 415–427.

JOHNSTON, D. W. 1975. Ecological analysis of the Cayman Island avifauna. Bull. Florida State Mus. 19(5).

KALE, H. W. 1967. Aggressive behavior by a migrating Cape May Warbler. Auk 84: 120–121.

KARR, J. R. 1968. Habitat and avian diversity on strip-mined land in east-central Illinois. Condor 70: 348–357.

———, AND R. R. ROTH. 1971. Vegetation structure and avian diversity in several new world areas. Amer. Naturalist 105: 423–435.

KLUYVER, H. N., AND L. TINBERGEN. 1953. Territory and the regulation of density in titmice. Archiv. Neerl. Zool. 10: 265–287.

LACK, D. 1933. Habitat selection in birds. J. Anim. Ecol. 2: 239–262.

———. 1940. Habitat selection and speciation in birds. Brit. Birds 34: 80–84.

———. 1954. The natural regulation of animal numbers. London, Oxford Univ. Press.

———. 1970. The numbers of bird species on islands. Bird Study 16: 193–209.

———. 1976. Island biology illustrated by the land birds of Jamaica. Berkeley, Univ. of Calif. Press.

LYNCH, J. F., AND N. K. JOHNSON. 1976. Turnover and equilibria in insular avifaunas, with special reference to the California Channel Islands. Condor 76: 370–384.

MACARTHUR, R. H. 1959. On the breeding distribution of North American migrants. Auk 76: 218–228.

———, AND J. W. MACARTHUR. 1961. On bird species diversity. Ecology 42: 594–598.

———, AND E. O. WILSON. 1967. The theory of island biogeography. Princeton, New Jersey, Princeton Univ. Press.

———, H. RECHER, AND M. CODY. 1966. On the relation between habitat selection and species diversity. Amer. Naturalist 100: 319–332.

MARTIN, A. C., H. S. ZIM, AND A. L. NELSON. 1951. American wildlife and plants. New York, McGraw-Hill.

MILLIMAN, J. D., AND K. O. EMERY. 1968. Sea levels during the past 35,000 years. Science 162: 1121–1123.

MOREAU, R. E. 1972. The Palaeartic-African bird migration system. New York, Academic Press.

MOREL, G. 1968. Contribution à la synecologie des oiseaux du sahel senegalais. Paris, Mem. Office de la Récherche Scientifique et Technique outre-Mer, 29.

MORSE, D. H. 1966. Foraging relationships of Brown-headed Nuthatches and Pine Warblers. Ecology 48: 94–103.

ORIANS, G. 1969. The number of bird species in some tropical forests. Ecology 50: 783–801.

RECHER, H. 1969. Bird species diversity and habitat diversity in Australia and North America. Amer. Naturalist 103: 75–80.

RICKLEFS, R. E., AND G. W. COX. 1972. Taxon cycles in the West Indian avifauna. Amer. Naturalist 106: 195–219.

ROBERTSON, W. B., JR. 1955. An analysis of the breeding bird populations of tropical Florida in relation to the vegetation. Unpublished Ph.D. Thesis, Champaign, Univ. Illinois.

———. 1962. Observations on the birds of St. John, Virgin Islands. Auk 79: 44–76.

ROOT, R. B. 1967. The niche exploitation pattern of the Blue-gray Gnatcatcher. Ecol. Monogr. 37: 317–349.

ROTH, R. R. 1976. Spatial heterogeneity and bird species diversity. Ecology 57: 773–782.

SCHOLL, D. W., F. C. CRAIGHEAD, SR., AND M. STRIVER. 1969. Florida submergence curve revised: its relation to coastal sedimentation rates. Science 163: 562–564.

SCHWARTZ, A., AND R. F. KLINIKOWSKI. 1963. Observations on West Indian birds. Proc. Acad. Nat. Sci. Philadelphia 115: 53–77.

SVÄRDSON, G. 1949. Competition and habitat selection in birds. Oikos 1: 157–174.

TERBORGH, J., AND J. FAABORG. 1973. Turnover and ecological release in the avifauna of Mona Island, Puerto Rico. Auk 90: 759–779.

TINBERGEN, N. 1957. The functions of territory. Bird Study 4: 14–27.

TOMOFF, C. S. 1971. Avian species diversity in desert scrub. Ecology 55: 396–403.

WATTS, W. A. 1971. Postglacial and interglacial vegetation history of southern Georgia and central Florida. Ecology 52: 676–690.

WETMORE, A. 1916. Birds of Puerto Rico. U.S. Dept. Agr. Bull. 32.

WILLSON, M. F. 1974. Avian community organization and habitat structure. Ecology 55:1017–1029.

WYNNE-EDWARDS, V. C. 1962. Animal dispersion in relation to social behavior. Edinburgh, Oliver and Boyd.

APPENDIX

Species Accounts

The material presented below provides a complete listing with annotations of the land bird species that I observed along the transect routes and elsewhere on Grand Bahama during the months of January through May of 1968 and 1969. Most of the ecological and population data are taken directly from tables and figures in the main body of the text and assembled here for ready reference under the species' names. Additional data on habitat distribution are presented in graphic form in Figures 19, 20, and 21. Birds of prey, not included in the formal list, consisted of a few wintering American Kestrels (*Falco sparverius*), a small resident population of Red-tailed Hawks (*Buteo jamaicensis*), one Barn Owl (*Tyto alba*), and a few dozen of Turkey Vultures (*Cathartes aura*).

The symbols denoting geographic derivation are taken directly from Figure 3, the letters indicating the source (C = Continental, A = Antilles), and the subscript numbers, the amount of evolution recognized (0 = no change recorded by taxonomists, 1 = subspecific change, 2 = full specific change). Geographic derivation is given for permanent resident and summer resident species only.

The coefficient of detectability (C.D. 412) for a species is the frequency (percent) with which birds were recorded in a band 824 feet (250 m) wide along the transect trails. Values were calculated by plotting the lateral distribution of all detection points along the trails, projecting the density of detections in a narrow strip near the trail, where full coverage is assumed, to 125 m (the wide band), and dividing the projected number by the number actually recorded in the band (Emlen 1971). C.D. values were used to translate the trail counts per km of transect (in the wide band) directly to density per km^2. All calculated densities were converted to metric units in this report. C.D. values for the species in this study ranged from 10% to 65%; data were inadequate to calculate meaningful C.D. values for the rarer species.

Under the heading "status" I recorded the seasonal occurrence of each species on Grand Bahama, whether a permanent resident, a winter resident, a summer resident, or an in-transit visitor (occurring only as a migrating transient) (Table 2). I then listed the mean density of the species for all census transects during the winter period, 1 January to 31 March (Table 2). The rank position of the commonest species is given in parentheses for the first 15. For rare species I indicated only the number of records obtained. For summer resident species I gave May densities where these were available.

Under habitat distribution I listed in order, the one or more (of seven) habitat types most heavily occupied by the species and gave the density in birds per km^2 for each of these types. In parentheses I added a J' value (H'/H' max) indicating the amplitude of dispersion of the species through the seven types. Values range from 0 (found in only one habitat type) to 1.00 (evenly dispersed through all 7). Data are taken from Table 5; they do not necessarily match those in Table 18 which covers only the 3 stands studied intensively for within-habitat distribution.

Distribution along seven selected habitat gradients is shown for most of the species in the diagrams in Figures 19, 20, and 21. The small circles in these diagrams represent the position of each of the 25 stands along the specified gradients, and the symbol within the circles gives the numerical status of the species in that stand. A key identifying the stands by position and explaining the symbols is presented at the head of each figure. Further explanations are given in the legend for Figure 11.

Under "habitat overlap" I listed a few species that share their habitats most heavily with the species under consideration. The value after a species' name is the percent of overlap with the indicated species through the 7 habitat types as taken from Figure 10. The number of species with overlap values greater than an indicated high level is given in parentheses.

Under "vertical distribution in pines" I simply referred the reader back to the species diagrams in Figure 32.

Under "compartment distribution in pines" I named the major compartments (among the 4 recognized: crowns, shrubs, trunks, ground) in which the species is best represented during the winter season and gave the calculated index of preference for that compartment

(4d/D) where the highest possible score is 4.0. The amplitude of dispersion through the 4 major compartments is presented as a J' value (H'/H' max) in parentheses.

Under "foraging guild distribution" I listed the one or several foraging guilds (among the 18 recognized in Table 20) in which the species is best represented, and then gave a J' value reflecting the amplitude of dispersion of the species in question through the 16 guilds. J' values run from 0 (all foraging is in one guild) to 1.00 (even distribution).

Under "foraging guild overlap" I listed the 2 or more species showing greatest similarity to the one under consideration in their choice of food and foraging methods. The values are the sums of tenths of overlap through the 16 recognized foraging provinces (Table 27). The total of overlap with all other species, given in parentheses, is an indicator of the overall level of foraging interaction with other community members; values range from 0 in the highly specialized Bahama Swallow to 88 in the eurythrophic Palm Warbler.

White-Crowned Pigeon, (*Columbia leucocephala*)
    Geographic derivation—A0.   CD412—30%.
    Status—permanent resident, 0.27 birds per km^2. Irregular.
    Habitat distribution—coppets. 3.9 birds per km^2 (J' = 0).
    Habitat gradients—Figs: 19.1, 20.1, 21.1.

Zenaida Dove, (*Zenaida aurita zenaida*)
    Geographic derivation—A0.   CD412—20%.
    Status—permanent resident, 3.4 birds per km^2.
    Habitat distribution—coppets—5.0, submature pines—4.2 (J' = 0.48).
    Habitat gradients—Figs: 19.2, 20.2, 21.2.
    Habitat overlap—Hairy Woodpecker—80, Cape May Warbler—79 (8 over 70%).
    Vertical distribution in pines—Fig. 32A.
    Compartment distribution in pines—ground—2.7, crowns—1.3 (J' = 0.46).
    Foraging guild distribution—ground seeds—9 (J' = 0.11).
    Foraging guild overlap—Ground Dove—9, Red-legged Thrush—4 (total 25).

Mourning Dove, (*Zenaida macroura carolinensis*)
    Geographic derivation—C0.   CD412—25%.
    Status—permanent resident, 1.68 birds per km^2.
    Habitat distribution—mangroves—15.0, submature pines—4.8 (J' = 0.28).

Ground Dove, (*Columbina passerina bahamensis*)
    Geographic derivation—C1 A1.   CD412—20%.
    Status—permanent resident, 4.1 birds per km^2.
    Habitat distribution—Coastal brush—41.5 (winter), submature pines—7.6 (J' = 0.33).
    Habitat gradient—Figs: 19.3, 20.3, 21.3.
    Habitat overlap—Palm Warbler—62, Common Yellowthroat—42 (3 over 30).
    Vertical distribution—Fig. 32B.
    Compartment distribution—ground—1.8, shrubs—1.6 (J' = 0.69).
    Foraging guild distribution—ground seeds—10 (J' = 10).
    Foraging guild overlap—Zenaida Dove—9, Red-legged Thrush—3 (total 16).

Key West Quail Dove, (*Geotrygon chrysea*)
    Geographic derivation—A0.   CD412—10%.
    Status—permanent resident, 0.80 birds per km^2.
    Habitat distribution—coastal brush—25.5 (J' = 0).
    Habitat gradient—Figs: 19.4, 20.4.

Yellow-Billed Cuckoo, (*Coccyzus a. americanus*)
    Status—in-transit visitor, 5 records, 6 May (1968)–25 April (1969).

Smooth-Billed Ani, (*Crotophaga ani*)
    Geographic derivation—A0.   CD412—60%.
    Status—permanent resident, 0.85 birds per km^2.

Habitat distribution—coppets—10.5, marsh—5.7 ($J' = 0.33$).
Habitat gradient—Figs: 19.5, 20.5, 21.4.

Chuck-wills-widow, (*Caprimulgus carolinensis*)

Status—winter invader, 6 records in March and April.
Habitat distribution—submature pines.

Cuban Nighthawk, (*Chordeiles minor gundlachi*)

Geographic derivation—C2 A0.
Status—summer resident (not recorded on transect counts), first spring record—29 April (1969).

Chimney Swift, (*Chaetura pelagica*)

Status—in-transit visitor, 4 records: 6, 7, 9 May, 1968, 27 April, 1969.

Cuban Emerald Hummingbird, (*Chlorostilbon ricordii bracei*)

Geographic derivation—A1.   CD412—14%.
Status—permanent resident, 93.6 birds per km^2 (2nd).
Habitat distribution—young pines—155, submature pines—99, coppets—90 ($J' = 0.81$).
Habitat gradient—Figs: 19.6, 20.6, 21.5.
Habitat overlap—Bahama Yellowthroat—72, Greater Antillean Pewee—72 (6 over 60%).
Vertical distribution—Fig. 27C.
Compartment distribution—shrubs—2.4, crowns—1.3 ($J' = 0.64$).
Foraging guild distribution—nectar—6, flower insects—3 ($J' = 0.35$).
Foraging guild overlap—bananaquit—7, Cape May Warbler—3 (total 29).

Bahama Woodstar, (*Calliphlox evelynae evelynae*)

Geographic derivation—A2.   CD412—12%.
Status—permanent resident, 21.2 birds per km^2 (15th).
Habitat distribution—young pines—72.5, coastal brush—54.0 ($J' = 0.59$).
Habitat gradient—Figs: 19.7, 20.7, 21.6.
Habitat overlap—Palm Warbler—59, Common Yellowthroat—55 (5 over 40%).

Belted Kingfisher, (*Megaceryle alcyon*)

Status—winter invader along waterways, 8 records. None seen on transect routes.

Red-Bellied Woodpecker, (*Centurus superciliaris*)

Geographic derivation—C1 A1.
Status—permanent resident (Bond 1971). None recorded in 1968 or 1969.

Yellow-Bellied Sapsucker, (*Sphyrapicus v. varius*)

CD412—22%
Status—winter resident, 3.2 birds per km^2.
Habitat distribution—coppets—22.0, submature pines—4.3 ($J' = 0.23$).
Habitat gradient—Figs: 19.9, 20.9.
Habitat overlap—Northern Waterthrush—89, Yellow-rumped Warbler—63 (7 over 40%).
Compartment distribution—trunks—2.8, shrubs—0.8 ($J' = 0.59$).
Foraging guild distribution—sap and cambium—5 ($J' = 0.41$).
Foraging guild overlap—Hairy Woodpecker—5, Brown-headed Nuthatch—4 (total 38).

Hairy Woodpecker, (*Dendrocopus villosus piger*)

Geographic derivation—C1.   CD412—35%.
Status—permanent resident 9.9 birds per km^2.
Habitat distribution—coppets—39.5, submature pines—14.1 ($J' = 0.60$).

Habitat gradient—Figs: 19.8, 20.8, 21.7.
Habitat overlap—Striped-headed Tanager—90, Black-and-white Warbler—87 (6 over 70%).
Compartment distribution—trunks—7.8, shrubs—0.6 (J' = 0.56).
Foraging guild distribution—Bark gleaner—4 (J' = 0.51).
Foraging guild overlap—Brown-headed Nuthatch—6, Yellow-throated Warbler—5, Yellow-bellied Sapsucker—5 (total 45).

Gray Kingbird, (*Tyrannus d. dominicensis*)
Geographic derivation—A0.   CD412—60%.
Status—common summer resident (two winter records 10 January 1968, 14 March 1969).
Habitat distribution—mangrove—0.80. Open pine woodlands around Freeport.
Compartment distribution—(breeding season)—crowns—2.5 (J' = 0.64).
Foraging guild distribution—air insect sallyer—8, ground insect pouncer—2 (J' = 0.17).

Loggerhead Flycatcher, (*Tolmarchus caudifasciatus behamensis*)
Geographic derivation—A1.   CD412—30%.
Status—permanent resident, 3.6 birds per km^2.
Habitat distribution—submature pines—6.7, coppets—3.9 (J' = 0.54).
Habitat gradient—Figs: 19.10, 20.10, 21.8.
Habitat overlap—Greater Antillean Pewee—89, Yellow-throated Warbler—89 (7 over 60%).
Vertical distribution—Fig. 32D.
Compartment distribution—crowns—3.6, trunks—0.4 (J' = 0.22).
Foraging guild distribution—air insect sallyer—6, ground insect pouncer—4 (J' = 0.27).
Foraging guild overlap—Greater Antillean Pewee—8, Stolid Flycatcher—7 (total 28).

Stolid Flycatcher, (*Myiarchus stolidus lucayiensis*)
Geographic derivation—C2 A1.   CD412—30%.
Status—permanent resident, 0.50 birds per km^2.
Habitat distribution—coppets—3.5, submature pines—0.3, (J' = 0.13).
Habitat gradient—Figs: 19.11, 20.11, 21.9.
Compartment distribution—crowns—2.4, shrubs—1.6 (J' = 0.49).
Foraging guild distribution—air insect sallyer—8, ground insect pouncer—1 (J' = 0.22).
Foraging guild overlap—Greater Antillean Pewee—8, Loggerhead Flycatcher—7 (total 41).

Greater Antillean Pewee, (*Contopus caribaeus bahamensis*)
Geographic derivation—C2 A1.   CD412—30%.
Status—permanent resident, 7.6 birds per km^2.
Habitat distribution—submature pines—11.0, young pines—9.3, coppets—9.0 (J' = 0.56).
Habitat gradient—Figs: 19.12, 20.12, 21.10.
Habitat overlap—Yellow-throated Warbler—83, Pine Warbler—80 (7 over 60%).
Vertical distribution—crowns—3.6, shrubs—0.3 (J' = 0.28).
Foraging guild distribution—air insect sallyer—7, ground insect pouncer—2 (J' = 0.31).
Foraging guild overlap—Loggerhead Flycatcher—8, Stolid Flycatcher—8 (total 42).

Bahama Swallow, (*Callichelidon cyaneoviridis*)
Geographic derivation—C2.   CD412—35%.
Status—permanent resident, 6.8 birds per km^2.
Habitat distribution—old fields—66.3, marsh—61.0, coastal—4.6 (J' = 0.42). Moved into submature forests for breeding in late April.
Habitat gradient—Figs: 19.13, 20.13.
Habitat overlap—Mockingbird—54, Common Yellowthroat—50 (4 over 50%).
Foraging guild distribution—air insect screener—19 (J' = 0).

Barn Swallow, (*Hirundo rustica erythrogaster*)
    Status—in-transit visitor. One record, 13 May 1968.

Brown-Headed Nuthatch, (*Sitta pusilla insularis*)
    Geographic derivation—C1.   CD412—25%.
    Status—permanent resident, 8.48 birds per km^2.
    Habitat distribution—submature pines—17.0 ($J' = 0$).
    Habitat gradient—Figs: 19.14, 20.14, 21.11.
    Habitat overlap—Cape May Warbler—62, Olive-capped Warbler—55 (4 over 40%).
    Vertical distribution—trunks—2.1, crowns—1.9 ($J' = 0.50$).
    Foraging guild distribution—bark insect gleaner—4, pine twig gleaner—3 ($J' = 0.49$).
    Foraging guild overlap—Hairy Woodpecker—6, Yellow-bellied Sapsucker—4 (total 49).

House Wren, (*Troglodytes aedon* ssp.)
    Status—winter resident, 1 bird present, 6–21 April 1969.
    Habitat distribution—submature pines.

Northern Mockingbird, (*Mimus polyglottos orphaeus*)
    Geographic derivation—C1 A0.   CD412—60%.
    Status—permanent resident, 4.15 birds per km^2.
    Habitat distribution—old fields—44.0, coastal—4.6 ($J' = 0.41$). Common in Freeport suburbs.
    Habitat gradient—Figs: 19.16, 20.16, 21.13.
    Habitat overlap—Grasshopper Sparrow—83, Common Yellowthroat—41 (5 over 30%).
    Vertical distribution—Fig. 32G.
    Compartment distribution—shrubs—1.7, crowns—1.2 ($J' = 0.91$).
    Foraging guild distribution—fruit and bud eater—6, ground insect pouncer—2 ($J' = 0.45$).
    Foraging guild overlap—Gray Catbird—7, Red-legged Thrush—5 (total 45).

Bahama Mockingbird, (*Mimus g. gundlachii*)
    Geographic derivation—A0.   CD412—60%.
    Status—permanent resident. One record, 18 March 1969.
    Habitat distribution—old fields—1.07 ($J' = 0$).
    Habitat gradient—Figs: 19.17, 20.17, 21.14.

Gray Catbird, (*Dumetella carolinensis*)
    CD412—18%
    Status—winter resident, 58.3 birds per km^2 (5th).
    Habitat distribution—coppets—251, old fields—249, marsh—54 ($J' = 0.61$).
    Habitat gradient—Figs. 19.15, 20.15, 21.12.
    Habitat overlap—Prairie Warbler—70, Bahama Yellowthroat—68 (4 over 55%).
    Vertical distribution—Fig. 32H.
    Compartment distribution—shrubs—3.0, crowns—0.4 ($J' = 0.52$).
    Foraging guild distribution—fruit and bud eater—5, ground insect gleaner—3 ($J' = 0.44$).
    Foraging guild overlap—Mockingbird—7, Red-legged Thrush—7 (total 62).

American Robin, (*Turdus migratorius* spp.)
    CD412—50%
    Status—winter resident, irregular. Five records (15–16 March, 1969).
    Habitat distribution—marsh

Red-Legged Thrush, (*Mimocichla p. plumbea*)
    Geographical derivation—A1.   CD412—18%.
    Status—permanent resident, 3.44 birds per km^2.

Habitat distribution—coppets—38.9, submature pines—2.0 ($J' = 0.20$).
Habitat gradient—Figs: 19.18, 20.18, 21.15.
Habitat overlap—Parula Warbler—95, Ovenbird—92 (7 over 70%).
Vertical distribution—Fig. 32I.
Compartment distribution—shrubs—1.7, ground—1.7 ($J' = 0.72$).
Foraging guild distribution—ground insect gleaner—4, fruit and bud eater—3 ($J' = 0.38$).
Foraging guild overlap—Gray Catbird—7, Northern Mockingbird—5 (total 51).

Blue-Gray Gnatcatcher, (*Polioptila c. caerulea*)

Geographical derivation—C0.   CD412—25%.
Status—permanent resident, 29.0 birds per km^2 (10th).
Habitat distribution—coppets—153, submature pines—31.0. ($J' = 0.45$).
Habitat gradient—Fig. 19.19, 20.19, 21.16.
Habitat overlap—redstart—93, Striped-headed Tanager—90, Cape May Warbler—88 (8 over 80%).
Vertical distribution—Fig. 32J.
Compartment distribution—shrubs—2.5, crowns—1.4 ($J' = 0.58$).
Foraging guild distribution—needle insect gleaners—4, shrub foliage gleaner—3, bark gleaners—2 ($J' = 0.51$).
Foraging guild overlap—Prairie Warbler—7, Black-throated Green Warbler—7, Cape May Warbler—6 (total 85).

Water Pipit, (*Anthus spinoletta rubescens*)

Status—winter resident on golf courses near Freeport—none seen on transect routes.

Cedar Waxwing, (*Bombycilla cedrorum*)

Status—in-transit visitor—flock of 50 seen in Freeport suburbs on 3–5 May 1968.

Starling, (*Sturnus v. vulgaris*)

Status—irregular winter visitor, flock of 100 seen 18 March 1969.

Thick-Billed Vireo, (*Vireo c. crassirostris*)

Geographical derivation—C2 A2.   CD412—36%.
Status—permanent resident, 22.6 birds per km^2 (13th).
Habitat distribution—coppets—133, marsh—35, Young pines—18.9 ($J' = 0.57$).
Habitat gradient—Figs: 19.20, 20.20, 21.17.
Habitat overlap—redstart—83, Blue-gray Gnatcatcher—82, Striped-headed Tanager—81 (8 over 70%).
Vertical distribution—Fig. 32K.
Compartment distribution—shrubs—3.6, crowns—0.4 ($J' = 0.25$).
Foraging guild distribution—shrub foliage gleaners—7, ($J' = 0.33$).
Foraging guild overlap—Parula Warbler—8, Black-throated Blue Warbler—7, Black-throated Green Warbler—7 (total 72).

Yellow-Throated Vireo, (*Vireo flavifrons*)

Status—winter resident, two records 15 March 1969, 25 April 1969.

Black-Whiskered Vireo, (*Vireo altiloquus barbatulus*)

Geographical derivation—C2 A1.
Status—summer resident, common. Arrived 3 May 1968, 5 May 1969.
Habitat distribution—restricted to coppets and around high shrubs and broad-leafed trees in disturbed open pineland.
Compartment distribution—shrubs—4.0 (breeding season).
Foraging guild distribution—shrub foliage gleaners—8, ($J' = 0.22$).

Bananaquit, (*Coereba flaveola bahamensis*)
    Geographical derivation—A2.   CD412—20%.
    Status—permanent resident, 55.0 birds per km^2 (6th).
    Habitat distribution—coppets—160, coastal—70, submature pines—62 ($J' = 0.90$).
    Habitat gradient—Figs: 19.39, 20.37, 21.31.
    Habitat overlap—Prairie Warbler—76, Bahama Yellowthroat—76 (10 over 60%).
    Vertical distribution—Fig. 27Z.
    Compartment distribution—shrubs—2.5, crowns—1.4 ($J' = 0.53$).
    Foraging guild distribution—nectar sippers—4, Flower insect probers—2, Shrub foliage gleaners—2 ($J' = 0.50$).
    Foraging guild overlap—Cuban Emerald Hummingbird—7, Cape May Warbler—6 (total 60).

Black-and-White Warbler, (*Mniotilta varia*)
    CD412—7%
    Status—winter resident, 4.5 birds per km^2.
    Habitat distribution—coppets—16.1, submature pines—6.3 ($J' = 0.30$).
    Habitat gradient—Figs: 19.21, 20.21, 21.18.
    Habitat overlap—Striped-headed Tanager—88, redstart—88, Hairy Woodpecker—87 (5 over 80%).
    Vertical distribution—Fig. 32L.
    Compartment distribution—trunks—4.0 ($J' = 0$).
    Foraging guild distribution—bark gleaners—10 ($J' = 0.07$).
    Foraging guild overlap—Yellow-throated Warbler (PR)—7, Brown-headed Nuthatch—4 (total 22).

Worm-Eating Warbler, (*Helmitheros vermivorus*)
    CD412—10%
    Status—Winter resident, 3 records, 8 May, 1968; 13 March, 1969; 25 April, 1969.
    Habitat distribution—submature pines—0.91 ($J' = 0$).

Golden-Winged Warbler, (*Vermivora chrysoptera*)
    Status—winter resident, one record, 10 March 1968.

Orange-Crowned Warbler, (*Vermivora celata*)
    CD412—12%
    Status—winter resident, 0.67 birds per km^2.
    Habitat distribution—mangrove—3.7, submature pines—0.6 ($J' = 0.21$).

Northern Parula Warbler, (*Parula americana*)
    CD412—12%
    Status—winter resident, 6.8 birds per km^2.
    Habitat distribution—coppets—56.9, submature pines—5.6 ($J' = 0.39$).
    Habitat gradient—Figs: 19.22, 20.22, 21.19.
    Habitat overlap—Red-legged Thrush—95, Ovenbird—90, Blue-gray Gnatcatcher—83 (6 over 70%).
    Vertical distribution—Fig. 32M.
    Foraging guild distribution—shrub foliage gleaner—9 ($J' = 0.15$).
    Foraging guild overlap—Thick-billed Vireo—8, Black-throated Blue Warbler—8 (total 55).

Yellow Warbler, (*Dendroica petechia gundlachi*)
    Geographical derivation—C1 A1.   CD412—20%.
    Status—permanent resident, 0.6 birds per km^2.
    Habitat distribution—mangroves—6.5 ($J' = 0$).
    Habitat gradient—Figs: 19.23, 20.23.

Magnolia Warbler, (*Dendroica magnolia*)

CD412—15%
Status—winter resident, 3 records: 15 January 1969, 21 April 1969, 25 April 1969.
Habitat distribution—coppets—2.3 ($J' = 0$).

Cape May Warbler, (*Dendroica tigrina*)

CD412—12%
Status—Winter resident, 6.75 birds per km^2. Abundant transient in early May 1968, late April 1969.
Habitat distribution—submature pines—9.3, coppets—6.0 ($J' = 0.33$).
Habitat gradient—Figs: 19.24, 20.24.
Habitat overlap—Blue-gray Gnatcatcher—88, Zenaida Dove—79 (4 over 70%).
Vertical distribution—Fig. 32N.
Foraging guild distribution—needle gleaners—4, shrub foliage gleaners—2, nectar sippers—2 ($J' = 0.58$).
Foraging guild overlap—Palm Warbler—7, Bananaquit—6, Prairie Warbler—6 (total 84).

Black-Throated Blue Warbler, (*Dendroica caerulescens ssp.*)

CD412—12%
Status—winter resident, 1.58 birds per km^2. Influx of transients in late April–early May.
Habitat distribution—coppets—48.8 ($J' = 0$).
Habitat gradient—Fig: 19.25.
Foraging guild distribution—shrub foliage gleaners—8 ($J' = 0.22$).
Foraging guild overlap—Parula Warbler—8, Thick-billed Vireo—7, Black-throated Green Warbler—7 (total 55).

Yellow-Rumped (Myrtle) Warbler, (*Dendroica c. coronata*)

CD412—20%
Status—winter resident, 66.5 birds per km^2 (4th).
Habitat distribution—marsh—146, coppets—121, submature pines—78.9 ($J' = 0.88$).
Habitat gradient—Figs: 19.27, 20.25, 21.20.
Habitat overlap—grassquit—80, Bananaquit—69 (5 over 60).
Vertical distribution—Fig. 32O.
Compartment distribution—crowns—2.3, shrubs—1.6 ($J' = 0.52$).
Foraging guild distribution—fruit and bud eaters—4, pine twig gleaners—3, ($J' = 0.51$).
Foraging guild overlap—Striped-headed Tanager—4, Gray Catbird—4, Northern Mockingbird—4 (total 62).

Black-Throated Green Warbler, (*Dendroica virens* spp.)

CD412—12%.
Status—winter resident, 0.67 birds per km^2.
Habitat distribution—coppets—7.0, submature pines—0.5 ($J' = 0.13$).
Foraging guild distribution—shrub foliage gleaners—6, pine needle gleaners—3 ($J' = 0.31$).
Foraging guild overlap—Prairie Warbler—8, Blue-gray Gnatcatcher—7, Thick-billed Vireo—7 (total 80).

Yellow-Throated Warbler, (*Dendroica dominica flavescens* (a) and *dominica* (b))

Geographical derivation (a) C1,   CD412 (a and b)—20%.
Status—(a) permanent resident (flavescens)—ca. 14 birds per km^2; (b) winter resident (*dominica*)—ca. 7 birds per km^2. Total 21 birds per km^2 (14th).
Habitat distribution—submature pines—30.5, young pines—15.9 ($J' = 0.45$).
Habitat gradient—Figs: 19.28, 20.26, 21.21.
Habitat overlap—Loggerhead Flycatcher—89, Olive-capped Warbler—85, Pine Warbler—84 (5 over 70%).

Vertical distribution—Fig. 32P.
Compartment distribution—crowns—3.1, trunks—0.5 ($J' = 0.49$).
Foraging guild distribution—(a) bark gleaners—7, twig gleaners—2 ($J' = 0.35$); (b) needle gleaners—6, pine twig gleaners—2 ($J' = 0.45$).
Foraging guild overlap—(a) Brown-headed Nuthatch—7, Black-and-white Warbler—7 (total 50); (b) Olive-capped Warbler—7, Pine Warbler—7, Blue-gray Gnatcatcher—6 (total 61). (Assignment to foraging guilds is very approximate since identification to subspecies was often impossible in the field.)

Olive-Capped Warbler, (*Dendroica pityophila*)

Geographic derivation—C2 A0.   CD412—25%.
Status—permanent resident—72.0 birds per km² (3rd).
Habitat distribution—submature pines—114, young pines—69 ($J' = 0.51$).
Habitat gradient—Figs: 19.29, 20.27, 21.22.
Habitat overlap—Yellow-throated Warbler—85, Pine Warbler—80 (4 over 70%).
Vertical distribution—Fig. 32Q.
Compartment distribution—crowns—3.96, shrubs—0.04 ($J' = 0.04$).
Foraging guild distribution—needle insect gleaners—9, twig gleaners—1 ($J' = 0.22$).
Foraging guild overlap—Pine Warbler—9, Yellow-throated Warbler (WR)—7 (total 52).

Blackpoll Warbler, (*Dendroica striata*)

CD412—20%.
Status—in-transit visitor; 15 April–13 May 1968; 21 April–18 May 1969.
Vertical distribution—Fig. 32R.

Pine Warbler, (*Dendroica pinus achrustera*)

Geographical derivation—C1.   CD412—30%.
Status—permanent resident, 27.9 birds per km² (11th).
Habitat distribution—submature pines—40, young pines—38 ($J' = 0.52$).
Habitat gradient—Figs: 19.30, 20.28, 21.23.
Habitat overlap—Yellow-throated Warbler—84, Pine Warbler—80, Greater Antillean Pewee—80 (4 over 70%).
Vertical distribution—Fig. 32S.
Compartment distribution—crowns—3.76 ($J' = 0.18$).
Foraging guild distribution—needle insect gleaners—9, bark insect gleaners—1 ($J' = 0.22$).
Foraging guild overlap—Olive-capped Warbler—9, Yellow-throated Warbler (WR)—7 (total 50).

Kirtland's Warbler, (*Dendroica kirtlandi*)

Status—Rare winter resident, never seen in 500 hours of field observation but one captured by Dr. Paul Fluck in April 1969.
Habitat distribution—Captured bird was in submature pine habitat.

Prairie Warbler, (*Dendroica d. discolor*)

CD412—15%.
Status—winter resident, 16.7 birds per km².
Habitat distribution—coppets—87, old fields—25, submature pines—15 ($J' = 0.66$).
Habitat gradient—Figs: 19.31, 20.29, 21.24.
Habitat overlap—Gray Catbird—90, Thick-billed Vireo—79, Bananaquit—76 (7 over 70%).
Vertical distribution—Fig. 32T.
Compartment distribution—shrubs—2.4, crowns—1.6 ($J' = 0.54$).
Foraging guild distribution—shrub foliage gleaners—5, needle gleaners—5 ($J' = 0.28$).
Foraging guild overlap—Black-throated Green Warbler—8, Blue-gray Gnatcatcher—7 (total 77).

Palm Warbler, (*Dendroica palmarum* ssp.)

    CD412—24%.

    Status—Winter resident 214.8 birds per km^2 (1st).

    Habitat distribution—Coastal brush—559, Submature pines—256, Young pines—197 ($J' = 0.82$).

    Habitat gradient—Figs: 19.32, 20.30, 21.25.

    Habitat overlap—Ground Dove—62, Common Yellowthroat—61, Bananaquit—60 (6 over 50%).

    Vertical distribution—Fig. 32U.

    Compartment distribution—crowns—2.7, shrubs—1.1 ($J' = 0.54$).

    Foraging guild distribution—ground insect gleaners—3, needle insect gleaners—3 ($J' = 0.80$).

    Foraging guild overlap—Cape May Warbler—7, Gray Catbird—6, Bahama Yellowthroat—5 (total 88).

Ovenbird, (*Seiurus aurocapillus*)

    CD412—12%.

    Status—Winter resident, 4.2 birds per km^2. Transient influx in late April and early May.

    Habitat distribution—coppets—63, submature pines—1.1 ($J' = 0.04$).

    Habitat gradient—Figs: 19.33, 20.31, 21.26.

    Habitat overlap—Red-legged Thrush—92, Parula Warbler—90, Blue-gray Gnatcatcher—75 (8 over 60%).

    Vertical distribution—Fig. 32V.

    Compartment distribution—Ground—3.6.

    Foraging guild distribution—ground insect gleaners—10 ($J' = 0.04$).

    Foraging guild overlap—Common Yellowthroat—8, Bahama Yellowthroat—6 (total 26).

Northern Waterthrush, (*Seiurus novaboracensis* spp.)

    CD412—15%.

    Status—winter resident, 10.3 birds per km^2. Transients in early May.

    Habitat distribution—marsh—125, coppets—49, mangroves—27 ($J' = 0.46$).

    Habitat gradient—Figs: 19.34, 20.32, 21.27.

    Habitat overlap—Yellow-bellied Sapsucker—87, Yellow-rumped Warbler—64 (2 over 50%).

Common Yellowthroat, (*Geothlypis trichas* ssp.)

    CD412—15%.

    Status—winter resident, 50.1 birds per km^2 (7th).

    Habitat distribution—coastal brush—341, marsh—228, old fields—216 ($J' = 0.79$).

    Habitat gradient—Figs: 19.35, 20.33, 21.28.

    Habitat overlap—Palm Warbler—61, Bananaquit—57 (5 over 50%).

    Vertical distribution—Fig. 32W.

    Compartment distribution—shrubs—2.9, ground—1.0 ($J' = 0.50$).

    Foraging guild distribution—ground insect gleaners—8, shrub foliage gleaners—2 ($J' = 0.17$).

    Foraging guild overlap—Ovenbird—8, Bahama Yellowthroat—7 (total 47).

Bahama Yellowthroat, (*Geothlypis rostrata tanneri*)

    Geographical derivation—C2.   CD412—20%.

    Status—permanent resident, 32.2 birds per km^2 (9th).

    Habitat distribution—coppets—80.1, old fields—53, young pines—46 ($J' = 0.78$).

    Habitat gradient—Figs: 19.36, 20.34, 21.29.

    Habitat overlap—Bananaquit—76, Cuban Emerald Hummingbird—72, Prairie Warbler—62 (9 over 60%).

    Vertical distribution—Fig. 32X.

    Compartment distribution—shrubs—2.7, ground cover—1.0 ($J' = 0.61$).

Foraging guild distribution—ground insect gleaners—6, nectar sippers—2 ($J' = 0.38$).
Foraging guild overlap—Common Yellowthroat—7, Ovenbird—6, Palm Warbler—5 (total 47).

Hooded Warbler, (*Wilsonia citrina*)

Status—winter resident, three records: 2 April 1968, 8 April 1968, 11 April 1968.

Wilson's Warbler, (*Wilsonia p. pusilla*)

CD412—12%.
Status—winter resident, 0.3 birds per km^2.
Habitat distribution—coppets—6.5 ($J' = 0$).

Redstart, (*Setophaga r. ruticilla*)

CD412—15%.
Status—winter resident, 8.5 birds per km^2. Transient influx in late April and early May.
Habitat distribution—coppets—49, submature pines—12.7 ($J' = 0.46$).
Habitat gradient—Figs: 19.37, 20.35, 21.30.
Habitat overlap—Blue-gray Gnatcatcher—93, Striped-headed Tanager—90, Black-and-white Warbler—88 (7 over 80%).
Vertical distribution—Fig. 32Y.
Compartment distribution—crowns—2.3, shrubs—1.7 ($J' = 0.49$).
Foraging guild distribution—shrub foliage gleaners—4, air sallyers—4 ($J' = 0.36$).
Foraging guild overlap—Greater Antillean Pewee—6, Stolid Flycatcher—6, Thick-billed Vireo—5 (total 69).

House Sparrow, (*Passer d. domesticus*)

Geographical derivation—XO.
Status—permanent resident.
Habitat distribution—Common in urban Freeport and around hotels. None seen on the transect routes.

Bobolink, (*Dolichonyx orizivorus*)

Status—in-transit visitor 27 April (1969)–11 May (1968). None seen on transect routes.
Habitat distribution—mainly in coastal brush and grassy areas behind dunes.

Red-Winged Blackbird, (*Agelaius phoeniceus bryanti*)

CD412—60%.
Status—winter resident, 5.8 birds per km^2.
Habitat distribution—mangroves—49, marsh—31 ($J' = 0.52$).
Habitat gradient—Figs: 19.38, 20.36.
Habitat overlap—Yellow-rumped Warbler—46, Bahama Swallow—45 (2 over 40%).

Baltimore Oriole, (*Icterus g. galbula*)

Status—winter resident. Uncommon in Freeport suburbs. None seen on transect routes.

Striped-Headed Tanager, (*Spindalis zena townsendi*)

Geographical derivation—A1.   CD 412—20%.
Status—permanent resident, 36.8 birds per km^2 (8th).
Habitat distribution—coppets—156, submature pines—44.4, young pines—24.9 ($J' = 0.45$).
Habitat gradient—Figs: 19.40, 20.38, 21.32.
Habitat overlap—Blue-gray Gnatcatcher—90, Redstart—90, Hairy Woodpecker—70 (6 over 80%).
Vertical distribution—Fig. 32AA.
Compartment distribution—shrubs—24, crowns—1.6 ($J' = 0.49$).
Foraging guild distribution—fruit and bud eaters—9 ($J' = 0.18$).
Foraging guild overlap—Northern Mockingbird—6, Gray Catbird—6 (total 41).

Rose-Breasted Grosbeak, (*Pheucticus ludovicianus*)
    Status—in-transit visitor, 4 records; 25 April to 9 May 1969.

Indigo Bunting, (*Passerina cyanea*)
    Status—in-transit visitor, 12 April (1968)—6 May (1969)
    Habitat distribution—Irregular at brushy sites near Freeport. None seen on the transect routes.

Black-Faced Grassquit, (*Tiaris b. bicolor*)
    Geographical derivation—A1.   CD412—15%.
    Status—permanent resident 24.0 birds per km^2 (12th).
    Habitat distribution—coppets—50.1, submature pines—37.7, marsh—34 ($J' = 0.76$).
    Habitat gradient—Figs: 19.42, 20.40, 21.34.
    Habitat overlap—Yellow-rumped Warbler—80, Bananaquit—72 (2 over 70%).
    Vertical distribution—Fig. 32BB.
    Compartment distribution—shrubs—2.4, ground cover—1.2 ($J' = 0.64$).
    Foraging guild distribution—stem seed pluckers—5, ground seed gleaners—2 ($J' = 0.47$).
    Foraging guild overlap—Red-legged thrush—4, Palm Warblers—3 (total 38).

Greater Antillean Bullfinch, (*Loxigilla v. violacea*)
    Geographical derivation—A1.   CD412—15%.
    Status—permanent resident, 2.1 birds per km^2.
    Habitat distribution—coppets—34 ($J' = 0$).
    Habitat gradient—Figs: 19.41, 20.39, 21.33.
    Compartment distribution—shrubs—2.0, ground cover—1.5 ($J' = 0.70$).

Savannah Sparrow, (*Passerculus sandwichensis savanna*)
    CD412—12%.
    Status—winter resident, 1.6 birds per km^2.
    Habitat distribution—coastal brush—34.5, old fields—11 ($J' = 0.28$). Also common in grassy lots in suburban Freeport.
    Habitat gradient: Figs: 19.43, 20.41, 21.35.

Grasshopper Sparrow, (*Ammodramus savannarum pratensis*)
    CD412—12%.
    Status—winter resident, 4.8 birds per km^2.
    Habitat distribution—old fields—51.7, young pines—1.0 ($J' = 0.05$).
    Habitat gradient—Figs: 19.44, 20.42, 21.36.

Lincoln Sparrow, (*Melospiza l. lincolni*)
    Status—winter resident. Two records: 6 May 1968; 8 February 1969.
    Habitat distribution—brush behind coastal dunes.